A Man's Reach

The Autobiography of Glenn Clark

WITH
A CONCLUDING CHAPTER
BY
Marcia Brown

Ah, but a man's reach should exceed his grasp,

Or what's a heaven for?

Robert Browning, *Andrea del Sarto*

GLENN CLARK

A Man's Reach

The Autobiography of Glenn Clark

ૅ

WITH
A CONCLUDING CHAPTER
BY
Marcia Brown

Macalester Park Publishing Company
AUSTIN, MINNESOTA

A MAN'S REACH

Library of Congress Cataloging-in-Publication Data

Clark, Glenn
A man's reach: the autobiography of Glenn Clark/Glenn Clark
p. cm.

ISBN 1-886158-19-3

1. Subjects: Clark, Glenn, 1882-1956.
Macalester College--Faculty--Biography.
College teachers--Minnesota--Saint Paul--Biography.
Evangelists--Minnesota--Saint Paul--Biography.

BV3785.C55 A3 (2004)
270/.09/2 B (2004)

Book cover and interior design by Justin Moreland,
Justin Moreland and Associates
www.jwmoreland.com

Printed in the United States of America

MACALESTER PARK PUBLISHING CO.
24558 546TH AVE.
AUSTIN MN 55912
USA
PHONE: 1-800-407-9078 OR 1-507-396-0135
EMAIL: macalesterpark@macalesterpark.com
WEBSITE: www.macalesterpark.com

CONTENTS

INTRODUCTION

A Man Passes By

FOOTSTEPS sound on the hot cement walk. The old lady on the corner pulls up the curtain and looks out. The man is going by.

Now the leaves are thick on the ground; they lie in little piles along the sidewalk, and the footsteps are swishing through them. At the sound, the old lady again pulls up the curtain and looks out. The man is still going by.

Deep snow, cold, crisp and dry as dust, has fallen during the night. Footsteps crunch upon the fine, white snow. Once more the old lady looks out. Still the man is going by.

That man is myself.

For thirty years I have walked the same walk, started from the same point, turned the same corners, reached the same destination, and thought little or nothing of it. Now I begin to see that the one thing to which I have given the least thought–this daily walk which has become so automatic and unconscious a part of my day–has perhaps been one of the most significant things in my life. As I look about me I find very few other men who have traveled the same path as often as I. Or, if they have traveled it, they have long ago availed themselves of labor-saving devices which, up till now, I have scorned–the automobile, the bus, the streetcar.

Now also I begin to see that this street has been rubbing pieces off me, absorbing something of me each time I go by. But I, too, have been absorbing the street, drawing in through my nostrils the odor of the

9

meals being cooked, the scent of gardens, of fresh-cut grass. Through my pores and through my lungs I have been absorbing the very dust of the road, something of the spirit of the road.

Thirty-five years ago I lived in another town and taught in another college. My home was directly across the street from the college. I arrived each morning in my classroom with lungs unextended; blood stagnant. In vain I tried to make up for the lack of exercise by walking up and down the classroom, shouting, gesticulating. But like a clock, unwound, the hands would lag, the main-spring would run down. In vain I made bold resolutions about getting up in time to walk seven blocks before the first class began. Each morning the resolution was recalled to my mind by the ringing of the first bell.

So when I came to the city I determined to correct this situation. I would get a house exactly the right distance from the college, and let necessity be the dictator of my conditioning.

The first question to decide was: what is the perfect distance for a college professor to walk each morning before his first class? A courageous idealist would probably have put it at two miles. But I could see the danger in overdoing any good thing. Two miles would make too easy a temptation to use the streetcar, steal a ride with a neighbor, or buy a little Ford of my own. Remembering the Greek adage, "Measure in all things," I measured off a distance both tempting and temperate—one-half mile. Half a mile one way would mean half a mile the other, and as I had classes both morning and afternoon, this would insure my getting the desired two miles on the hoof.

But where to find a house located at the exact distance required? I began my hunt by patiently stepping off a half mile straight north. This brought me into a noisy, unhomelike streetcar district. One vacant house, bleak and bare, leered out at me. This would never do. North was not the only direction in the world. I still could go east or west or south. So, attaching an imaginary string exactly one-half mile in length to the center of the college campus, and the other to myself, I started forth in much the same manner as a mathematician draws a compass around a sheet of paper. When I had completed the entire circuit and had returned to the bleak house to the north, I had found not a single house to rent or to sell that met my peculiar requirements. Only one vacant lot.

There was an idea! If the right house was not waiting for me to come to it—didn't Mohammed do something of the sort? I bought the lot as a Christmas present for my wife. Surprised her with it. I hoped she would be satisfied when I told her of my perfect plan. And to my surprise she was. Then together we planned the house. I mean my wife and the architect together planned it, and it was built. To our delight, when we were about to move into it, a picture of the house appeared in the morning paper under an advertisement of the architect, labeled, A DREAM HOME COME TRUE.

At that time we had been married several years and had had no children. Therefore, we built the house just a little too large for two—that represented Hope; but not quite big enough for five—that was Prudence. Within a few years we had three children, and since then, the house has been full to the bursting point. However, my advice in all facets of life is to err on the side of Hope rather than on Prudence.

The most permanently active objects along this half mile I traveled daily were the children and the dogs. Many of the dogs, large and small, showed their devotion to their masters and their solicitude for the little children in their care. One dog, however, did not show his singleness of attachment in so attractive a light. He was a short, stocky bull of very vicious, jealous disposition. At times, for no apparent reason whatever, he would go nipping viciously at my heels, or place himself stubbornly in front of me and insist on my coming to a perfect halt. And even then he would not budge in spite of my nice-dogging him in dulcet tones, until the little daughter of the home would come out and call him to her.

But while little dogs nipped at my heels or let me pass with proud indifference, little girls treated me otherwise. Three romances illuminate these years. About every seven years a two-year-old maid would appear along the walk and adopt me as her fairy godfather for a while. At the age of four each little sweetheart would become most fascinating and at seven begin to sweeten and grow sedate, but at ten or twelve she would vanish into the awakening self-consciousness of girlhood.

I believe our friendships should always have the zest of newness upon them. The interchanges of conversation between me and the little girl of the year were simply crammed with this newness. Every meeting was a positive exhibit of newness—new bonnets, new overcoats, new mittens, new shoes, once a new petticoat. At the Christmas season it was always a new toy, never all the toys, always just one, the one closest to the heart. I was always granted the great compliment of being omniscient. Cousins I had never seen were discussed with me, relatives mentioned by their first names. Always I accepted these honors with the benign acquiescence of my all-encompassing intelligence. Elizabeth, Natalie, Evelyn—three little graces, eternally young in my mind.

But of course I have seen people grow older along this road. I was interested to discover between what ages people seemed to change the most. One would naturally imagine that the period between five and twenty-five would reveal the greatest actual transformation and development. But to me the youngster I first knew at five, when he became twenty-five, still had the freshness of childhood clinging to him like the fuzz of the peach. The greatest change seemed to come between twenty-five and fifty. In this period the warmth of youth is replaced by the approaching chill of age. And there is a sadness. As one turns the corner between forty and fifty, so turns the tide of one's life that reveals failure or success.

Then there have been echoes along this road, echoes from another world. Ministers have come along the walk that people might be married. People have died, people have been born. Walt Whitman says, "You road I enter upon and look around, I believe you are not all that is here, I believe that much unseen is also here."

Among the unseen things there were the singing footsteps of Fremont Taylor, the lamplighter. Fremont was one of that group of boys and girls who awaited me at the college end of the walk each day. I was aware that every evening after I had gone into the house and closed the door after me, a lamplighter would come by and light the lamps along the walk. I was aware that every morning before I got up, the footsteps of the same lamplighter passed by as he put out the lights. But I did not know to whom these mysterious footsteps belonged until one day

I asked my boys and girls to write an original verse. Then it was that I found a sheet of paper on my table in Fremont's handwriting.

> I am the wight that lights the lights on the
>   streets and lanes,
> And I patiently tramp from lamp to lamp in the
>   sleets and rains;
>
> All day at the college I seek for knowledge
>   and work like one possessed,
> And then with my torch it is forward march
>   when the sun is low in the west;
>
> At five in the morning at Big Ben's warning
>   I rise up from my bed,
> And hustle about to put the lamps out
>   ere the morning sky is red.

And then the World War broke out, and Fremont took the last long road alone. Others, too, who once walked my road have taken the final trek.

The old lady who first raised the curtain to see the man going by has long since raised the curtain for the last time. If there are others who still lift curtains at the sound of footsteps along the walk, let me give all fair warning. They are not seeing what they think they are seeing. Not just an insignificant, graying man, walking from a house to a college. They are looking upon a still-hopeful lamplighter marching determinedly from lamp to lamp in the streets and lanes.

BOOK ONE

I Assemble My Universe

CHAPTER I

I Assemble My Ancestors

EACH of us is a son of God.

Each of us is a son of Man.

As the former, we are each a focal point through which the infinite resources of God Himself may flow. As the latter, we are each related to every other human being on the face of the earth. Therefore, in writing these pages from my own life, I am actually reporting the experiences of every life. In writing this *auto*-biography of *me*, I am in reality writing a *bi*-ography of *you*.

A famous author when asked to address a group of descendants of the *Mayflower* felt impelled to explain why none of his own ancestors came over in the famous boat:

"I had two grandfathers and two grandmothers," was the purport of his remarks. "Four great grandfathers and four great grandmothers, and back in 1620 I had sixty-four great, great, great, great grandfathers and sixty-four great, great, great, great grandmothers. When it came time for the *Mayflower* to sail, all these great, great, grandparents packed up and came down to the dock, fully intending to come to America. But when they reached the ship, the skipper told them that the *Mayflower* would hold only one hundred and one passengers. Then my sixty-four great, great, great, great grandfathers said they would not go without the sixty-four great, great, great, great grandmothers, so they all picked up their bags and walked straight back to their homes."

I have traced my own parentage back in this fan-shaped way, and then traced my descent, also fan-shaped, from all these forebears, and the general effect of the two fan movements—one back and up, and the other forward and down, is to reveal that I am at least a thirtieth cousin to every Anglo-Saxon man and woman. I have no doubt whatever that should I trace these genealogical fans back to the Ark instead of the *Mayflower*, I would find myself a one-thousandth cousin to all mankind upon the face of the earth.

And so, Cousin, this front door autobiography of me that you think you are reading is really a back door biography of you.

In assembling my own great-grands, I am not going to assemble all of them. I admit that I am doing a lot of picking and choosing. Out of the past there looms one picture which I treasure above all others. It was brought to me in the words of Herbert Booth Smith, former Moderator of the Presbyterian Church of America. "The black plague that devastated London was sweeping over Scotland," he writes. "The people of Dundee saw it approach from the west in the form of a great black cloud. They fell on their knees and cried to the cloud to pass them by, but it came ever nearer. Then they looked around for the most holy man among them to intervene with God on their behalf. They wanted a holy man—somebody whose prayer-handwriting God was acquainted with—somebody who didn't have to be introduced to God. All eyes turned to George Wishart and he stood up, the old account tells us, stretching his arms to the cloud, and prayed, and it rolled back."

This "holy man," who later became the teacher of John Knox, the founder of the Presbyterian Church, was described in the words of Knox, as a "man of such graces as before were never heard of within this realm, yea, and are rare to be found yet in any man."

One night he and John Knox were driving to Dumbarton together. Arriving there, he turned to Knox. "Good-by forever," he said. "I go to where danger awaits me. If I should die, I shall ask the Blessed Savior to give all Scotland to you."

The young man never saw him again. But from that time on, Scotland belonged to John Knox.

George Wishart became the first martyr to the Protestant church in Scotland. What did he think about as he was lashed to the stake, as his eyes looked far off, south and west? May he not have seen dimly in the prophetic light which had come to him so acutely in the past few hours, a new, daring race! I can almost hear him saying, "Lay fast on God," as he saw that new land unfolding into its own across the seas; "Lay fast on God, lay fast on God," and so he died.

He did not see tiny me–three hundred years away–across that sea, across that time. All he saw that hour was God. Only as I grow close to God will he ever see me. It matters not that there was blood in him that day that is now flowing in me. Only as the love of Christ that was in him that day is now flowing in me are we truly related. For who is my mother and my brother and my sister and my descendant but he that doeth the will of the Father?

Another ancestor whom I treasure highly is Jonathan Edwards, not because of his masterpiece, *The Freedom of the Will*, which has been called "the one large contribution which America has made to the deep philosophic thought of the world," not because he was the first president of Princeton, but because of his beautiful home life and the profound love and devotion husband and wife had for each other. The Edwards' home has been described as one of the very few examples of a spiritual leader whose wife was in perfect accord with her husband in all things. Socrates had his Xanthippe and Charles Wesley had his Sarah, and in between comes a long list of saints, whose martyrdom did not always consist of the lions or the burning stake. The love of Jonathan for his wife was just a little less than his love for God, and she in turn merged herself into his life with absolute devotion. The children from such a union, conceived in the love of God as well as in the love of man and woman, are the kind of children who will ultimately nourish the life and spirit of their nation unto the thousandth generation.

These ancestors were not perfect. They had their faults; they made their mistakes. Much of the persecution they encountered, they undoubtedly brought upon themselves. Wishart's condemnation of beauty of form and of ritual, Edwards' sermons on the horrors of hell, awoke revolt not only against the speakers, but against the entire religious and spiritual program of their day. Every effort to define, to limit, to corral, to point judgment, was as barren as dead stalks of corn after the grain has been garnered. But now that they are gone, nothing but the seed corn need be treasured.

Three "cousins" of mine sat in the White House: John Adams, John Quincy Adams, and Rutherford B. Hayes. Each one got in by the skin of his teeth, and each one went out with a bang. Not one was re-elected.

Of these three, it is my cousin Rutherford B. Hayes, whose administration I would especially commend to every incoming president as a fitting model upon which to plan his administration. He had the distinction, according to all historians, of appointing the most perfect cabinet that any president ever gathered around him. His biographer, H. J. Eckenrode, writes:

> He brought to an end the scandal of the reconstruction period. He cleansed the government of the pervasive corruption which had established itself during the Grant administration, he re-established the authority of the president over the Congressional oligarchy, he put the war-inflated currency back on a sound money basis, he introduced the previously scorned element of good faith into the nation's dealings with the Indians, he defied and vetoed the attempts of California to exclude the Chinese until after a mutual treaty with China had made such a policy accord with international fair dealing, and he brought sadly lacking standards of morality into public life. Of course, in doing all this he made his re-nomination for a second term impossible. But that seems never to have bothered Hayes. He was that rare phenomenon—a public man who always did what he thought was right simply because he thought it was right and without the least regard to personal consequences. Hayes was beyond question one of the half-dozen great presidents of the United States.

When I was a boy there was only one man I wished I had descended from but couldn't because he never married. He was George Rogers Clark. But this bachelor hero of mine had an uncle who married twice, and had thirty children, *twenty-eight* of whom were boys. As my great, great grandfather Clark came from the same county in North Carolina where these twenty-eight grew to manhood, and as this county at that time was sparsely settled, I don't see how I could have escaped being related to them! True, this is what the courts would call circumstantial evidence, but here I believe that the "circumstances" are somewhat numerically in my favor.

Because I am deeply interested in the spiritual welfare of this nation, I am deeply grateful to God for letting my ancestor, James Wilson (with the aid of Gouverneur Morris) write the final draft of the Constitution of the United States. Few people know that he used the Constitution of the Presbyterian Church founded by John Knox under the guidance and inspiration of George Wishart, as his chief model, making comparatively few and only minor alterations necessary for adapting a religious document to a political situation.

Another ancestor of mine who sat with Wilson and Adams in the famous Continental Congress was Roger Sherman of Connecticut, the only one who signed all four major documents in American history, the Articles of Confederation, the Declaration of Independence, the Constitution, and the Ordinance of 1787.

I like to think of myself, and of you, my cousin reader, as born with our bodies swathed and supported by sinews made strong by the energy of forebears who created with ax and plow a new nation, physically and materially, and with our brains, grooved by brain paths made by forebears who had carved and created a new nation mentally and spiritually.

But before I came into this world, an amazing interlude occurred between the period of the founding of the nation and the creation of the modern world into which I was to be born. It was one of the most startling reversions of history that the world has ever known.

People reared in a civilization of the very highest, bred and nourished in a culture that had created a Shakespeare, a Spenser and a Milton, were plunged again into a darkness of the wilderness. Having once emerged from the forest trails of the Goths and Saxons and from the Viking ships of the Scandinavians, these pioneers rose to the heights of the Elizabethan civilization and produced in the British Isles a highly enlightened Empire. Then suddenly a whole section of that population was plunged again into the wilderness of a new world where most of the old cultures were cast aside. Those of them who found their way into the southern mountains remained in this semidarkness for several hundred years. Those who took the northern trails in covered wagons were lost in the shadows for only a century.

As I look backward over the time that has elapsed between the establishing of the Constitution and now, this is what I see:

A splendid, cultured group of folk stepping from the very highest known sphere of literature and culture of England and Scotland into the forest frontiers of North America. I see them discard all their delicacies, refinements, and cultures as a man sheds a garment before he takes a dip in the sea. Then I see these adventurous folk a generation or two later emerge with big rough hands, a primitive callousness to blood, their own or another's, cutting the throat of their swine, shooting down the wolves that preyed too near their cabins, laboring in grease and sweat, vigorous, tremendously vital and alive. I see them receiving as a beggar receives, the stint of religion doled out to them by the coarse-grained, good-intentioned circuit riders who followed in the footsteps of the Wesley disciples. These riders with the Bible in their saddlebags were lean, earnest devout men, but without their leader's culture and restraint and charm. Theirs was a shouting, emotional religion much like the strong cider that in those days found its way to the stomach and veins of the pioneering men.

I can picture one of them, a pioneer sitting in the back of a country store, talking politics with a gathering of his neighbors, telling stories or listening to them—wincing just a bit at times as echoes of his cultured ancestors wakened in his nervous system little twitches of rebellion against the coarseness and crudeness of it all, but compromising slowly with his environment, coming down, down, down to the primitive, a little closer each day.

And his wife, bending over the kitchen stove, using far too often the frying pan, a crime against digestion and sound judgment unknown to the simpler Europeans, expressing her frustration in impatience, sharpness and driving energy as she worked away her life—a life consisting chiefly of breeding and rearing many children. I can see my own Grandmother Clark with her suppressed craving for higher things receiving her only intake through the Bible and *Saint's Rest* while all about her was nothing but grinding toil. I never saw this grandmother of mine who descended from George Wishart, tied in holy matrimony to my grandfather who was related to George Rogers Clark, but I have seen a daguerreotype, and oh, how the Hamlet cried out in the face of that suppressed grandmother of mine!

There they came, my ancestors, my father's and my father's fathers', like creatures crossing the Stygian pond, while the devils of their primitive and savage environment fly above them with three-pronged forks to thrust down their heads whenever they try to lift them high enough to catch a glimpse of the blue sky of culture and vistas of beauty and the arts.

CHAPTER II

I Assemble My Parents

My GRANDFATHER, Glenn Clark, was born in Kentucky April 2, 1800. Nine years later, almost within a stone's throw of where he lived, Lincoln was born. A year later, in the same locality, Jefferson Davis was born. Thus my grandfather acquires geographical distinction.

The first of the three to leave this locality was Abraham Lincoln, and, by a throw of fate, he moved north into Indiana. Next the family of Jefferson Davis left this territory, and by a throw of fate, moved south into Mississippi. Finally in 1825, my grandfather with his wife and a little newborn baby moved across the Ohio into southern Indiana not far from where Thomas Lincoln, a poor carpenter with a kit of tools and several hundred gallons of whisky and a little child named Abraham, had previously moved. Grandmother rode in the wagon, driving the horses, with the cow tied to the tail gate, and grandfather walked, driving a small bunch of sheep. Five years after grandfather reached Indiana, Abraham Lincoln moved on into Illinois. Years later Abraham Lincoln and Jefferson Davis were destined to lead the two halves of this great nation into the bloodiest civil war of all history. And while the four brothers-in-law of Abraham Lincoln chose to march under the banners of Jefferson Davis, the four sons of my grandfather chose to march under the banners of Lincoln. So closely interwoven are the lives of all Americans and yet so far apart!

Grandfather had saved a little money with which he bought one hundred and twenty acres of land from the government for two dollars an acre, fifty cents cash down and the balance over a long time. When the family reached their land they were alone in the forest, only one other family within ten miles.

To build his cabin grandfather cut logs out of trees the same size, twelve feet long for the ends of the cabin and fourteen feet long for the sides. He laid the two first end logs at the proper places, trimmed or edged the upper side near the ends, so as to fit perfectly a corresponding notch cut on the underside of the first two logs for the sides. When these four logs were thus placed in position the foundation for the cabin was complete. He then prepared logs enough for the entire house with edges and notches to fit into each other when the cabin went up. When all the logs were thus prepared, he mounted a horse and struck out to find men to come to his first house-raising.

After the house was up, grandfather split or rived boards three feet long and six inches wide with which to make a roof. There were no shingles or nails. The first course of boards was laid and a straight pole placed on them and tied or secured in position to hold this course firmly in place. Then the second course was laid lapping six inches over the first and secured in like manner with another pole, and other courses were laid until the house was completely covered. The floor was mother earth. The chimney was built of sticks, but plastered on the inside with mortar made of yellow clay and water.

The windows were square holes cut in the walls and covered with thin paper or thin white muslin. The single doorway was an opening cut in the wall, eased with a slab of wood secured by wooden pegs driven into the ends of the logs. The door was made of split boards, which was hung on wooden hinges and swung out. It was fastened by a wooden latch which fell in a notch in the inside, and was raised from the outside by a string which always hung out.

A necessary article of furniture for this cabin was a bedstead. Only one post was required. It was set up four feet from one wall and six feet from another wall. Two large holes were bored into this post two feet from the ground; and two holes opposite these in the walls, and into these holes were inserted two poles, smoothed with a drawing knife, one four feet and the other six feet long. This structure constituted a frame upon which were placed split boards for the bed to rest upon.

With a cabin for shelter and a bed to sleep on, the next indispensable thing was bread. My grandfather knew his bread was in the ground, beneath the forest where he was to dig for it. In digging for that bread he began by cutting out the underbrush and cutting down all the trees that were eighteen inches or less in diameter. When the timber was cleared off and the ground ready for planting, the stumps were so close together that the hoe was the only instrument with which to plant and cultivate the first crop. This was the heaviest timbered region in all the state, and the labor of clearing the ground was my grandfather's absorbing work for many years. When he had finally got a little patch cleared and raised his first crop of corn, then began a fight with the squirrels and raccoons to save his hard-earned grain. He kept his loaded rifle always close at hand, and shooting squirrels in self-defense furnished plenty of squirrel meat for the table. The coons ravaged the corn at night, which made it necessary to provide himself with dogs to hunt them down. Thus coon-hunting by men and boys at night with their own coon dogs furnished fun and excitement. No need of theaters and moving picture shows when a coon hunt was in sight!

After my grandfather had a little farm established, he built a log blacksmith shop. He drove one hundred miles to Lawrenceburg, a trading station on the Ohio River, and secured the tools and iron for everything he needed. He made horseshoes and horseshoe nails. He shod his own horses and those of his neighbors, made plows, harrows, hoes, shovels, forks—in fact, everything necessary for use on the farm. He also brought home from Lawrenceburg a shoemaker's outfit. During rainy days and evenings he made shoes for grandmother and the girls and boots for himself and the boys. When he found he needed a good deal of leather for shoes, harnesses and other things, he constructed a tanning vat, gathered the kind of bark necessary to make good leather, collected a few hides and made the leather required for all the needs of the farm.

Grandmother took the wool which my father sheared from the sheep, dyed it with the walnut ooze, carded it by hand cardboards into rolls, spun it on a large spinning wheel into yarn thread, wove it on a hand loom into a web of durable jeans cloth. She then cut this cloth and made of it winter garments for each member of the family, including headwear for males and females. From the yarn she knitted stockings and socks for all alike in the family. She also wove blankets for all the beds from this homemade yarn.

To provide sheets and summer wear, my grandfather each year raised a patch of flax. When the flax was ripe, he pulled it by hand and spread it in rows or swathes on the ground for the straw to dry and rot. He then broke and hackled it, thus producing a quantity of clear, clean fiber. This fiber grandmother spun on a small spinning wheel into fine linen thread. From this thread she wove great webs of strong, durable linen cloth, from which she made sheets and summer clothing for everyone of the family. From this thread she also knit summer socks and stockings for all. Also from hemp grandfather made rope of different sizes for clotheslines, bed cord and other purposes.

The winter caps were made out of the jeans cloth and the summer hats were made out of oat straw, braided into narrow strips and sewed into wide-brimmed hats fitted to the heads of little and big girls and boys and parents.

The artificial light in my grandfather's home came from the open fireplace, or from a rag in a saucer of lard. Tallow dips or molded candles were a later innovation. Bread was made from a coarse corn meal, produced by a hand grater. Wild turkeys, squirrels and an occasional deer furnished the meat. The only drink was milk and water, with now and then a tea made from spice brush or sassafras.

There was always, once a year, a "hog-killing time" when meat was provided for the entire year. That day was followed by the putting up of sausage and the smoking of the hams, shoulders and sides in the old smokehouse until they were beautifully cured and browned, so that they kept sweet and good until hog-killing time came again the next December. That day was an event each year. From eight to ten young hogs were required for the family. It was a hard and exciting day's work, commencing before daylight and closing after dark—leaving a row of white, clean porkers hanging in perfect line to become cold in the frosty winter night.

Suspended to the joists in the cabin hung a framework of nicely smoothed poles one foot apart. On these, in the early winter season, rich golden pumpkins hung in long thin slices to dry for pies and stewing. And later on, when the orchard trees began to bear abundant fruit, the roof was covered with apples and peaches nicely pared and cut into suitable sized pieces for sun drying, and in quantities sufficient to last until the fruit season came around again. Thus grandfather and grandmother, always frugal and forehanded, provided dried pumpkins, dried fruit, and filled the cellar with apples, potatoes, turnips, cabbages and other vegetables, besides a barrel or two of cider, a quantity of popcorn and other things needed for winter use.

For years corn meal was the only provision for bread. Kentucky corndodgers and hoecake furnished the staple bread supply. Mush and milk, which provided the evening meal for the family, was a luxury after a hard day's work, and was sufficiently soporific to make sleep sound and restful. Later on a grist mill was set up, at which wheat could be ground into flour. Then the family began to raise wheat in small quantities. A fine grove of sugar trees was found in the wood pasture and from the flow of the sap in the early spring they made sugar and syrup enough to last the family through the year. Thus my grandparents could have built a Chinese wall around their farm and have lived comfortably within its boundaries, asking favors of no man.

Twelve children were born into this home (besides the one who died in Kentucky), eight daughters and four sons. About every fourth or fifth year another log cabin was added on to make room for the new arrivals. But by 1851 the family had outgrown the little farm of one hundred and twenty acres, and by that time they began to hear of beautiful prairie lands in Iowa with its rich acres ready for the plow, where there were no forests and stumps and rocks to contend with. And so in 1855, selling his little farm for $100 an acre, and putting in a claim for Iowa land that could be purchased for $1.20 an acre, Glenn Clark put his little family consisting now of eight—as most of the oldest daughters had married as soon as they reached the age of fifteen—into two covered wagons and an open buggy, and joined the great caravan going west. They started the journey in August and reached their destination in October of that year, a two-months' trek which in a modern, six-cylinder "covered wagon" would require one day.

By the year 1860 both my grandfather and grandmother had died. Then my father, nineteen years old, sold his only belongings– a calf and a saddle–and with that money as sole asset entered Iowa Wesleyan where he worked his way through a year of college. That spring he answered Lincoln's first call for volunteers and took part in the first Iowa regiment's march to Wilson's Creek to save Missouri for the Union. After participation in seventeen battles, during four years under Grant and Sherman, he took part in the last battle of the Civil War, the charge on Fort Blakely, fought several hours after Lee had already surrendered to Grant on the same day.

It was not until his regiment marched into Selma, Alabama, on the 21st day of April, over a week later, that news reached him of the surrender of Lee's army and of the truce between Sherman and Johnson. Father was not well, and a kindly gentleman invited him to occupy a room in his house. That day news came that Lincoln was assassinated, and in the evening father's host revealed the fact that he was Colonel Todd, a brother of Mrs. Lincoln, and an officer of the Southern Army. He spoke of Lincoln's assassination with great grief, and then in that courtly, cultured Southern fashion of the day, quoted from Macbeth, substituting the name of Lincoln for that of Duncan:

> Besides, this Lincoln
> Hath borne his faculties so meek, hath been
> So clear in his great office, that his virtues
> Will plead like angels, trumpet-tongu'd against
> The deep damnation of his taking-off:
> And pity, like a naked new-born babe,
> Striding the blast, or heaven's cherubin, hors'd
> Upon the sightless couriers of the air,
> Shall blow the horrid deed in every eye,
> That tears shall drown the wind.

At the same identical hour, on the same identical day, in the little town of Carlinville in southern Illinois, my grandfather Egbert Page closed his store for the day and secluded himself in his room in a day of mourning for his beloved friend.

Eight years before, Grandfather Page and Lincoln had met for the first time. One day my mother, then a little girl of five, was looking out of the window and saw her father, who was a tall man of six feet two, talking with another man taller than he. Grandfather brought his guest into the house and left him seated in the front room with my mother while he went to the kitchen to bring his wife in. While he was gone the stranger picked my mother up on his lap and told her stories. When her parents returned, grandfather introduced him to grandmother as Abraham Lincoln.

In 1942 I visited Carlinville for the first time and in the front yard of my mother's childhood home I saw a huge rock with the inscription, "Here Abraham Lincoln addressed the citizens of Carlinville in 1858 in his campaign against Douglas for the Senate." Mother told me how the people crowded her front porch and of the deep impression Lincoln made upon them all. When the war broke out a few years later she vowed that when she grew up she was going to marry one of Lincoln's captains and she renewed the vow at the time of his death. Little did she know that the captain that God had selected for her was in that very hour mourning the death of Lincoln in the home of Lincoln's brother-in-law in Selma, Alabama. This background partly accounts for the fact that in my boyhood home the name of Abraham Lincoln was revered only second to the name of Jesus of Nazareth.

But where do I come in? That came about in this wise: My mother's family moved from Illinois to Iowa City, and my father, instead of returning to Iowa Wesleyan after the war, went to Ohio Wesleyan where he graduated in 1868. But finally he came to Iowa City to study law and graduated as valedictorian in the first law class ever to graduate from Iowa University. After he graduated he married a Miss Hutchinson and to them a child was born, Robert Glenn. Then his wife died of childbirth fever, and a few weeks later little Glenn died.

Then a girl named Fannie Page moved to Des Moines at the time when father was investigating the comparative merits of Des Moines and St. Louis as possible places to hang out his shingle. I can never forget when I was a boy with what awful suspense I read through that part of my father's diary. A great fear came to me that he would not select Des Moines where Fannie Page was living. Probably because I was up in heaven–waiting–watching–pulling–drawing them together. I accomplished the job, but what a hard job it was! However, I have this much to say for myself: after the job was finally accomplished it turned out to be one of the best, if not the very best, jobs I ever did. For the marriage proved to be marvelously happy and the home that resulted was one of the most heavenly homes ever established on this earth.

It was the year of the Centennial of America's Independence, when father and mother were married. Their wedding journey took them to the Philadelphia Exposition. Then they set up their home in Des Moines. Their first child was named Laura, but we called her Dot. The second child came on the 13th of March, 1882, and they called him Egbert Glenn for his two grandfathers, just as the first Glenn had been named for *his* two grandfathers.

Next came Page, then Helen, and then the twins, Mabel and Morton. That made six, but father and mother wanted twelve. However, when the next one, little Jamie, died at birth, they took that as a sign from heaven that perhaps six were enough.

Father had a good income as a member of the law firm of Cole, MacVey and Clark, and had invested his captain's savings in real estate that rose in value as settlers continued to arrive. Moreover, cooks in those days could be hired for three dollars a week and nursegirls for two dollars a week, so that mother very rarely spent any time in the kitchen. Darning stockings, planning meals and cleaning house, besides looking after her six children, kept her time well occupied.

A revolver cracked in an eastern railroad station, and President Garfield fell fatally wounded; a terrible cyclone swept through the nearby college town of Grinnell; and while the entire nation was getting excited over these important events, I was born. No horns were blown and no bands played. It is at this point that my autobiography really begins.

CHAPTER III

I Assemble My World

I SHALL never forget what difficulty I had assembling my world. First of all, my world was pretty well made up of quadrupeds. At the age of two I have one of my first vivid memories, seeing father bring home a small thoroughbred Jersey cow. Brocade was her name, and as the years went on she grew somewhat in stature and tremendously in output until she was producing eight gallons of milk a day, one-third of it rich cream, not a drop of it wasted by our ever-growing family. Each year she had a calf, and all but one of them were heifers; and if each one of her fifteen heifers produced off-spring in the same ratio and milk in the same quantity, I dare say that half the butter produced in Iowa today bears the Brocade trade mark.

Fascinated, I watched my father wash her udder and teats carefully before he applied his strong, deft fingers to wringing forth the milk to the tune of the vibrant singing bucket, nor did he stop till the four gallons night and morning were ready to pour into the crocks. The great bubbling creamy top was always enticing to my childish tongue, and father often took a cup and dipped off a mug full of its foaming surface for us to drink, in all its warmth and sweetness.

Then there was old Charley the horse, flicking the flies from his white sides as he munched the corn in his stall, occasionally turning a casual eye upon the clustering tots looking up at him. The reading of *Black Beauty* finally "canonized" Charley and he moved in a mist of quadruped sanctity for years.

Kittens came into our lives, and finally a pup named Dandy, who grew into a Scotch terrier. When we returned home from any journey he welcomed us not by letting his body wag his tail but by letting his tail wag his entire body. For us he was distinguished from all other dogs by his human way of unsheathing his teeth in an actual smile.

Then there was the world of insects. We loved to catch butterflies and put them in little cages, not knowing that the flutter of their wings against the inhibiting screens reduced their period of life in this world. Nor did we know that their full allotted span of life was measured in hours and days. Had we known that we would not have interrupted them even for one short hour. Grasshoppers were fun to catch and squeeze gently till they would spit tobacco, after which we would permit them to go. But our chief absorption was in ants which we loved to watch building their homes, and in flies which continually seemed to be waging unequal war with the spiders.

Spiders and spider webs, especially thick in the barn, were our special nightmares, and their webs, spiraling back into deep, dark grottos, were our particular infernos. We would gaze hypnotized with horror into the deep, curling labyrinth in their thickest webs, down deep, deep into a corridor where sat the grim old villain awaiting his prey. And when the luckless fly got entangled and the hairy monster rushed out to throw his meshes over him, how we shuddered, transfixed with horror! Often we liberated the fly, but usually it died very quickly as a result of some hidden poison the spider had injected into it. Some nights I would awake in a sweat after a dream of being caught in some tremendous net, and from which I would wiggle into consciousness just in time to escape the gigantic crawling creature which tried to envelop me.

The geographical world into which I was born was a difficult and baffling world to get acquainted with. Of course we assumed, as all sensible men from Ptolemy down to Columbus had assumed before us, that the world was flat. When one of our elders first told us that the world was round, we refused to believe him. Then when we found that all our elders agreed with this heresy we naturally inferred that we lived on the *inside* of the ball, as otherwise we would certainly fall off.

But when we were told the reverse was true, we began to believe that wonders would never cease. After my sister Helen heard that we were upside down at night she used to hang on to her bed very tightly with her chubby hands, lest she fall off and never get back again.

"And on the other side of the world, just through the ground on which we stand, is China," we were told. This set us off into a wild scramble of adventure. A rock in our pasture intrigued our imagination. We dug and dug, and finally got down to where, with enough levers, we might possibly roll the rock out. All aflutter with excitement over the certainty that through the hole made by the removal of this rock, we were sure we would be able to peer into China. We had more fun exploring China in imagination than we ever expect to get from actually seeing the land of Cathay in the flesh. But, alas, the rock was too heavy to move and to this day not one of us children has ever seen China.

Thus we struggled with this old world, until gradually bit by bit we began to assemble it in order as it properly belonged. But while I was adjusting myself to this outer world, I was also encountering an inner one, which was equally absorbing and intricate and difficult to understand.

From the time I was two I had the gift of creating and bringing forth images as vivid in the darkness as any figures in broad daylight. I could wish a dog to appear and he would appear. In fact, I could visualize and produce any person I wished at will. As I grew a little older, this power gave me a wonderful opportunity to recreate past ages whenever I so desired. Men in doublet and hose, swashbuckling nobles, armored knights, all had their day. But it was more often the animal world I conjured forth than the human one. However, I found to my consternation that my skills had one limitation. I could control my puppet's entrances, but not their exits. Therefore when in a burst of adventurous or morbid curiosity I invited a bear to enter I could not make him depart. My next discovery was that my fears were as powerful as my wishes, and when I feared that a bear might look at me he invariably would. And his gaze would transfix me with horror! Such experiences usually ended by my calling my mother and in response to her kindly words I would explain that there had been a bear in the room. At this she would smile and say, "It is just your imagination,

Glenn," but she had no idea how vivid and real my imagination was. No one I ever met in life or literature until I read De Quincey's *Confessions of an Opium Eater*, could know how vivid my imagination was.

I finally devised a method for ridding me of the bear who would not leave. I would conjure up a lion and set them upon each other. All then went well unless the morbid fear would creep into my mind that they *both* might stop fighting and look at me. Invariably this fear became father to the fact. Then both mother and father would be summoned double-quick! However, I learned the lesson early that what you want comes true if you want it strongly enough, and also the corollary of this fact, that what you fear comes to you, if you fear it strongly enough. Fear, according to my experience, is merely the opposite expression of desire.

The next world we explored was the world of books. *Black Beauty* was the first book to ease us into this world of make believe. Then *Little Women*, *Robinson Crusoe* and *Swiss Family Robinson* carried us into the world of social and physical adjustment. After that came the *Oliver Optic* books which opened the Civil War in story. Father had already made it real by his tales of Wilson Creek, Vicksburg and Mobile. And then began a parallel development: Cooper's *Leather-stocking Tales*, read around the evening lamp to the family as a whole, and Henty's books, read by ourselves alone. I read *In Freedom's Cause* by Henty seven times until I could shut my eyes and reproduce each title of each chapter from memory, and could expand each chapter into every incident and adventure, almost word for word. This story of the fight of Bruce and Wallace for Scotland's freedom thrilled my boyish blood, but more than all, the story of the boy hero, Archibald Forbes, who trained his boy friends into capable wielders of the sword and spear so that when they became lads in the teens their prowess was irresistible, especially thrilled and inspired me. The theme that it touched off in me was this: *train for something in secret when you are young and when the crisis comes in later life you will be ready.* So in my imagination I began to train myself for possible situations, and saw myself emerging in the next war as a major general, riding at the head of many battalions.

With Charley MacVey, the son of my father's law partner, I made swords out of lathes and shields out of boards; we trained ourselves in the most arduous combats for weeks and weeks. I believe I could step into an Olympian fencing contest tomorrow and come off with glory, so thorough and so intense was the training Charley put me through. Finally he and I organized a band of boys known as the "Knights of Sparta" and all of us read *Rupert of Hensau* and *The Prisoner of Zenda* which in different ways we dramatized and acted out among ourselves.

When it came to the *Leatherstocking Tales* the world took on its first great unfoldment. Without my knowing it I presume I had been living over in chronological sequence the whole history of our nation, and in Natty Bumpo, hero of *The Deerslayer*, I found myself launched into the dark virgin forests of my own native land where my brothers and sisters and I trecked over narrow paths and broke through forests and found tracks of bison and redskins, as our own forefathers had done. Our family moved at this time into the country where the oak trees shut out the sky, with a deep ravine on one side and a little glen on the other. Through the dense jungles of the ravine and through the forests that skirted it we lived over and over again the stories of *The Last of the Mohicans*, *The Pathfinder* and *The Pioneer*.

Out of these books I assembled for myself my own spiritual ancestors. If it is true that we take on the traits that we admire in our childhood, and if Alexander the Great *did* sleep with Homer's story of Achilles under his pillow, and if Napoleon slept with the story of Alexander the Great under *his* pillow, then the books under my pillow and the characters that strode across the pages of the books I loved were my true lineal ancestors just as much as Jonathan Edwards and George Wishart.

Why shouldn't we choose our ancestors? Personally, I think there should be a course required of every pupil in the public schools, in the art of selecting his ancestors. In this course it should be made clear to each one that the great men of history whom one admires have more to do with the forming of one's character than the men who just happened by some accident of proximity to be his actual forebears.

Now there happen to be two ancestral ingredients that go to make up "me."

The first ingredient is admiration for the courage that protects the rights of the oppressed. Gideon is my first ancestor. I do not know whether I admire him with his three hundred the more, or Leonidas with his three hundred, but I am sure that one of my four grandparents descended from some hero who fought with three hundred men at his back. But into this line of heroic patriotism there is just a dash of the old Nick too, and a dash given expression to by Sertorius who defied Rome, William Tell who defied tyrants, and Robin Hood who defied the rich.

These spiritual ancestors of mine came from nearly every country under the sun but they all came to a focus in the dashing figures of Wallace and Bruce of our own beloved Scotland. Under the spreading branches of my family tree I find that I do belong to the line of these Scottish heroes, although by no means as directly as my beloved friend and colleague, Dr. James Wallace, whose father actually was a Wallace and whose mother actually was a Bruce.

The other class of spiritual ancestors that I chose to love and admire were those men of such high integrity that "their word was as good as their bond." Chief and foremost of these was Cato the Younger, who was so honest that when his enemies had a suit against him they preferred to have him act as judge, trusting his fairness above all others, even in a case in which he himself was involved. Alfred the Great, King Arthur and our own Honest Abe Lincoln belonged to this line.

Coming nearer home, George Rogers Clark in his audacious capture of Vincennes had that perfect combination of patriotism and jaunty adventurousness that appealed so much to my boyish imagination. The pioneer-hero fiber came down to me through my father's line—my hero-captain whose boyhood exploits of breaking wild horses and out-wrestling all the champions of his county were music to my ears. The integrity-fiber came down through my mother's line. Her father, my grandfather Egbert Page, after cashing a large check one day in the Carlinville Bank, returned to the cashier and reported that a big mistake had been made.

"I am sorry," said the cashier, "but no corrections can be made after you have left the bank."

"But," remonstrated grandfather, "the mistake runs up into

hundreds of dollars."

"I am sorry, but you heard what our rule is. I can do nothing for you."

When grandfather reached the door he turned and remarked, "You might be interested to know that the mistake was in my favor."

"Oh!" exclaimed the bank cashier, his manner completely changed, "I am sure that the correction can be made. Come back and we will see what can be done about it."

Years later when grandfather's merchandise store failed he refused to take advantage of the newly-passed bankruptcy law, and through years of industry and careful economy he finally paid his creditors to the last cent.

In my own life, upon many a football field and later as a coach, I had plenty of opportunities to lead the attack in the spirit of Gideon, or the defense in the spirit of Leonidas, depending upon which way the score was going. And three times when rival teams had difficulties in finding a competent referee, they asked me to act the part of a modern Cato. The distinction, I claim, really belongs to my assorted ancestors whose tough fiber can sustain the generations.

CHAPTER IV

I Assemble Myself

I WAS around seven when a question slapped me squarely in the face.

Why was I, I? When I pinched myself I could feel pain; when I pinched my sisters I could hear them squeal but I had no positive knowledge that they really could feel pain. I couldn't feel for them, and so far as my own conscious evidence went, I was the only person in the universe able to feel pain. Maybe I was the only conscious person in the universe. The only person I felt sure of existing beside myself was God.

So far as I knew, all the people I met might be just as unreal as the people in books or as the people in my dreams. Meg and Jo and Beth and Amy in *Little Women* were very real to me, and when my heart was broken over the death of little Beth, my parents told me not to grieve too much, as she was only make-believe. If the characters so vivid in books were all make-believe, and if the people in my dreams were merely phantoms, how did I know that people I saw on the street were not just fantasies and make-believe?

If that were so, why wear myself out over other people's suffering when it might all be a dream? Why ache over other people's aches when I couldn't be really sure that their aches were real? All I was sure of was that God existed and I existed. He had to exist because He made me.

But why did He make me, me? Why didn't He make me the little ragamuffin who had a drunken father and never had enough to eat? Why didn't He make me Harry, who got drowned? If I got drowned, all the sunlight would go out of the world so far as I was concerned. So far as I was concerned, the world would end when I ended. All alone in the world with God made me feel very lonely.

If I was I, God must certainly have some great and mighty work to do through me. As I could not answer these baffling questions, I had better at least get busy and do whatever I could for God.

Later in life the thought occurred to me that perhaps there is only *one* consciousness in this world, and we are *all* parts of that one consciousness. Perhaps all that does exist is God and I. And God and you. And God and everybody, each an individual human soul, made perfect in that Oneness of which we are all a part.

I know now I had touched at the age of seven a great beam of cosmic consciousness. I had seen a great light. Boylike, I didn't hold it, but it reappeared to me from time to time, and that light has lighted my path more or less ever since. And that light spelled out six illumined words: *I and my Father are One!*

I was early introduced to three great realities–Life, Death and the Creative Imagination.

One day when I was two years old I was sitting in the lap of my nursegirl playing with toys. Growing tired, I leaned against her bosom to sleep. She, too, was sleepy. I suddenly started back with fright and stared at her. My impression was that she must be dying. Her placid face did not share my concern. Her breast, or something inside of her, was heaving, heaving. Again I touched her. Up and down she went in slow, mighty swells. Now she nodded and her eyes were shut. I feared she was going to burst, explode. I slid down quietly and hurried to tell my mother of the impending catastrophe. To my surprise, she only smiled and replied, "Anna is breathing, that is all." Then followed another explanation, and I was initiated into the mysteries of the human system, especially the function of the lungs. Still unconvinced that the sleeping Anna was not in dire danger, I tried by mighty inhalations to make my own little breast heave up and down. Only a mild response could I obtain. But it was sufficient to prove to me that my mother was right. Surely I–and Anna–and the world–were wonderfully and fearfully made. That was Life!

Hardly more startling was my introduction to Death. One day I was taken by mother to a home on Eighth Street on the hill. It was the first time I remembered being in another home. I believe I could retrace my steps to it now, although I have never been there since. In the house was a little girl playing on the floor. I don't know if she could talk much or if I could at that time, for we didn't say anything to each other as I recollect, but played silently and watched each other out of big, wondering eyes. I thought she was the prettiest sort of creature. It probably hadn't occurred to me that such sweet little creatures existed. I was flattered by her offer to let me use her playthings.

Several weeks afterward I asked mother if she wouldn't take me to see the little girl again. She hesitated and then said, "You can never see the little girl again," I asked why. She replied, "Because she is dead." I asked what that meant. Then followed a long explanation. I went off to my little bed that night with the terrible mysteries of life and death, mysteries of the earthly and eternal life, throbbing in my temples. I felt a suffocating sorrow for my little friend of Eighth Street hill, not now there, but somewhere else. I was also filled with a new and majestic sorrow for myself–and a fearful shrinking of my warm body from the ice-cold fingers of the dread intruder, Death. This was only the beginning of many nights of fearful dreams and haunting fears. A vast fact–immense, incomprehensible, unbelievable, expressed in an offhand, casual way–had come tumbling into my little childish brain, and for days I could not get over the injustice, the wastefulness and the awfulness of it–but above all, the unbelievableness of it. Then it slid deep into my unconscious and I thought no more of it until it came three times to knock upon the door of my dreams. But I must reserve these dreams for a later chapter.

All these experiences prepared the way for the awakening of my creative imagination. One day after looking at pictures–a pastime which always thrilled me–this same nursegirl picked up a sheet of newspaper and taking a pair of sharp shears, proceeded before my very eyes to cut out some wonderful butterflies pictured thereon. The deed was done while I looked on—life created by the stroke. Piece by piece the little creatures were liberated, first a wing, then the head, then another wing, then the tail, from their prison pages, and fell fluttering into her lap.

The effect upon me was overwhelming. I was intoxicated with a new sensation. My brain swam. I picked up each little paper butterfly tenderly, felt the outlines of its body, and then placed it in different positions in relation to the others. The carpet suddenly became a forest, the rug by the fire a secret garden, the table by the nurse's chair became a plateau. The room suddenly became peopled with living creatures. I remember she lifted me up on the table—me clutching feverishly my new-found playfellows, my firstborn imagination children. There I could let go of them and watch them go fluttering to the floor one by one. I was in ecstasy. To this day I can recall those first exquisite sensations of an awakened imagination. Nothing could separate me from those new things. I remember I was whisked off to bed far too early, while still the fever of my joy was at full height.

And now to the merging of life and the creative imagination.

Having discovered that a pair of scissors could release living butterflies from an old newspaper, it was not long before a greater discovery was made, that a pencil could place these living creatures on white sheets of paper. Long before I could read I began to draw but never did I draw a design or a picture of still life, but always a living thing in *action*. Life swarmed all over the blank white pages of the big blank books which my father brought home from the office and gave to me—old, half-used ledgers which his bookkeepers had discarded. Cabins opened their doors and let out cowboys, jungles opened and exploded forth animals and African Hottentots. Vast prairies were swept with feathered Indians on bareback ponies chasing stagecoaches that were constantly being rescued by daring cowboys. A sense of geography was missing—to me the earth remained flat until my seventh year—but it was very convenient to have one place like Africa where all the dangerous things came from, and a land like America where all the heroes were born. I was the special hero, of course, although presently my little brother Page joined me. From then on there were two heroes. Under this joint partnership the adventures grew more and more exquisitely exciting.

In this little laboratory of spontaneity I made a discovery of great use in my later life—how legends and tales, the very masterpieces of literature came into being. I discovered that all great literature is more or less a shared process, that the simplest tales always grow spontaneously in the presence of an audience. The song of Troy, improvised by the traveling bards, laid the foundations for the great epics of the *Iliad* and the *Odyssey*. In our case, we alternated: I was the bard and Page was my audience; then Page was the bard and I was the audience. If Homer or Chaucer had been sitting by surely they would have gathered material enough for a dozen books from the tales that grew out of this legendary past of ours.

A great raft that we sketched in the white pages of the ledger had side-wheels which could be easily turned by hand lever when the wind abated too much to fill the sail. When a villainous pirate ship attacked us, shot and shell could do no damage save make a few holes in our planks. Meanwhile we had attached a sheet-iron, razor-sharp edge to its front side, and putting on full speed, we crashed into the pirate ship and cut it in half. After these arduous exploits were over what contentment we experienced when we touched at an island and ate our fill of breadfruit and drank coconut milk and rested under the palms.

In these journeys on the raft we visited all countries under the sun, which led us to a more intensive study of geography than any mere schoolteacher could ever have driven us to. One teacher could not conceal her wonder at a story I wrote of an imaginary trip through South America. Said she, "I would have thought you actually had been there." Little did she know how often I had explored its inlets and bays!

I feel constrained to tell of one of our fairy tales because it came welling up within us with such force and recurred so often that I know it was not something that was made, but was something that was "born." It is a living legend—how it ever escaped the collection of

Hans Christian Andersen or of the Brothers Grimm I do not know. The great tales of fairyland are symbols of our own subconscious nature—allegories of truths too profound for words. They lie deep in the subconscious mind of the race, even as coal and gas lie in the understrata of the earth. When a man digs up coal on his land he does not claim to have *made* it. Neither should a man who discovers a fairy story lying deep in his subconscious memory claim that he created it. *It was already there.* It merely awaited someone to dig deep enough to bring it forth. For instance, the legend of *The Sleeping Beauty*, a legend which recurs in every land, is nothing more than the allegory of the awakening of the soul.

This story which Page and I had such joy in creating began with a discovery of the Island of the Soul. Boylike we called it something else. But what is an island separated from the mainland by a body of water but a symbol of the subconscious mind of man in which is hidden all the mysteries of the race consciousness? Once we find that island, untold wealth is surely ours.

Upon this island we found three races of people—strange people, looking much like other people, save that one-third of them were black, one-third red, and one-third brown. We found this color division very convenient later in illustrating battles with our little box of crayons. Each of the three groups had one marvelous, unexplainable gift, and all three of the gifts were different. The brown men could see a mile as distinctly as they could see an inch, and what is more, when we put a gun in their hands we discovered that they could hit a fly on a tree a mile away. The black men were tough as iron. No bullet or explosive could penetrate their skin. And finally, the redskins could run like the wind.

None of these three tribes had ever seen a white man, and upon the arrival of my brother and me they accepted us as though we were gods. They at once made me king and my brother general-in-chief of the armies. Immediately we set about to organize three hundred chosen men for some great and wonderful exploits. On the ship which had brought us, which, by the way, had foundered on a reef just out of sight of the island, were plenty of guns to arm a hundred brown men whose shooting eyes were so extraordinarily accurate, a hundred swords to give to the blacks, and plenty of ropes to give to the reds.

After we got our three hundred men well trained a world war broke out, in which Russia and Germany were marching upon helpless little France and Belgium and England with intent to conquer the world. We arrived on our remodeled ship with our three hundred one late afternoon in the month of May in the fair land of France.

"What can you do with three hundred men?" we were asked.

"Wait and see," was all we answered. "Give us a dangerous post near the front." This, to our delight, was granted.

Then the greatest event in military history took place, perhaps the only event which topped David's defeat of Goliath and Gideon's defeat of the Midianites. As the enemy advanced in solid phalanxes the hundred brown men hidden in treetops let go their fire. Not waiting to see the whites of their eyes, not even waiting till they came within ordinary gunshot, these extraordinary precursors of the modern range-finding machine guns began picking off the enemy. When the field was pretty well piled with carcasses the hundred black men made a brave charge right up to the cannon's mouth unmindful of the shot and shell which left them unscathed. When they reached the enemy lines they hewed into them right and left, shedding the bullets that rained upon them as though they had been so many raindrops.

In consternation over this strange phenomenon the enemy very naturally turned and fled, the generals leading the way. But alas for the generals! Little did they know the ace we had up our sleeve. For it was not time for the redskins to sally forth. Running like Wyoming antelope they simply swept over the ground, bagging general after general, tying each one fast and bringing him back on their shoulders.

Needless to say, the war soon came to an end. Against such heroes, what was the use? Even had the enemy wanted to continue the fight, how could they after one hundred leading generals had been tied up and carried away as hostages.

Beneath this simple story of our childhood imagination lies a tremendous allegory, all the more wonderful because the creators were so unconscious of any of its deeper implications. The spontaneity with which it welled up out of our childish imaginations is its best guarantee of authenticity. The island we had discovered was the island of the Soul, that God-point in everyone's consciousness. The men who could see so far and always hit the mark represented the spirit of divine *omniscience*, the all-knowing mind and the all-seeing eye of God. The men who could overcome any opposition and whom no outside force could penetrate were the spirit of God's *omnipotence*. The men who could run like the wind were the spirit of God's *omnipresence*. In this imaginary world crisis all the evil forces of the world were helpless the moment the omnipotent, omniscient, omnipresent powers of the Soul were released upon them. Indeed, is there anything that can stand before the power of the Soul when its power is utterly released? "Love is strong as death. . . . Many waters cannot quench love, neither can the floods drown it."

Little did I know that someday I should see these infinite powers engage in mortal combat with sinister forces very similar to those that our old ledger had once recorded. Gandhi was the first one to demonstrate in actual history what Page and I have here recorded in allegory, that *soul force* can liberate a people from oppression more effectively and more permanently than all the conspiracies of diplomacy and all the instruments of war combined. Children sense this soul force. The popularity of *Superman* and other similar comics among the children today is undoubtedly due to the hidden, unconscious symbolism concealed within them of an omnipotent Mind greater than ourselves, working through us and instantly available the moment the need calls.

In those days I was stepping constantly into the mind of little Page on these deep unconscious levels of the spirit, and he was constantly stepping into mine. The link that grew between us was like the link that bound Damon and Pythias and David and Jonathan. It had something that was not of this world. We began planning our future lives together. When we grew to be men we would spend our days drawing pictures and writing books and perhaps raising chickens, and maybe a few coconuts and a little breadfruit on the side. I sometimes think that my friend James Norman Hall and Charles Nordhoff on the Isle of Tahiti stepped into the dream which my brother and I set rolling in the early nineties.

BOOK TWO

Backgrounds

CHAPTER V

The Backgrounds of Childhood

MY LIFE moved on from that point as rhythmically as a cycle of Greek dramas with the central characters in command of the stage, but with a chorus always in the background. The central characters were the members of my own home; the choruses were the relatives that appeared from time to time, the school life that was steadily with us, and the gangs of boys with whom my life became more and more involved.

In the chorus which accompanied that early cycle was Grandfather Page, six feet two and straight as a pine tree, with a white beard that made him look exactly like Robert E. Lee. He was always an object of great reverence to us all. But his little redheaded wife with her tremendous opinions, always finding fault with the grandchildren to their faces while she loved them to death behind their backs, was an object of fear and foreboding.

Into their home Aunt Jane soon returned–beautiful Aunt Jane, mother's youngest sister, called by many the most beautiful girl in Des Moines. Earlier in her life she had had the pick of a dozen young men and out of them had finally chosen a debonair and dashing chap, adept at repartee[1], a charming dancer, but unfortunately a spoiled only son. When my father and mother had cautioned her that he was an alcoholic she had scorned their warning as malicious gossip and had

---

[1] Banter, lively conversation

49

gone ahead and married him; and then she was in for a life of hardship and grief such as she had never dreamed possible for anyone to suffer. One night she arrived at her father's home with her three little babies and said, "It's all over." Thereafter the quality of wistfulness and at times envy with which she surveyed our family happiness added to the emotional background of our lives.

She and her two brothers, Uncle Will Page from St. Paul and Uncle Morton Page from Fargo, constituted a fascinating trio of conversationalists when they dropped in from time to time. In the presence of this remarkable trio, our own mother, who completed the family quartet, became a little gray wren among a nestful of orioles.

Arriving unexpectedly at times there were also the country relatives from my father's family, bony, rangy men with immense Abraham Lincoln hands, hands that were eternally brown, calm and motionless. Easy, quiet, sedate voices rumbled over our heads for days following their arrival, the men speaking seldom but always out of gentle, resonant throats, the women speaking continuously with voices pitched much higher, not unpleasant save as the steady monotone of their prattle sometimes grew weary to the ears.

There was much gossip to pass along on these visits: How Mary Anne's daughter had married the Sheriff of Clay County; how Sarah had twins; and how Uncle Walter died slowly of dropsy developed years ago in the war. Someone was always dying in this big contingent of country cousins, and how these aunts, much, much older than my mother, did dote on telling all the morbid, minute details of the "last illness" and the treasured "last words." A few days of these old wives' tales and my eyes were well-nigh popping out of my head.

Once the gossip was all spent, then it was my mother's turn to gather up the threads, and while the others listened she steered the talk into a slightly higher channel. The conversation now began to center around problems and issues instead of the ceaseless run of personal facts. The morbid dropped out, creative values came in. Strange how the men listened to mother. They would gather in from the outer edges of the room or from the barn and garden, whither their man-talk about short horns and threshing machines had often taken them, and draw about this little woman of sympathy and culture. The women, too, thawed out of their ruts and, after a day or two, their voices grew less monotonous and their thoughts took higher flights. Undoubtedly some of the rough places in their past lives were ironed out and some of the flat monotony of their toilsome days was being refreshed and brightened by the contact with this sweet little lady whom they all called "Aunt Fannie."

Sometimes a tall figure stooped and picked me up and sat me on his or her lap, and I became aware of the warmth that emanated from the capacious body and of the hardness of the strong arms, or the softness of the great bosom that I was pressed against. Or again how chilly and hard might be the cheeks that contacted my tender cheek. How irksome they all became if they did not shortly let my feet touch the ground and scamper away.

The aunt I remember most vividly was Aunt Nancy Barngrover, who was not a regular aunt, as my mother explained, but a great, great aunt. She was very old and exceedingly deaf. It wore mother out to talk to her because she had to shout so loud, and it was equally wearing to have Aunt Nancy talk to mother, because she talked so long. So when Aunt Nancy Barngrover came we children would gather around her when mother asked us to come in and "spell" her a bit. Aunt Nancy was equal to this relay system, and such amazing things out of the past that her tongue would bring us! Her last visit was in 1892. She was ninety-five. That would make her born in 1797 while George Washington was still president.

"I loved to talk to my great aunt, your grandfather's grandmother, when I was you children's age," she would say. "She used to tell of how she accompanied your great, great grandfather in all the Washington campaigns. The Colonial soldiers took their wives with them to do their cooking and nurse them when they were sick or wounded, and how I shuddered at their hardships at Valley Forge. And the Continental money your great, great grandfather was paid wasn't worth a Continental, so after the war he got in a covered wagon and went farther west."

When the relatives were not at hand, we took stock of our neighbors. The most active neighbor we had was General Weaver. Almost any day our cousin Ralph might call to us, "Come out, boys,

General Weaver is exercising his horse again." And sure enough, there was General Weaver, in his big vacant lot, holding one end of a long rope while his spirited horse was trotted and raced around and around in the circle traced at the end of the rope.

In those days General Weaver was too busy attending political meetings of the new-formed People's party to do much pleasure riding. We never saw him ride that beauty of a horse, but he was getting him conditioned for a long ride in celebration of the victory the Populists would someday win. One Saturday afternoon when father was sitting on the porch with us General Weaver stopped and chatted with him as he went by.

"There," said father when he had left, "is a man who could have been governor or senator if he had stayed in the Grand Old Party. But he got mad at the Republicans one day and joined this crackpot Populist crowd."

The people's revolt was sweeping the Middle West, the revolt against high taxes and inflated money. Democracy was looking to its future. Edward Bellamy's *Looking Backward* had just come out. William Jennings Bryan was even then preparing his "Cross of Gold" speech. In the years to come General Weaver's name was often spoken in our home, the man who ran as candidate for president oftener even than William Jennings Bryan, and just as futilely. Or was it all futile? Many of the reforms he advocated have since become laws.

Another chorus that gave background to my life was school. Mother was afraid of the public school system so she sent to Germany for some of Froebel's books and conducted a sort of kindergarten in the home. In 1889 she finally relinquished her fears and started Dot, now nine, in the first grade and me, now seven, in the kindergarten. In missing kindergarten, Dot lost something which she was never able to replace—the play spirit of education. School was a duty to her instead of a joy. Being a conscientious girl, she always stood near the head of her class and yet she was always bored by schoolwork. The result was that she, the best student of the family, never cared to finish college.

I was eight years old when I completed kindergarten and started to learn to read. A late start, you may think, but it turned out to be a very good start. I have since met a number of people who did not start school until they were eleven. Their parents taught them to read and gave them some tools and turned them loose in their own back yards, a fine way to conserve whatever modicum of originality may be in the endowment.

My school life became a sort of cycle affair; one year my chief interest was focused upon one subject, and the next year upon another. In the first grade I became distinguished for my drawing, although drawing was not in the curriculum. The teacher, after discovering my propensity to illustrate my reading lessons by sketches, often had me put these sketches on the blackboard for the others to see. I was once overwhelmed by a teacher from a higher grade inviting me into her room to do a similar illustration in front of all her pupils.

In the second grade I was the best reader, putting "the most expression" into the task; indeed I was a far better reader then than I am today. In the third grade I was the best speller, being able to spell the whole room down, but I regret to confess I have been a poor speller ever since. And—my friends won't believe this—in the fourth grade I excelled all in penmanship. It seemed that I had to get all these good things out of my system, and, unfortunately, after getting them out they stayed out. However, when I was in the fifth grade, I developed a flair for creative writing and that gift, in contrast with all the others, did not completely leave me when the year came to a close. At last my stream of imaginary "ledger-stories" and my conventional schoolwork began to flow together.

In school, no matter how prosy the teachers, I was never bored, for when I had finished getting my arithmetic lesson and had read for the third time all the stories in the reader, and the seat began to irk me, I would lean back and gaze at the ceiling and ponder on what a vast, roomy place the ceiling was, unlittered with desks, unencumbered with children. Then I would straightway rub my Aladdin's lamp, order some fly-foot shoes, put them on, walk straight up the walls, and dance and gyrate upside down on the ceiling. The pupils would stare up at me, and when I would deign to come down, with what awe and wonder Miss Hawkins would behold me! One day I was so absorbed in this ceiling diversion that I was not aware of the teacher's voice and the fact that all the pupils this time actually were staring at me. When I finally came down from the ceiling I found that the teacher had called upon me three times to take my part in the reading lesson which had started while I was cavorting around those vast, open spaces.

To be a famous novelist became my next daydream. In this dream there was no wish whatever for crowds of people to acclaim me. There was no thought of glory. There would be glory enough and to spare in merely writing the book. So I would sit for hours musing upon the glorious big-printed pages it would contain. A large book with a picture, drawn by the author, on every left-hand page. When I was nine I could wait no longer. I must write a novel. So I sat down and wrote the tale of "Lost Gilbert." The teacher, Miss Everett, found my novel one day and was so pleased with it—or was she amused?—that she insisted on my making a copy for her. Nothing bored me more than being set to the cramping task of copying in cold blood what I had already created in hot blood. However, I complied with the request, stifling my inner rebellion, but for one moment thought the rebellion would get the better of me when she selected the original and left with me the inferior secondhand copy.

When I was in the first grade my cousin Ralph and I both fell in love with Bernice Greefe, the daughter of the local grocer. Then Page fell in love with beautiful little golden-haired Helen Stephenson in his room, and I fell in love with her sister Katie Stephenson in my room. When the plague of diphtheria struck the city that winter, both died. I remember how our grief was dulled by the tremendous wonder of the event. The overpowering mystery of death carried its own anesthetic and the chief sorrow we both felt was not for ourselves or for the girls but for the mother whom we had never seen, whose only children had been taken from her.

The third and most perilous background of my childhood were the gangs of boys, my peers, the little savages and barbarians of my own age.

My father, knowing from experience the perils of this jungle age, bought for my eighth birthday a set of boxing gloves and a book of indoor games, which included one chapter on the "Manly Art of Self-Defense." Then he remarked, "The Spartan mothers used to say to their sons when they started away to war, 'Return bearing your shields or borne upon them.' By this they meant that they wanted their sons to come back victorious or dead. It was a saying among the Greeks that if a man met one enemy he must defeat him; if two, fight with him; if three, stand them off; but if four, then there would be no disgrace in running away."

"Return bearing your shields or borne upon them," Page repeated to me as we put on our caps the next morning and sauntered over to school. And as we entered the school grounds we found a great crowd of boys clustered around the side entrance, talking fiercely. A glance showed they were divided into two camps—the dirty little boys from the low-lying mine districts along the river, and the boys from the paved street districts—boys whose mothers tied their neckties and brushed their hair before they started for school. It was common knowledge that the necktie bunch had no fighters and the other gang had legion. Page and I naturally gravitated to the group which contained most of our own associates, the necktie crowd. To do so we had to press through a ragged skirmish line of the other group.

Three boys bustled up to me at once, fists clenched, yelling angry words at me. I stood my ground with a certain quietness and coolness, at least I put up that appearance, although somewhat quaking within. But the inner quaking was being marvelously steadied by the slow, rhythmic chant ever intoning in my ears, "Stand your ground with three, stand your ground, stand your ground." My courage came not from myself but from something that vibrated clean down deep inside me. My example seemed to stir the retreating white-faced lads of the necktie boys and with a wild yell they surged forward. Jostling began all along the line, but no blows were struck before the bell rang to call all to their rooms.

Immediately after school that evening, however, the two lines formed again. The grimy crowd pressed forward a powerfully built lad named Fred Schuler. Their opponents pushed me forward to represent them. Next thing we knew we clinched. Then we wrestled to a draw which meant that both sides claimed the victory. From that day forth all the altercations between the two groups were settled not by mass battles but by pushing forward a champion to represent each side. When a dispute was to be settled by wrestling, Fred Schuler was always their representative; when it was to be settled by boxing it was always Jud Dempsey. I preferred wrestling but rarely came out better than a draw with stout Schuler. In boxing I usually won, but no one but myself knew by what a slender margin. That margin was almost altogether psychological. When Jud Dempsey came forward with his doubled fists at his side, I always stepped forward with more alacrity than he and always with a calm smile upon my face.

"Come on," I would say, edging up to him sideways, my formidable looking fists hanging relaxed at my side, "why don't you come on? Are you afraid?"

"No, darn you," he would exclaim, but everyone noticed that he always backed away from me as I edged forward. Half the time he retired before my forward march without either of us even striking a blow.

Another lad I loved to wrestle with was Moffet Weaver, tall and sinewy, but on more friendly terms. One muddy day in the schoolyard we started to tussle. He clutched me in his long arms. We swayed back and forth in the deep, sticky mud, and then both slipped and went down on our sides. With one hand braced to keep our bodies from touching the ground, each began a slow, steady, defensive battle to keep the other from turning him over in the mud. Then something strange came clear to me, and that was that in this particular position I could, because of my length of back, bring greater power to bear on Weaver than he could on me. And it dawned on me that if I kept up my courage and confidence, I could press him into the ground. But when I looked down at the mud my heart failed me. I could never throw anyone into that mud! He would not quit, and neither would I, so when the bell rang I knew one would have to go under before either got up. Finally his pressure tightening a bit, I let myself slip down on my back. Instantly we were both running for the door, he clean except for his shoes and hands, I with a terribly smeared back. I hurried breathlessly straight to the teacher's desk.

"Please, may I go home and change my coat? I got it covered with mud."

"Yes," she said.

And as I ran over to the house no shame was in me, but a quiet, newborn confidence. I KNEW at last that I could throw Moffet Weaver, but in the mud I wouldn't. And the strength that I wouldn't use to hurt another gave me greater confidence than the strength that I could have used to win that day.

In the fall of 1892 all rivalries were temporarily buried and every boy in school from kindergarten to eighth grade united to do honor to the discoverer of America. Old Crocker School was suddenly set aflame with patriotism—one big happy family. Boys in my grade that I didn't know could use fife and drums were suddenly organized into a fife and drum corps. Our spelling time we used gloriously for practicing "Columbia the Gem of the Ocean" and "Hail Columbia, Happy Land," and all the other hymns of patriotism. At recess we practiced marching about the graveled schoolyard behind the drum corps, singing songs in honor of the four-hundredth anniversary of the landing of Columbus. And when the great day came our little Crocker regiment marched proudly through the streets of Des Moines with all the other schoolboys of the city.

At recess time my favorite game was one we called "Blackman." I have never heard of this game by that name anywhere else. Its nearest counterpart is "Prisoner's Base." From two goals on opposite sides of the schoolyard the boys would run and the "Blackman" out in the center would try to catch them and pat them three times on the back. Then they would help him catch the rest. Finally when the yard was swarming with catchers and only a few runners remained there came a high test of dodging. This game was a constant thrill to me, for I was often the last one to be caught. It was for me a dynamic expression of perfect rhythm as my body wove and swiveled through the surrounding hands in a dance of combat, a thrilling exercise of one's entire being in friendly rivalry. It proved to be my kindergarten training for the later excitements of football.

And behind all these lesser backgrounds was the broad, all-encompassing background of the city of Des Moines, with its wide lawns and leisurely tempo, its hot quiet summers, punctuated by the pleasant chime of the lawn mower that made the dusk smell green as evening approached. Des Moines was a perfect city in which to spend one's boyhood, for it ranked then and ranks now as the city of

America that has the greatest number of vacant lots. Its people, like its architecture, have always been unpretentious and friendly. It never had a society of the four-hundred type. A college education and a double-breasted suit were credentials enough. Its schools and churches were its pride and few illiterates could be found in Des Moines. But alas, the coal miners along the Des Moines River uncovered the softest of the softest coal and the blackest of the black. A widely traveled hobo once described Des Moines to me as "A slovenly housewife gossiping with her neighbor on the back stoop."

While I was a boy, Des Moines was rapidly becoming the publishing center of the west through the quiet work of "Uncle Henry" of *Wallace's Farmer*, Jim Pierce of the *Iowa Homestead*, and E. T. Meredith of *Better Homes and Gardens*, Gardner Cowles and Harvey Ingham of the *Register*, and J. N. Darling, the noted cartoonist, who stuck to Des Moines in spite of golden lures to go to New York. The Hulbells and Rawsons and Nollens in life insurance, and my father in fire insurance, saw the city become the insurance center of the west.

But to me, the high points of Des Moines were the annual Seni Om Sed parades (Des Moines spelled backward) and the Iowa State Fair. The Iowa State Fair is the Mardi Gras of the prairie country, and a blue ribbon is said to be the Iowa version of the Order of the Garter. Here the old soldiers of the Civil War had a special tent and meeting place, and while father met with his cronies, we children, munching popcorn and drinking pink lemonade, wandered all morning through the great barns between rows of pigs, sheep, ponderous cattle and horses and in the afternoon peered over the fence at the trotting horses racing by. Moreover, we had a quarter apiece to spend!

CHAPTER VI

The Backgrounds of Page

THE family was growing in those days, and the little faces and personalities of my brothers and sisters were forcing themselves deeper and deeper into my consciousness. There was my sister two years older, a thin, pale, peaked face, with beautiful long black hair falling to the shoulders. She was quiet, at times strangely listless, and in the nights sometimes I woke to see my mother and father with their arms around each other, standing looking down into her bed. She was patient, and never collided with my desires when I sought things in my play that belonged to her.

There was my brother Page, two years younger than I, his face a little globe of sunshine, with two large, bright eyes shaded by long lashes, a long expressive upper lip that was wont to break into a smile whenever I came near. He had a habit of chewing his food in his front teeth like a little chipmunk, and when he was happily excited he would dance up and down and trot around the room. From the time he was a toddling two-year-old boy that face worked its way into my heart so wholly and completely that I can to this day shut my eyes and see it near me, day or night.

Plump Helen came next, the one in the family that never was undernourished, never got sick, never had to be coddled or protected. She romped and ran with the boys, and outran them and outplayed them. She loved every game, every story, and was the first to catch the point of every joke. She had a rippling laugh that I have never heard duplicated. When her sisters were sick she envied them, especially when neighbors showered them with flowers and gifts. Once she confessed her secret dream was that some day she would experience the novelty of being sick in bed, and when guests would come to the door to inquire how she was faring, mother would say softly, "No better, no better."

Then came the twins, Mabel and Morton. They posed a problem at first as to whether they would live. In those days when a mother hadn't milk enough it was customary to hire a wet nurse. Since none was available and the babies grew "no better" every day, a kindly Mr. Horlick invented a process known as Horlick's milk, in the nick of time. From then on the twins posed another problem. Instead of being too lifeless, they now became too lively. Father finally solved the problem by getting two nursegirls. Those nursegirls posed for us children the biggest problem of all. For Katie Lynch was a Roman Catholic and Zenna Mohler was a member of the Holiness sect, and between these religions there was no compromise. As we children listened to their debates and then perused Dore's terrifying illustrations in Grandma's immense, illustrated edition of the *Divine Comedy*, we became more and more convinced that the Inferno and Purgatorio would someday be yawning for us children who did not fit into either brand of salvation.

After supper, mother and father often gathered us together around the evening lamp and read to us. We derived our greatest thrills over books that today are very little known, *Five Little Peppers* which seemed to have been written especially for us and the *Barnum Book* in which Jack Harvey, Bob Marshall, Dick Brownell and Mr. Godkin brought the wild animals back alive for "The Greatest Show on Earth."

Besides the illustrated fairy stories that Page and I were constantly creating, these literary hours exploded in us a whole repertoire of improvised drama. The sliding doors between the dining room and sitting room made an ideal Little Theatre. *Rip Van Winkle* and *Fantasma* became our chief masterpieces. We also produced *Punch and Judy*, *Rupert of Hentzau* and other creations of our own imagination.

When I was nine, the family moved for the summer to the Sunnyside woods in Oak Park, a suburb of Des Moines. A forest of great oaks and little ironwood trees was spread out for acres around us; a winding glen led us down to the flood plain of the Des Moines River on one side of the property, and a deep mysterious ravine, dark and jungly with tall trees and tangled underbrush, led to the same destination on the other side; and to cap the climax, a little forest of trees loaded with hickory nuts, walnuts, butternuts and wild berries furnished food for the hungry little Indians and hunters when they gathered around the Council Ring.

From listening to the reading of novels I passed easily to the writing of novels. I have already mentioned the title of my maiden venture. I know now why I took for the title of my first novel, *Lost Gilbert*. It was because I was so completely "unlost," so completely "found," so completely secure and safe in a charming, protective home circle, that my instinctive method of appreciating that security was vicariously to step out of it to discover what loneliness might be like, and from that point of lost-hood, fight my way back home. So at nine years of age, I described how nine-year-old Gilbert was lost in the wilderness and made himself a bow and arrow, shot squirrels and wild ducks, gathered berries and other fruits, built himself a cabin, lived for several years close to nature, and finally discovered people who took him back to his home for a gladsome family reunion.

Following this creation I daydreamed of writing a long novel about deer, profusely illustrated with beautiful fawns and does and antlered stags. At that time I assumed that my capacity to draw would develop as fast or faster than my capacity to write, and I visioned an immense folio as large as Grandma's *Divine Comedy* with my illustrations rivaling Dore's pictures but with a more cheerful theme. For several years I had this craving to draw beautiful deer; why, I do not know, unless there was in it a seed thought of the hind's feet that were someday to set me on high places.

When Page and I started raising chickens, I tried my hand at writing a novel about a chicken, following the model of *Black Beauty* and *Beautiful Joe*, but after three or four carefully written chapters the story came to an end. Chickens' mentality, I discovered, was not particularly inspiring, and the drama of cock fights did not equal horse races or the romantic combats in the courts of King Arthur and his knights.

So I turned my imagination, long fed upon the Civil War stories of my father and *The Blue and Gray Series* of Oliver Optic, to the writing of a mighty novel of the Civil War. I was twelve when I started this work and for the first time I began to get the thrill of living with my characters. The story was too big for a child untrained to the marathon of a full-length work of fiction, so I found myself at night thinking out chapters far ahead. When I found the writing was beyond me, the notion came to me that merely the thinking of the story might be good training to prepare me to be a novelist when I grew up.

My boyhood compositions finally came to an end with an unfinished masterpiece of brotherly love. When Page was eleven and I thirteen, I started this masterpiece which was to be an idyll of two brothers in ancient Corinth. Many chapters were written with the most artistic illustrations of my childhood career. The Olympic games in which we were to excel were just starting in the story when Page, the model for one of the chief actors, was suddenly called off the stage—and I never wrote one line more. I shall keep these unfinished chapters with their illustrations among my treasures as long as I live.

One summer, my father, who had invested unwisely in a Wyoming ranch, gave me the thrill of riding to Chicago in a caboose attached to a load of shorthorns. I felt sorry for the poor creatures who were destined to be slaughtered, but I was not prepared for the shock of reading in the Chicago papers that three laboring men who had been too violent in their appeals for higher wages were to be slaughtered also. All my flesh grew faint at the thought of the grim gallows that was to hang them by the neck until they were dead. The Chicago *Inter-Ocean* ran terrible cartoons of Governor Altgeld with horns like Satan himself and with fork and tail because he tried to pardon the three men. I did not know then that Altgeld was fifty years ahead of his time, a man who might have been president had he not deliberately chosen to follow his conscience. He, like General Weaver, believed in the common man. I knew nothing about property rights then, how sacred they were, and how powerful.

Back home again, it took days for me to recover the normal interests of boyhood. One day Colonel Ibex, a veteran with a wooden leg, called on father. He took a great fancy to me. "You must come and see me sometime, my little man," he said. "I own a big Shetland farm. If you come I will give you a pony."

But my entreaties fell on mother's deaf ears. Of course I couldn't pay a call on Colonel Ibex. And of course he was only joking. "Little boys must learn to take these promises of men of the world with a grain of salt."

But to this little boy in his dream world, all men kept their promises. Suppose, though, that I never could have a real pony? I could at least have a dream one, and dream ponies were almost as much fun as real ones, especially when Page and I spread them all over our blank books. So I took this promise that began as a grain of salt and turned it into a grain of mustard seed.

Many weeks later a boy came galloping up the street on a Shetland pony. All nine cousins were outdoors playing in our big vacant yard. I had a certain yearning as I saw the boy glance up at our house and slow his pace and then go galloping on. Presently he came galloping back.

"Does Glenn Clark live here?"

"Yes. Why?"

Without answering he went clattering up the driveway, straight into the barn, and while we all stared dumbfounded, he presently emerged from the barn, carrying a bridle, and strode off. Had he been the Angel Gabriel leaving Nazareth after the Annunciation he could not have stirred up a greater sensation. Two seconds later, nine pairs of childish eyes were staring into the soft, mischievous eyes of Daisy. Immediately I knew that this gift to me would be equally shared with Page.

After the fourth summer in the woods of Sunnyside, father and mother decided to build a great mansion and live there permanently.

"I have ordered a dozen Plymouth Rocks from Aunt Lizzie," father said, "so Glenn and Page can start in the chicken business if they so desire."

If we so desired! Heaven surely was coming to earth! Father advanced the money which we would pay back in eggs. The twelve hens cost twenty-five cents apiece, and the rooster fifty cents. The debt of \$3.50 looked very formidable, but we could sell eggs to mother for twelve cents a dozen, and that would soon pay for the outfit. Father would furnish the lumber if we would furnish the labor and build the chicken house. Shades of Swiss Family Robinson! Those were indeed heavenly days.

Every hen had a name, Mrs. Speckle, Mrs. Biddy, Mrs. Yellowfoot, Mrs. Wattle, and every name fitted the character just as the names in the Bible did. The talkative hen we named Mrs. Magpie. We felt like Adam when he named the animals or almost like God Himself when he changed Jacob's name to Israel. The first rooster we named George Washington. The following year George Washington was succeeded by John Adams, and he by Thomas Jefferson. Benjamin Franklin had long spurs and one afternoon when we were away he engaged Abraham Lincoln in a duel to the death. Our martyred Abraham Lincoln was the most beloved rooster we ever had.

Now that we had moved to the new school district, Page and I had to prove our mettle with an entirely new set of gangs. I had been growing at a stupendous rate and was the largest boy in my room. Because I had started school late, I was a year older than most of the boys. In our battles I discovered that I could now throw any two boys at the same time. So our place was established permanently.

What disturbed us was the new kind of stories the group was passing around—such ribald, vulgar tales as we never had dreamed possible. One day father told us of a banquet that he had attended in honor of General Grant. General Custer, who was on the program, began his speech with a series of ribald stories. Grant rose and remonstrated.

"What's the matter?" Custer asked with a grin. "There are no ladies present." Grant replied, "But there are gentlemen present."

So the next time the boys started on the old line, I told them there was to be no more of that talk in Page's and my presence.

"What's the big objection?" exclaimed the ring leader of the gang. "There aren't any ladies around."

At once Page spoke up. "Don't forget that there are gentlemen present."

This started a guffaw and a threat to topple us off our high perch.

"Whoever saw such a pair of sissies?" cried one.

"Who called us sissies?" I asked.

"We all did," they shouted.

That was the day that Page and I relived the experience of Jonathan and David with the Philistines and of Samson with the jawbone of the ass, and of Gideon and the Midianites all in one. From that day forth the boys of Oak Park School had a new respect for the word "gentlemen" and there were no more dirty stories.

At the age of twelve and ten, Page and I began to daydream of an entirely new form of education. Here are some of the reforms we decided on:

We would have schools hold sessions only in the mornings. The afternoons could then be turned into the most valuable part of our school plan. Hikes in the woods would give opportunity to study the habits of birds and ants and bees at first hand. Occasionally the afternoons should be given over to folk dances or pure games. In winter the boys could spend the afternoons in the shop and girls in domestic science kitchens, with occasional visits by all to art galleries, museums and factories.

We would put the play spirit into everything, such as rigging up a little store in one end of the room to teach arithmetic where the girls could do their marketing and the boys insure their belongings and do their banking. Geography could be taught by imaginary trips in which big maps and blank books and lots of pencils for drawing would have a place. History could be turned into pageants and acted out. At one end of the room should be a miniature stage where works of fiction could be dramatized.

Examinations should be taboo but reviews could be given in the form of quiz games—for fun, not for grades. Books should never be assigned with cut-and-dried book reviews required. The teacher should read the first three chapters aloud and get the students all excited about the story and then she should hide the book and make them hunt for it. No library in the city would be safe, and no bookstore free from invasion, until that book had been discovered and read by every pupil in the class. I still think that these spontaneous ideas of ten and twelve year olds could make a big improvement over much of our education today.

Our home was on a majestic bluff overlooking the flood plain of the Des Moines River. A broad lawn lay spread before our house, beyond that an entire acre of garden and orchard, and then the steep slope to the plain below where the tenant's garden farm began. A quarter of a mile beyond that was the heavily wooded pasture where the tenant's cattle and horses roamed and where Brocade and Daisy had pleasant company. Beyond the pasture was the flowing river, mingling its blue water with the brown and green of the opposite banks. On the other side of the river above the rip-rapped banks rose the city of Des Moines. All we could glimpse through the trees was an occasional steeple. But to the southeast, high amid the treetops like a picture framed in a circle of branches, hung the gilded dome of the Iowa State Capitol, a brilliant golden spectacle that put all other architectural achievements in the state in the shade. When overgrowing trees threatened to shut out this vision, I would climb the trees and saw away the intruding branches in such a way as to make a perfectly circular frame of shrubbery for what I considered to be the most glorious sight in Iowa.

About this time I had occasion to recall three dreams that had come to me on three successive nights and which I could not efface from my memory even though they had all occurred before I was out of my fifth year.

In one dream I saw little Page in the current of a great river calling to me for help just before he sank out of sight. In the next I saw him swallowed up in a great crowd of people and all my searching for him proved in vain. In the third he stumbled down an areaway leading to the basement windows of a large new house that was in the course of construction. The sides were too steep for him to climb out and my arm was not long enough to pull him out. The shock of awakening before I had recovered my little brother and the crushing loneliness that followed each dream was as real as if the catastrophe itself had actually happened.

After coming to the new home within easy walking distance of the river, father often took us boys swimming. We were sufficiently secluded so we could leave our garments under the trees in the pasture and go into the water in the garment nature gave us at birth. One day as Page's naked little body slipped into a deep water hole, memories of an old dream seized me for a moment like a nightmare, to vanish instantly when father pulled him out.

Another day when we were at the Zoo Gardens adjoining our farm we lost Page in the crowd and after a frantic search we found him crying, and another old memory asserted itself.

Another day Page ran under the latticed porch of our new home when we were playing hide-and-seek; we had trouble finding him, and I found a catch in my throat when he finally emerged safe and sound.

"New houses are damp," said an old lady. "You folks will get sick your first winter, see if you don't." Page was the only one who got sick. It was a mild case of quinsy, nothing to be concerned about. For years he had worn a truss for a rupture which was the result of strain from coughing during a siege of the measles I had brought back to him from my Chicago trip. The rupture was cured but now he was threatened with an ailment newly recognized in the 1890's, called appendicitis. I had just reached the age of fourteen on March 13, 1896, when his quinsy was followed by an acute attack of appendicitis and he was put to bed. I hurried home from school every afternoon to read to him. One day the doctor said, "This is serious. We must operate." Page could not be moved, so I had to help father nail the boards together to create an operating table. The appendix was perforated in six places, and the doctors removed a quart of pus. When the long operation was over, Page was a terribly sick boy. The most beautiful nurse I ever saw, wearing a gray dress with white collar and cuffs, was sent from the hospital.

One morning at five o'clock father, clad only in his nightgown, was standing in my room.

"Dress fast, Glenn, and hurry up to the fire station and phone for the doctor. I think Page is dying."

The fire station was a mile away. I fairly flew. That morning the three grief-shattering shocks of my childhood dreams united in one final shock of stark reality.

My grandmother broke the news. "Your little brother is gone."

We children gathered in the hall. Father and mother came out from the room and father put his arms around us all, his great figure shaking with sobs. "We can thank God that we have each other." Yes, I thought, we have each other, but no one can take the place of Page.

That night I heard someone say, "He passed away at nine o'clock this morning." I shed no tears. Why should I? None would come if I tried. I was the only one who shed no tears. A few days later the house was filled with people–neighbors, schoolmates. The pastor gave a kindly message. Page was a good boy, he said. People said many things, offering consolation to my parents. Most of the people passed me by. I was glad they did. The family rode in two black carriages drawn by walking horses clear through the city to Greenwood Cemetery. When one's soul is asleep it can stand such things.

A day came when the preacher's voice was a memory. I stood in the gathering dusk contemplating the garden and orchard. The same, and yet never again the same. It was Page's twelfth birthday, but he was dead. "He passed away," I heard them say, "he passed away at nine o'clock in the morning." Great oak trees stood like silent sentinels about the big house, and it grew dark within. They were lighting the lights inside; the shadows from within came out to mingle with the shadows from without and both hung in the branches that swayed in the wind.

Have you noticed that in the face of a great overpowering calamity the mind of man grows very still? In its presence there are no tears, no cry. When the Higher Power speaks, man listens as though in a trance. He turns to his doom and awaits it calmly. I cannot explain it, but I know it is true. Danger creeping near like the tiger about to leap spurs man to fight or flight. But in the face of sure and overwhelming disaster, he folds his hands for a last prayer and stands still.

So I turn from the light in the house and look into vacancy. Is it the limitless expanse of the flood plain of the river that stretches before me? Or is it the trackless heavens that have never been charted? I do not know–but it is something vast, something beyond the measurements of man, something that cannot be compressed into the confines established by the human mind. It is vacancy, space, something so large that it is awful. Why can I not grasp this thing that has come into my life? Why do I gaze stupidly into this little earthly room whose walls retreat and vanish and disclose that awful something that I cannot understand, but that seems to be without end, empty, measureless, encompassing all eternity within its grasp?

Dead? Was that what they said? Is that the message that the night wind is bringing me—dead? No, the casual word I heard was not *dead*. "He passed away at nine o'clock in the morning." Yes! Yes! *Passed away*. I begin to understand it. He, the one whom I loved above all others, has passed away, passed out of my life.

I will grasp this thing in a while. I will understand it, realize it. I will come back out of this limitless flood plain of meditation, my mind will forsake the trackless sky that has never been charted—and I shall understand that this soul that I loved has only passed away.

The twilight deepens. A belated bird, hurrying home on wearied wing, flutters past the great oak under which I stand. A new moon hangs high in the sky, and the light lies sparkling across the breast of the distant river.

CHAPTER VII

The Backgrounds of Self-Discipline

IF HE WOULD cry, it wouldn't cut so deep," I heard one of my elders say. After almost a year had passed, I still did not weep for Page. Then there came a time when many a night I awoke sobbing. And as I felt the empty pillow where my comrade's head would never lie again my sobs redoubled. The soft footsteps of my mother were nearly always the answer. Before she went away the sobs subsided.

Then one day a great resolve was made. After that, peace came, a great peace. I never wept again. The resolve could be stated very simply. But it was made with all my being:

I shall henceforth do the work of two men.

Page's life would not now be in vain. The dreams he and I had dreamed I would carry out alone—and yet not alone. In some strange way beyond my own capacity to explain, he would be helping me. A great work lay ahead. What and where I did not know. But in the meantime I would be getting ready.

After that decision was made a new kind of dream came to me. It was not a night dream, this time, nor exactly a daydream. It was not something I thought out; perhaps it was something that Somebody thought out through me. For want of a better word, I might call it a vision. Call it what you will, here it is:

A program was all laid out that I was to follow. It came to me as I was ending my fourteenth year. During the seven years between

70

fourteen and twenty-one I was to concentrate all my energies on developing myself, regardless of what others would think. The seven years between twenty-one and twenty-eight I was to mix and mingle with the world and adjust myself to people and events. From twenty-eight to thirty-five I was to interweave the inner and the outer threads in as perfect an integration as possible in preparation for my life's work. From thirty-five to forty-two I was to start my life work. And from forty-two on—no, there the vision stopped. Was I to die at forty-two, step from this mundane earth into heaven; or was I to rise to some heights in this world above what my boyish vision could at that time glimpse? After finding that the lens of prophecy could not penetrate the mists any farther, I settled down to the immediate task of obeying the vision as far as I could then see it. Somewhere I had read a passage of Lincoln, "Prepare yourself and the opportunity to use that preparation will come."

Prepare yourself for writing. I searched my father's library and found Blair's rhetoric. Such a smooth-flowing style, such felicitous phrases, such stately, balanced sentences! Even while reading what Blair had to say about the rules of rhetoric, the rules were made alive and real to me in the sentences themselves. How different, how refreshing in comparison with the dry-as-dust, pedagogical, pedantic rhetorics given me when I reached high school.

From that time on I not only read books, I noticed the rhythm and swing of their sentences and the choice of words. Henty and Oliver Optic now paled. I turned to Washington Irving and Hawthorne. Strange to say, the chief thing I noticed—the new, unusual thing—was the use of semicolons. Long sentences could be held together and get their meaning across if properly pinned together with semicolons. This device, now out of fashion, almost sidetracked me from my main purpose. My letters suddenly became salted and peppered with semicolons.

The sudden realization that the style of great writers was something that could be cultivated in oneself almost overwhelmed me. I resolved to spend a few minutes each day cultivating my style. But all this was done in secret. My teachers didn't know I was learning far more about writing in my lonely browsing than they could ever teach me in their regimented classes.

And I trained myself in speaking. I had read how Henry Clay trained himself daily by reporting the contents of some historical or scientific book to his cattle and pigs. I substituted chickens instead, and scattered corn while "orating." I am led to remark that never since have I had an audience half as responsive to my gestures as these descendants of proud Plymouth Rock families of the barnyard.

But above all, I tried to cultivate my thinking. When riding on streetcars I looked at the vacant faces around me and wondered how many of the passengers were really "thinking." I would take a theme such as *Love* or *Habits* or *Compensation* and concentrate my mind upon it to see if I could think of analogies or parables that would illustrate it. I did this sometimes till my head would ache. Then one day I picked up Emerson's essays and discovered that he had thought most of my ideas before me. For the next few years Emerson became my teacher.

An opportunity finally presented itself for applying my thinking habit and my writing practice to some definite purpose. The Des Moines *Daily News* offered a prize of a framed picture to the school of the pupil who wrote the best essay. The theme for this particular week was "The Curfew." The curfew in Des Moines rang at nine to warn children under fourteen to be at home. Home–the ideal home–the conservation of home values–that was the one thing I knew about. So I sat down, pencil in hand, and the words flowed through me. Finally my essay was finished. Sunday afternoon I took a long walk by myself. On a lonely street I dropped the precious envelope in a mailbox, looking furtively from right to left lest anyone should see me.

Days went by and then a letter came.

"Your essay has won the prize and a picture suitably framed will be sent to your high school to be presented with proper ceremonies." That night at supper my sister Dot, who had overheard my reading the letter to mother, broke the news to the family in a circuitous way by relating how an unnamed young man once upon a time wrote an essay. But while she was still a long way from the end, I contrived to slip unnoticed from my chair and when she reached the climax of "unveiling the author," the author was safely concealed beneath the table.

A few days later, when presenting the picture to the high school, the principal enlarged more upon this table episode than he did upon the essay or upon the picture itself. And so for the first time I saw my writing in print, and found myself being heralded as an embryo author, whose talents were outdone only by his modesty. Those were sweet and heavenly days. I was content now to relapse into obscurity for the next twenty years until I might have a real message to bring the world. What that message would be I did not know, but when the time came the message should be ready.

One day I found an old, dog-eared book in the attic, filled with pictures of heads, chins and noses, and I asked father what it was all about. He said, "That is Fowler and Wells' *Phrenology*, the book that gave Edison and Beecher and your Uncle George and me our start in life. It encouraged us as it did many others in our day to become what we are." Immediately I became immersed in a study that made me look at people. We might debate to our heart's content whether it is true that creatures such as cats and bulldogs whose heads are wide through the ears are more pugnacious than creatures such as rabbits and sheep whose heads are narrow through the ears, but this much I can say: there is a value in any study that makes one look at people. Because this "ology" had not as yet been accepted in the schools I studied it only in secret. Finally there came a time when I did not need to look at people's heads to read their characters, for I had found an even better way, and that was to look into their eyes to read their souls.

The shock of Page's death just as I entered adolescence and the unresting activity to improve myself which this event had stimulated in me had affected my health in many ways. My eyes developed a severe astigmatism that only glasses could correct. I submitted to nine cauterizations for catarrh of the nose. I was given physic for my digestion and iron for my blood, until I was nothing but a bundle of nerves. All this developed in me a tremendous self-consciousness. I became a very awkward member of the little social groups I was thrown into, and doubly awkward in the presence of girls I admired. Being such a failure I took refuge in my dreams of the future. Nothing in the present mattered. It was merely a marking-time place. "Someday my associates will be proud of me," was my thought. "Someday they may be surprised to find that I amount to something!" And so I accepted everything with a patience and humility that finally impressed my friends. It awoke pity, surprise or sometimes admiration, depending upon who the person was. All thought I was a good boy; some a goody-goody boy; some feared I lacked spine.

This last conception was a mistake. I was full of spine. I bristled with ambition, with self-confidence, with conceit. I was constantly reading the lives of great men and trying to find what made them great. I lived in an atmosphere of greatness. The fact that I failed at so many points made me humble but did not crush me. I was holding back for a future time—MY TIME!

I had always thrilled over the stories of the great west. Father had sold his shares in the Wyoming ranch, but my cousin, Lon Condit, thirty-six years old, had a ranch, and would love to have young Glenn spend a summer with him. My parents saw an opportunity to put a bridge between the past so full of memories of Page and the unfolding future; therefore one fine spring day I found myself riding the stagecoach from Claremont to Buffalo. There Cousin Lon met me with a buckboard drawn by two broncos and drove me the remaining seventy-mile journey to the Great Red Wall on the southern fork of the Little Big Horn.

Here I was given the fastest horse on the range to ride and was rapidly initiated into the routine of the rough-riding cowboy. In our long mountain trips in search of our cattle for salting or branding, I was puzzled by the uncomfortable gait the cowboys chose for their horses. Instead of the pace or the gallop I had seen in the horseback riders in the city of Des Moines, the invariable gait they used was the trot. And instead of rising and falling in rhythm with the bounce, what is called posting, the cowboys turned in their knees and stuck like a burr to the jouncing horse. When I asked the purpose in this, the reply was, "We believe in saving the horse, not the rider." In time I became an expert in this form of riding and became very proud of my skill.

On these plains where there were no fences and no limits or barriers anywhere of any kind, not even trees to block the eye as it scanned the horizons, I learned the meaning of the word "Infinity." It became a word that could be attached to any other word one chose to use. If I looked about I was looking into Infinity. If I discovered a thought it was an infinite thought. If I loved anyone it was with an infinite Love. If I had faith in God it became an infinite faith. I could see why Elijah and John the Baptist and Jesus went out into the desert to pray.

Out there I got the perspective of my life–of all life. Life no longer consisted of what a man *thinks*, but rather of what a man *is*. I determined then and there to make the central aim of my life the development, not of my talents, which were very limited, but of my soul, which was as unlimited as God was unlimited.

There were two Wyoming scenes I shall never forget. One was of a wolf stealing upon a herd of cattle, with its eye focused intently on a little frisking calf. The cattle sensing the approach of danger shepherded their little ones into an inner circle, and then formed themselves in a larger, encompassing circle, heads and horns facing outward. Against this formidable array the wolf had no chance. Another time I saw a cavalcade of wild horses when menaced by danger form a similar ring, but this time with their faces toward the center and their heels facing outward. The living message these two unforgettable pictures left me was that any group centered in love, completely dedicated to the purpose of mutual aid, assures the most perfect protection anyone can find when his heart seeks refuge from the stings and arrows of life.

Returning from the cowboy days I regretted that I could ride the plains only one summer. That set me to wondering how I could transplant my "rough-rider" experience to the civilized land of Iowa.

A young lad carried our morning paper on horseback, galloping down our driveway every morning about five o'clock on a pony that was skin and bones. One day when I was out early I asked him if he would sell his route. The next day he and his father came to see me. They would trade their horse and route for my pony and cart. The trade was made. Father had a western saddle up in the attic. I found the route very long, twelve miles to ride every morning, and the horse very thin and overdriven. The weekly pay was three dollars. It cost me fifty cents a week for corn and hay. My actual clearance on my investment would be $2.50 for six mornings of hard riding. In those days there were no Monday morning papers; newsmen rested on the Sabbath.

But hurrah! I should have two years for extending my cowboy experience before I had to leave for college. The first miracle I wrought was on my horse. Every rib showed in her. Sticking in my knees, cowboy fashion, I clung like a burr while she *trotted* the twelve miles. In a few weeks she became plump and slick, the admiration of all the newsboys whom I met on my travels.

Those were long, beautiful mornings. At three-thirty every morning I slipped into shirt and overalls in summer and into the deep sheep-lined ulster and double overalls tucked into heavy riding boots in winter. Stepping out into the morning air under the stars with all the space in the universe thrown wide open to my will was like stepping into heaven. Once in the heavy saddle, the thrill of trotting and jolting along the rugged Oak Park roads seemed to stir up a whole new type of circulation, which I have never experienced in my life since.

To start out in a world where no one was awake brought me a great sense of peace and inspiration. I rode alone those mornings and yet I was not alone. I wondered what the unconscious thoughts were that flitted through the slumbering minds of those whose homes I passed. In that released atmosphere of early morning I liked to let my thoughts go forth and mingle in the unconscious thoughts of the sleepers. What appealed to me these mornings was the absolute purity of such thoughts. I was not in love at that time although I was seventeen and attuned to love. Little did fair maidens know what blessing a youthful knight of King Arthur's Round Table was laying at their doorsteps. But to this day I believe my thoughts could reach and bless them.

These years of riding built up my constitution for athletic games. I had a rhapsodical interest in our high school athletics, and each football season was like the return of the golden age of history. During the years that I played tackle on the football team my chief thrill was in weaving through the opponents' line and tackling the man with the ball. When I was promoted to halfback the thrill was in dodging through the opponents' line and making touchdowns. Our best team was Avery Cooper at center, Sam Peterson and Tommy Hilman at guards, Ernest Cree and Glenn Clark tackles, Tad Harris and Archie Ring ends, Ben Tracy quarter, Jim Tracy and Will Thornburg halves, and Garner Felt fullback. My senior year I organized the track team and had my first success at winning the half-mile run. But I must not tarry on this theme or I shall out-rhapsody Isaiah and the ballad of Beowulf combined!

My last year in high school I wrote the high school song, the school yell, and the senior class play, *Jack Donaldson's Revenge*, in which the class insisted that I play the lead. Oak Park High School was a small, three-year school of fifty or sixty students. Father was president of the school board for eight years, so was the official to give me my diploma at graduation time.

CHAPTER VIII

The Backgrounds of Sunnyside

T HE idyllic atmosphere of our home was severely altered after Page's passing. Something he represented that could not be replaced, was gone. An almost overwhelming sense of loss seemed to project me into the past and into the future, everywhere but into the immediate here. The family felt my withdrawal. It was almost as though they had lost two sons. Instead of the Glenn they knew, there appeared a moody, silent young Hamlet, living in a dark wood shot through and through at times with heavenly light. Gradually as a new world formed itself around me, a world that was so full of needs and opportunities that at times it seemed breath-taking, I resumed my place, but as a new man. The boy Glenn and the boy Page had both gone forever.

With the death of Uncle George and Aunt Sadie in Washington and the coming of their three children into our home, the spirit of Sunnyside was even more drastically changed than by the passing of Page. Had we searched the globe we could not have found a greater contrast in backgrounds, disposition and upbringing than these "Washington cousins" represented. They came out of an environment of extreme worldliness, as sophisticated as ours was simple.

Edith was almost six feet tall, erect and proud, with deep-set mysterious eyes and a stylish swing in everything she did. Strong, vigorous men fell in love with her, but she never returned their love. Later she had many opportunities to marry, but she chose not to give up her freedom. Her striking face and figure made her known as the "Gibson Girl" and she was often portrayed as such in her college annual.

Clifford was something of a problem child. Raised in a home of wealth, an only son to whom nothing was ever denied, anything he wanted he just took. At times this habit of appropriation became a serious problem bordering on kleptomania, but we managed to weather it. He had a tremendous dramatic sense and was continually improvising new plays, new acts. This was the only bond between him and me. He finally decided to seek expression for his romantic temperament by living on a Western ranch. Off he went. On a trip west to visit her brother, Edith attended a Western barbecue and danced with the president of the school board who promptly offered this sophisticated Gibson Girl out of the east a job in a country school. She accepted it and for a year taught a handful of ranchers' children, then got a job in the Sheridan schools, then was elected county superintendent. She selected a horse so spirited that most women would not have dared to ride him and made so romantic a figure riding the trails to her county schools that when the Republicans sought someone to run for state superintendent of schools, she was nominated. She outran the entire ticket, winning by such a big majority that her election was a sensation.

When the Hughes party stopped at Cheyenne on their canvass of the nation, she and the governor met them, and all the reporters fell for this striking new figure on the political scene. She had something of the Rooseveltian political acumen in her veins. One of the reporters for a national magazine wrote her up profusely, his story illustrated with pictures of her cowboy horse and outfit, and entitled "The Coming First Woman President of the United States." The year he prophesied for her election to that high office was to be 1936. That turned out to be the year she died. Clifford had already died of the flu in World War I.

Eleanor was the compensation, the redeeming feature, of the trio. Everything the others did sprang from thoughts of self; everything Eleanor did sprang from thoughts of others. A little nine-year-old girl who had been raised among servants and never taught to do a lick of work in her life, she watched with big wondering eyes the way my sisters regularly did their hour or two of chores, sweeping, dusting or making beds. One day as I sat curled up in a big chair in the library reading, I saw Eleanor come in and without noticing me, pick up a dust cloth and dust every chair and table in the room with little tentative, wistful wipings, as one training herself in a new art that she craved very much to master. I reported her actions to mother, who listened with tears in her eyes. From that time on Eleanor was one of us, bone of our bone, blood of our blood. In many ways she grew to resemble her "Aunt Fannie" more than her own daughters did.

Through little Eleanor the old idyllic quality of Sunnyside gradually re-emerged in a new focus. Eleanor was exactly two weeks older than the twins. They compromised and observed the three birthdays on the date halfway between the ninth of August. Soon they were dubbed the triplets, and they remained that through their grade school, high school and college life. Mabel and Eleanor soon became inseparable pals.

The triplets and I loved to take long walks. Coming home from college, I found Mabel and Eleanor more interesting companions than any other girls I knew. I was nineteen, and they thirteen, but that made no difference. They looked up to their big brother, and I loved their adoration and their fresh curiosity.

The day of the kerosene lamp was over. Gas burners were now in every room. During winter months we were too busy studying or going to parties to assemble as a family. But in summertime when we were all together again the great front porch was our gathering place. This porch was twelve feet wide and extended along the front of the great house, and halfway around the side. The long summer evenings found the entire family sitting there on the south side where, ten feet above the ground, we caught any south breeze that blew. With all the flood plain of the Des Moines River below us, many were the breezes which found us out. There the lights of the distant city and the still more distant stars were all the illumination we needed as we talked of past; present and future.

When Dot spoke in her gentle voice, never too often and always to the point, I felt that a certain kind of perfection was present. When

Helen's voice burst forth in laughter, I rested back in the stream of humor which carried us all along. Mabel, usually at my side, joined the conversation in her soft contralto, with a little laugh usually at the end of a sentence. Morton shot in a clever piece of repartee occasionally and when he spoke at length it was always with a shy, apologetic laugh at the beginning and ending. Father was usually content to be silent and when he did speak we all listened. He liked to have mother talk. If she had attended the Women's City Club or the Northside Club that day, father insisted on her telling all about it. And little Eleanor, the adopted one who seemed more like ourselves than we who were born there, brightened and sparkled up the talk more than anyone else.

Sometimes that porch was shared only by Mabel, Eleanor and myself, when on bleak or rainy nights we found ourselves walking arm in arm, parading the full length of the porch for hours, talking and planning away to our hearts' content. So genuine and so profound was the atmosphere of love and harmony in these family porch gatherings that when I later attended student religious conferences at Lake Geneva or other places—gatherings that were pronounced Utopias and mountaintop experiences by other young people—they always seemed something of an anticlimax to me.

One evening as we sat on the porch contemplating the stars in their courses there suddenly came to me a realization that this spirit which so pervaded the family circle was the greatest proof one could ever ask for immortality. Whatever else might pass away in that group, one thing would forever remain, and that was the love that was present. This idea did not come as a fleeting impression. It stabbed my deepest consciousness with such force that I knew at that moment that we live forever, that the real self within us is something permanent and eternal.

With my sisters and brother I regularly attended the Christian Endeavor Society. I responded to the fellowship I found there and to the something that lay deeper than fellowship, which I could not completely grasp or explain. And then one day the full force of that something deeper came to me. I had been thinking of Page and striving to get the deep peace that comes only with complete relinquishment, when an overwhelming statement came to mind: "Acknowledge Him in all thy ways and He shall direct thy paths." I found myself actually believing that promise to the very inmost center of my subconscious self. Immediately I began to act on it. I gave myself to it utterly. Self-consciousness fell from me, selfishness fell from me, I ceased to worry, or to think forward to the consequences of my actions. I seemed to have knowledge that if my intention was right I could do anything, leaving the outcome entirely in God's hands. I never was happier, never healthier, never had more power for work and more enjoyment in play and never had more influence for good upon my associates than I had during the few short months I kept this confidence as my attitude of life. I felt like the man who had been always turned around in his directions who awoke one morning to find that north was actually north to him, that his compass was for once straight with the world and the universe.

But like the man who once gets this straightening out of his world and tries elaborately to fix landmarks so as to make it permanent, only to forget his vigilance one day and suddenly revert to his old misdirections, so I became absorbed in some little self-centered problem and grew self-conscious again, worrying about the outcome of every move I made, afraid of losing my popularity, depressed about my health. From a magnetic, happy adolescent I became a self-conscious, calculating, timid, eccentric introvert, groping my way along, missing much of the joy in the world. But now I knew that the compass existed; no one from that time forth could make me believe that north was south, and I knew that sometime my directions could be permanently set right. Someday, somewhere, somehow, I would realign myself with that compass.

BOOK THREE

Education

CHAPTER IX

Grinnell College

AROUND the evening lamp at Sunnyside the family read together Ike Marvel's little book, half autobiography, half fancy, entitled *Dream Life*. It cast on us all a mesmeric spell. Now it so happened that Ike Marvel was a landscape artist and among his works of art was the campus at Grinnell. I was still under the charm of his book when I walked upon his campus, and as I walked the cinder paths those first days, I was walking down cloistered Oxford or Cambridge. Every boyish face concealed behind it a soul of Tennyson or a mind of Emerson.

At Grinnell I found a daily chapel which no one was required to attend and to which everyone went—a tradition of voluntary attendance that made this college unique among the colleges of America. I found an athletic tradition where every track athlete finished his race whether he won or lost, and every football team played better the second half than the first. Dramatic, last-minute victories had built up a legend known as "The Grinnell Spirit" which was headlined in the sporting pages year after year.

I found, in addition, a little city of the New England stamp, where everyone kept his lawn cut and his place beautified for the good of all. And at the particular time I went to Grinnell, I found a highly cultured and scholarly group of teachers.

I loved the school from the first. Oak Park High School was only a three-year school; I had taken summer school work in Latin and Greek at Highland Park College, hoping thereby to qualify as a freshman at Grinnell. Great was my dismay when I found that I must register in the Senior Academy. But I became reconciled when I realized that five years, after all, would not be too long to spend at so satisfactory a place. There were no men's dormitories in those days, so I was guided to "Soapy" Williams' house, where I had a room across the hall from two lads named Parker Fillmore and William Parker. Immediately I set to work to arrange my room to suit me. It pleased me to do things as I wished and to arrange my time as I wished. One of the first things I did was to exchange my one rocking chair for another straight-backed chair. I wanted to live as Spartanlike as I could. Nevertheless, I put a tennis net on the wall and into it stuck all the pictures I had accumulated in the past few years, family, friends and high school classmates. Then I arranged the schedule of the day, and adhered to it faithfully. Knowing my tendency to insomnia ever since Page's death I arranged my time so I would never have to study after nine o'clock in the evening. Faithfully I set aside the late afternoon hours for athletics. It was an essential for me to keep in good condition.

That first year I was an irrepressible idealist. When I was invited very early in my first year to belong to a "secret seven" of personal workers to look after the spiritual life of the college, I felt highly honored. I represented the Academy, Chauncey Chapin the freshmen, Charles Burnside the sophomores, Ernest Crabb the juniors, and Tom Ziegler the seniors. Morton Macartney, president of the Y.M.C.A., met with us occasionally, but he was rather the power behind the throne. To me, this group took on the aura of the twelve disciples. Tom Ziegler was John the beloved disciple, Ernest Crabb, Peter the Rock, Sam Williams, Andrew who brought people to Jesus, and Charley Burnside, Nathaniel, in whom there was no guile.

Gradually I became aware of the college tapestry made up, warp and woof, of human personalities. Every year the college itself was a new tapestry, each year different from the year before. Obviously, outgoing and incoming students helped to make the change. But chiefly it was created by changes going on within myself. It was as though I were a different personality each year. As my sister Helen would say, "The grub was becoming a butterfly."

Dreams come true, but they are often deferred. The summer I was seventeen I had decided that Oak Park School should support a literary magazine. Because of the dearth of writers in so small a rural school I was positively sure that if we started one I would be the logical editor-in-chief. So consistent had been my faith that if one prepares himself the opportunity will come, that during the summer following my junior year in high school I had sat down each morning after my chores were done and written an editorial. When high school convened that fall I presented the proposition of a school magazine to the fifty members of the school and it was unanimously adopted. But despite our best efforts the paper flourished but for a few months and then died.

But do dreams ever die? Another law I believed in was that whenever a door is closed there is always a sign on it pointing to a better door on ahead. I had prepared myself that summer to be an editor. When would my door open?

Seeing that a prize was offered for the best story for the Grinnell literary magazine called *The Unit*, I wrote one, and to my great joy, won the prize, and in the spring was elected an associate editor. At the close of my freshman year I was elected editor-in-chief and was re-elected every year following. This gave me opportunity month after month to write editorials that had some influence in shaping the policy and spirit of the school, a privilege I took seriously.

I still had a great passion for self-improvement, to make myself an all-round, balanced, heroic, creative soul. To that end I spent much time in the library reading philosophy and dramas completely outside the required curriculum. And to that end I went out for football and track teams and kept up the training without intermission for the five years I attended the college.

Athletics continued to be the rhapsody of my soul. At tackle and end I was usually the lightest man on the football squad and on the second team had the privilege of playing every Tuesday, Wednesday and Thursday in scrimmage against the first team. I was not a sprinter but was exceedingly fast on the start. Getting the jumps on my heavier opponents many a time I rifled through in time to make a tackle behind the lines. How easy it is to conquer when we catch our opponents flat-footed. How hard after they get their full momentum up.

One afternoon the coach stopped the entire first team and said,

"You haven't stopped this scrub tackle once all afternoon from getting through and smearing all the plays along this side of the line. If you don't get something started soon to stop him you'll all be fired from the team."

"Get something started!" Did they? When they got through with me that afternoon I was ready for the Old Veterans Home.

The man who looked after the conditioning of the football team was Jack Watson, and he, more than any other, was responsible for the remarkable endurance of Grinnell's fighting teams. At that time Jack Watson was the greatest track coach in the Middle West. Although a small college, Grinnell belonged to the "Big Four" which dominated Iowa athletics for years. The other three were Iowa University, Drake University and Ames Agricultural College. Grinnell won more track championships than any of the others and rarely fell below second place at any time. When I graduated, Jack had gone to Ames, and several years later he accepted the coaching job at Iowa University. Wherever he went, championships followed. To him I owe my own success as a coach. The greatest gift he gave me was never to send a man into a contest overtrained. "Little and often" was his password. "Never too much."

As I look back upon my record as a student I find I was below the average in grades but somewhat above the average in grasping the basic principles of the subject, an achievement which did not manifest itself in grades. But the one unique thing which I brought to every subject of the curriculum as well as to every extracurricular activity, was that I related it to everything else in life as well. In a Unit editorial I wrote:

> The ideal college course should be one which traces relations
> of each study to the others. To do this it would be well for each
> individual to select the study or studies which to him are the most
> vital and into these to focus all the others, tracing the relations of
> all the main studies until he is enabled to see the true bearing of
> each on his own personal life. Such a course would use biology as
> the physical basis of psychology, history as the evolution of ethics,

literature as an enveloping background for French and German, Greek as the fountain-head of literature and philosophy. By bearing in mind these inter-relations it would be possible that the notebooks in one course would resemble almost to identity the notebooks of another. Such a system would vitalize every study by investing it with the interests of all the others. Like the Brooklyn Bridge which is so constructed that a man's weight on one trestle is equally distributed to every other part of the structure, so no excess of enthusiasm could be bestowed on any one subject, to the detriment of others. A college should not divide a man into a dozen separate little compartments; it should not isolate him, whenever he undertakes a task, from all the rest of the world. A true college education is one that enables a man to step into his laboratory or into a book or into a corn field or into the ball grounds and at the same time step right into God's broad expanse of life.

Grinnell had a remarkable faculty when I was there. The most real teacher I ever had was Miss Clara Millerd, who taught Greek and made it alive. She also taught the history of philosophy in such a way that Thales, Socrates, Plato and Spencer became the audience and the students in the class became the philosophers. Mark Hopkins on his end of the log never drew out the student on the other end more effectively than Clara Millerd drew out the creative thinker in us.

Seldon Whitcomb, half Saint Francis, half Thoreau, the man with a frail little body but with hands and head of a master, was both an inspiration and an enigma in the field of literature. He was always frightened of his classes and he always kept them frightened of him.

Allen Johnson's classes in history were examples of pedagogical art. His lectures made history link together like a chain of cause and effect. Dean Maine, who taught advanced Greek, gave me much, mostly because of what he *was*. A quiet, reserved man, almost inarticulate in expressing himself, he later amazed those who didn't know his inner resources by the way he became one of the great college presidents of his time. I can never forget the way he paused before me one day, his six-feet-four towering over my little five-feet-seven, and laying his hand on my shoulder said, "I have unbounded faith in you, Glenn."

Those words alone were worth the price of five years at Grinnell.

Dr. Edward Steiner, distinguished authority on the emigration problem, came to the Chair of Applied Christianity at the beginning of my last year. He opened the world of today to me and related it to the world of the prophets. His Jewish background leading into Christianity gave him a stimulating point of view and his eloquence was outstanding not only in the Middle West but across the nation.

Before Dr. Steiner came to Grinnell there had been an interim when there were no classes in religion in the college. Religious needs were looked after by the Y.M.C.A.'s voluntary classes on Sunday. I volunteered to teach a class in the life of Christ and continued teaching it for three years. When I graduated I wrote a book entitled *The Art of Living,* "a little silhouette portrait of the life of Christ," as Lyman Abbott described it in *The Outlook.*

I learned as much from my extracurricular reading, from my experiences on the board of editors of *The Unit,* from my conversations with DeWitt Sprague and George F. Richardson as I ever learned in the classroom. I was an idealist to the end of my college days. My last two years I roomed with three men, "Teddy Roosevelt" Schilling, and across the hall, "Ralph Waldo" Sprague and "Thomas Carlyle" Richardson. These last two were philosophers at whose feet I often sat. When they debated free will versus predestination, I listened to the philosophers of all the ages wrangling through them. My room became a Parker House of Hawthorne and Holmes and the New England writers, or a Coffee House of Sam Johnson and his crowd.

My senior year marked the climax of my athletic career. When the year started I was still on the scrubs. I took for granted that I always would be. All other seniors who had not made the team had long since dropped the game to younger, more ambitious beginners. However, to me football was not a matter of making the team; it was still my autumn rhapsody. It was a part of my zest for living. It was my poetry of body and soul.

At the close of the first week, Clint Harris, the coach, gathered the team together in a corner of the new cement grandstand and gave them a pep talk. "It is the spirit that counts in football," he said. "This year we shall have to depend upon the Grinnell spirit as never before.

There is one man on the squad who typifies that spirit. Glenn Clark back there has been out every year of his college course, and has never made the team. That's what I call the Grinnell spirit. Never say die. That is what we need this year. A team that knows no quitters, no matter what the reward."

Then to my surprise he put me on the first team. I still weighed only 135. No good for the line. He tried me at left halfback. In the first game our team opened a hole for me. I was quick to get under-way–that was my forte–and shot through the hole like greased lightning. In the open field there were eleven opponents who could overtake me. I listened for their footsteps. As I turned I found some of these overtaking footsteps were my own team. My opponents found me clever that day in ducking in and out among my own interference. There was another art I had–I could follow my interference. Perhaps I could still hold my place on the team. I made a touchdown.

The score remained 6 to 0 till late in the game when an opposing player scooped up a fumble of my running mate and started for the goal, I after him. Out of the corner of my eye I saw that I was alone in the pursuit. The fate of the game depended on my speed–and I had no speed. The first ten yards I held my own, but then the gap widened. The longer legs of the adversary were making better time than my short legs could make. Over my shoulder came the breath of the captain of the opposing team, the speediest man on the field, maneuvering to block me out of the running completely. In disgust he gave me a shove with both arms, being in position where the umpire could not see the unfair play, a shove so vicious and tremendous that it sent me completely off my feet. Knowing I was going headlong I immediately churned the ground with my feet, utilizing the shove to send me in a grand arching leap, landing within reach of the flying ankles of the ball carrier, which sent him spinning to the ground. That accident saved the victory which my long run had won. For a slow runner to make a touchdown himself, and later prevent an opponent's touchdown by making a record-breaking leap through the air and bringing down his man, built up my reputation no end with the coach that day. This game is a picture in little of my entire life, the story of a slow runner catapulted by his very limitations and the accidents of circumstance into victories which he by his own endowments never deserved to win.

When the big game of the season against Drake University was played in the great Drake Stadium, I had the thrill of knowing that I was being watched by my father and mother and three sisters and my kid brother, Morton, who was destined someday to become one of Grinnell's immortals on track and gridiron. Bleamaster, the right halfback, was much heavier than I. He could hit the line harder, run the ends faster, stiff-arm better, do practically everything better. But there was one thing I could do better than he—I knew the art of following my interference. Between halves Coach Harris said to the quarterback, "They have Bleamaster's number. They are stopping everyone but Clark. This half give him the ball every other play."

The second half was more than half over when I began to realize that I was making all the gains but Bleamaster was getting all the cheers. Even when thrown for a loss they cheered him. And all because he was dodging and dashing out in the open where all could see him, while I was always so encircled by my interference that no one knew when I was carrying the ball. On the next play, therefore, I determined I would go out into the open where everyone could see me. I too would get my glory!

My mother described what happened more accurately than the sporting editor of the *Des Moines Register* did the next morning: "I thought it was terrible the way those twenty-two big wicked men all jumped on my poor little boy at the same time." That was certainly the way it felt. And how often have I cited this incident to drive home the truth that "the moment you put yourself into the picture you get bumped." On the other hand, if you can follow your Captain so closely that those in front cannot see anyone but the Captain, you can keep on going as long as the Captain wants you to go!

When I was in the Senior Academy, Louise Miles was in the Junior Academy. From the very beginning I felt drawn to her as the girl I would someday like to marry. It was not until I was a sophomore that I got up courage enough to go with her "steady" and then I was so shy I think I must have bored her to death. We were both shy and lacked the audacity and spontaneity of the other "steady couples" moving around the campus in the springtime. When the year ended I told her that I felt it was not fair for me to monopolize her social hours and that the next year I would stay out of the picture and give her a chance to go with other boys. For a year and a half I took a different girl every time I "stepped out" and I was glad to see that Louise herself never lacked beaus. But the last of our senior year we found ourselves gravitating toward each other again and this time with a background and a maturity that enabled us to bring infinitely more to each other than we had before. My mother had given me a slogan: long courtships but short engagements." I believed there was wisdom in her advice so it was three years after we graduated before I proposed to the woman who was to be my wife.

There were no social dances permitted at Grinnell in those days, but the four classes held separate discussion meetings every Saturday after supper. And everyone went. After a song and a prayer there followed some very vital discussions. These gatherings also furnished excellent opportunities for little groups to get together afterwards, or for some to stroll off in pairs; and in a very wholesome way laid foundations for the best kind of social life. There were some magnificent folks in my class of '05: Herbert Templeton, Walter Spencer, Irving Davis, Paul Trigg, Mary Raymond, Ada Hopkins, Ruth Roberts, Edith Swan, Esther Seaman, and a score of others. One hundred and five came in as freshmen and fifty-five went out as graduates.

The Congregational colleges, Oberlin, Beloit, Carleton, Colorado and Grinnell, were then, and still are, outstanding in the Middle West. They all stressed social service as championed by Josiah Strong and Walter Rauschenbush, but alas, they greatly under-stressed mysticism and the inspiration my soul craved. In the student Bible class which I was leading we concentrated on the life of Jesus. I became tremendously enamored of Jesus. In my boyhood he had been someone too far away for me to grasp. As a God there was an impassable gulf separating us. But when I "imagined" that I was reading the records for the first time, or better still, when I imagined that I was with the crowd around John the Baptist when he suddenly pointed to a silent figure coming down the hillside from the shops of Nazareth, that gave me—and my little group of college boys—a real experience. The college seal was Christi

Duce, "Christ the Leader." I soon found myself translating Jesus' command, "Follow me" to "Be like me." It became my passion to be like Jesus. By seeing him more human and less divine it spurred me on to follow him in every way that I could. In one respect alone I was not satisfied—I could not pray to the Father with the faith that Jesus had.

About that time I read a new book entitled *In His Steps*, which had a deep influence on my life. From that time on, everything I studied centered around Jesus. All history was dominated by his figure. Hardly a department of our life, I noted, but has been touched and profoundly modified by him. Literature, music and art I found were all saturated with his influence. In short, it was impossible to understand the history of two millenniums without reference to him. So taking him as the center, I proceeded to unify all my college courses around him.

However, at the same time that I was trying to understand the life of Jesus, I was also majoring in Greek, history and philosophy. And when I came to read Maeterlink's *Buried Temple*, something he said made me believe that the faith of humble people in immortality had been the chief lever by which the favored few kept the great mass content in their poverty, and I suddenly had to admit that from an entirely *human* point of view, from a material standpoint alone, I could not honestly say there was any proof of God or of immortality. With one sweep of the pen, as it were, all my inherited religion, based upon authority, all my faith, built upon hearsay, were swept away.

Life suddenly became grim and gray. That grayness lasted for over a year. I became an agnostic. A miserable agnostic. Only an absolutely genuine spiritual experience could ever sweep that agnosticism away. I did not know it at the time, but this was the best kind of a foundation for the greatest reality I ever could have experienced to come to me. I wonder if it was on a foundation of such honesty that Saul of Tarsus' revelation came to him? But of that awakening I shall write later. Indeed, it is the chief excuse for the writing of this book.

When we were freshmen I had been elected president of the class. When a senior I was elected class poet. My final message to my classmates as well as to the dear old college can be summed up in this stanza from my graduation poem:

For we once had a theory what the world should have been,
A message to startle the slumbering dead,
A fame to snatch from the lions den.
Till we learned that greatness was daily bread,
Transfigured with love of man.

Next to Jesus, Browning had become my passion. Browning's poem "Paracelsus" was the inspiration of my college days. Naturally I was impressed by the fact that this poem was written in Browning's youth when he was even younger than I was then. On my twenty-first birthday when I recalled the Divine Plan of my life that had been revealed to me when a lad of fourteen, I found singular inspiration in the words:

I go to prove my soul!
I see my way as birds their trackless way.
I shall arrive! What time, what circuit first,
I ask not. But unless God send his hail
Or blinding fireballs, sleet or stifling snow,
In some good time, his good time, I shall arrive:
He guides me and the bird. In his good time!

As I left college halls in June, 1905, I carried the ringing challenge of Paracelsus when he left the security of his college town.

Are there not, Festus, are there not, dear Michal,
Two points in the adventure of the diver,
One—when, a beggar, he prepares to plunge,
One—when, a prince, he rises with his pearl?
Festus, I plunge!

And more and more as I traveled through life I have felt the truth in the precious lines:

Truth is within ourselves; it takes no rise
From outward things, whate'er you may believe.
There is an inmost centre in us all,
Where truth abides in fullness; and around
Wall upon wall, the gross flesh hems it in,
This perfect, clear perception—which is truth.

A baffling and perverting carnal mesh
Binds it, and makes all error: and, to KNOW,
Rather consists in opening out a way
Whence the imprisoned splendor may escape,
Than in effecting entry for a light
Supposed to be without.

CHAPTER X

I Learn to Teach

IT HAD always been a dream of mine to come back and teach in my home-town high school. This dream came true when I was elected principal of my old Oak Park High School of Des Moines at a salary of fifty-five dollars a month for nine months. The superintendent of the grade schools had a few classes and I had two experienced teachers under me. I was to teach each day three classes in English, two in history, coach the debate team, the senior play, football and track. The only subjects I felt qualified to teach well were football and track.

The triplets were now seniors. They called their big brother "Glenn." All the pupils called me "Glenn." Discipline, when its need did arise, was a problem. I managed to keep one step ahead of the classes in preparation and one step behind in discipline. But the outside activities thrived under my direction. Morton starred in the class play, Mabel on the debate team, and Eleanor in the classroom. I starred only in the athletic coaching. Although we were the smallest high school in the city, we ranked third in both football and track. My brother was captain of the football team and the outstanding star on the track team. In convocations the students sang the school song I had written (to the tune of "Mandalay") and at the athletic contests they yelled the yell I had composed seven years before. But thank the Lord, they chose "Esmerelda" for the class play and not "Jack Donaldson's Revenge."

This year at Oak Park rounded out my life at Sunnyside and made it complete. I felt the need of this final year with father and mother and the beloved triplets before I was ready to go ahead. The memory I shall always treasure most was the opportunity to pal with my little brother, now towering above me in height, in this fellowship on the athletic field and in the classroom. I came within a hair's breadth of losing him just before the school year began. That summer he and I occupied the same bedroom, the original room meant for Page and me. One night I awoke with the strange feeling that I was next to a furnace. I reached out and touched my brother. His body was so hot I drew back my hand. A fever of at least 104, I guessed.

"I won't waken my parents now," I thought, "but I'll tell them the moment morning comes, and we'll have the doctor."

But when morning came, Morton seemed as well and jolly as anyone at breakfast and all memory of my night experiences faded from my mind. The next night I awoke again with the same impression of burning heat. And when morning came I again completely forgot the fever. It was just as though I had dreamed it up, and just as dreams fade away like morning dew unless clutched firmly at the moment of waking, so these experiences faded completely.

Late that second afternoon Morton said, "My stomach doesn't feel good." Suddenly the memory of the two night awakenings came to me. I felt his forehead. Burning hot! When the doctor came he said, "This boy has typhoid. The fever is 105. He must have had it for three days. I'll try to get a nurse. This is serious." But it was impossible to get a nurse.

"I'll sit up with him tonight," I said.

A great peace came to me. I positively *knew* the Lord would not take my last and only remaining brother. He had taken one. I had a divine right to keep this one. I don't always get this sense of Destiny, but whenever I do, I find it more powerful than prayer itself. When all the family had retired and I was alone in the sick-room, this peace and conviction became so strong that merely my *knowing* was more powerful than any prayer I could have offered. Every hour my mother came tiptoeing in, in her wrapper and slippers, and I sent her straight back, assuring her with such calm and confidence that all was well

that she caught the contagion in spite of her motherly concern. The
Power in that room that night was actually tangible. Sure enough, the
quick recovery of my brother was so amazing the doctor could not
understand it. In two weeks he started school. In four weeks he was
playing on the football team!

It is fascinating to watch a boy of sixteen or seventeen learn the
mysteries of muscular coordination for a new athletic event. In the early
spring my brother Morton could leap four feet eleven inches. Rumors
reached us of four boys at West High who could do five-four.

"Don't worry," I told Morton, "I am going to bring you along
gradually. You will outjump them all when the state meet arrives."
How thankful I was now for my training with Jackson Watson. We
had no track equipment. With three hurdles, handmade, I trained
Morton at this event also. "Three hurdles are all you need for practice,"
I comforted him. "We have plenty of room for you to train for speed
and endurance. If you have those two things when the meet comes off,
ten hurdles will be as easy as three."

He ran second in the hurdles and first in the high jump. He also
tied for first in the latter at the state meet. On a toss of the coin he won
the right to represent the state at the famous Stagg Meet in Chicago.
My dreams of athletic prowess which were never completely fulfilled
in my own life began to be fulfilled in the life of my brother.

The succeeding fall Mabel and Morton went to join Helen, who
was now a senior at Grinnell, while Eleanor, who was the outstanding
student in Oak Park High School, had won a free scholarship at Drake
University and remained in Des Moines. The following year she joined
the other two at Grinnell where they all graduated. When my first year
of teaching was over I was offered a position in every high school in the
city at greatly advanced salary, which would not have been offered if
they had known what a poor teacher I was. I chose North High. And
here it was that I made atonement for all my previous mistakes. For
here I learned at last the fine art of teaching.

Miss Emma Case Moulton was head of the English department.
"Teach the sophomores the *Idylls of the King*," she said, "and if you do
it the right way you can actually change their lives."

"How?" I asked.

"At the right time have them memorize the Knights' Oath in 'Guinevere.' It will do more to purify their souls than all the preaching in the world."

She was right. At another time she said, "We aren't allowed to teach religion in the public school, and above all we mustn't preach. But the best door to building spiritual character is the English department. My father was a minister but I have preached five sermons for every one he ever preached. I will show you how." And she proceeded to show me how poetry lifts, whether it be by Wordsworth or David, by Edwin Markham or Isaiah.

In my English classes I devised the system of putting sentences on the board, like *Grandmother Grey sat knitting in the back yard under the old apple tree*, and letting the students shut their eyes, visualize the picture and then reproduce it in words.

"Don't bother about neatness, spelling or punctuation," I said. "The picture comes first."

The little freshmen did more brilliant work than my composition teachers at Grinnell had succeeded in drawing out of college students. At last I had found the secret of writing which is alive, the secret which, ten years later, found its way into my *Manual of the Short Story Art*.

My two sections of American history I called the Senate and the House of Representatives. Each student represented a state. At the end of each month we took the chief problem before the nation in the form of a bill set before Congress and had a great debate upon it. The senator who presented the bill led the defense of it. All the other senators fought for the floor to defend or attack the measures. Inhibitions, self-consciousness were all cast out the window. Shy pupils became brilliant orators. Personal names were forgotten and state names substituted. American history became a living thing.

I coached track that spring and the school ranked fourth in the state meet, higher than ever in its history. I can shut my eyes now and see Crawford coming down the 440 straightaway, Kenneth Hunter and McCreight sweeping the low hurdles, and Fat O'Brien breaking all records in the hammer. The art of getting men into the pink of condition at the right time which Jack Watson had taught me worked surprisingly well.

Theodore Roosevelt was the man in the public eye in those days. His emphasis on large families was lifting the role of motherhood to a new height. That winter my mother was called upon by her church to give a talk on the "Teddy Mother." She was such a marvelous mother herself, I knew it would be a success if she could in some way let *herself* flow into it. One day I walked into her room as she sat at her desk preparing the speech she was to give. I can never forget that hour. It was my last year in the old home, as I was leaving next year for Harvard.

Suddenly my mother looked up from her writing. "Would you like to hear my speech, Glenn?" she asked.

Even before she began to read her speech I had already composed one in my own mind about her. But now I stopped my thinking and began to listen. Had she been Lincoln speaking at Gettysburg she could not have held me more enthralled. The closing lines were as follows:

> Having loved her parents, she loves all old people. Loving her children, she loves all children, and desires to help every unfortunate child. There are lines upon her face that sorrow has left there, and as we look closer, we see gaps in the family circle that have bound her closer to all humanity.
>
> This mother knows there is something more to do than pray with and for her children—necessary as that is. She knows Bible texts and Sunday school will not save her children. To make her children God's children she must prune, and weed, and hoe. She must live with her children, be young with her children, stand by them in time of temptation as a pilot stands by his wheel in a storm. She believes in fun and frolic, in making home attractive, and is not willing to give anything to the devil that will make young people happy.
>
> She never worries. Why should she? God made the world—she did not—and she knows God is capable of taking care of His own. She does not sink under responsibilities; she only does her part each day and leaves the rest to the Great All-Father.
>
> She knows this world is only a prelude to Eternity, and that the broken sounds of illy-touched flutes and harps here will there unite in one grand harmony.

"Wonderful!" I breathed, when she had finished, "It is the one masterpiece I always wanted you to write. I know that it will ring the bell." And sure enough, nothing ever spoken in Plymouth Church in my day created such a sensation as this talk of my mother's. The pastor had it printed and distributed to his entire congregation the following Sunday.

None of her children ever saw their mother when she did not have white hair framing her strong, tender face. It was as though nature was here trying to exact compensation for the extraordinary youthfulness of her heart. I never heard a quarrel nor even a heated argument between father and mother. This atmosphere of complete harmony naturally extended itself to the children so that there was seldom any discord in the home; but on those rare occasions when one of the children did go to bed nursing a grievance, invariably after the lights were out and all was quiet, he would hear the familiar footsteps that were so dear to him, and his mother's arms were soon around his neck while she pleaded that he forgive the one that had hurt him. I know of nothing that has done so much to make life sweet and worthwhile to all those who have gone forth from that home as that attitude of trust and love and mutual forbearance that was fostered and inspired by that mother's love.

The following winter she and father moved to La Jolla, California, with Helen. The children had flown the coop and now the parents fled also. In La Jolla, the gem of the sea, they set up their "Villa Arden" and established a new sanctuary for their children. But the happy days of Sunnyside were over.

CHAPTER XI

Europe and Harvard

"COME with me on a bicycle trip through Europe," Wilbur Schilling wrote to me. He was teaching history at Parson's College. "Shake the dust out of your bones and listen to the call of the open road. I will review my knowledge of European history and you review the backgrounds of English literature and together we shall lick the platter clean."

"Aye, aye, Mate!" I replied. "Get the bicycles and the tickets and I will join you in Quebec."

Thus a new chapter opened in my life, in perfect accordance with the second period of the Divine Plan, widening my contacts with the world and its people.

Wilbur applied for an agency of the Columbia Bicycle Company in the little town of Fairfield, Iowa, where he was teaching. The company replied that he would have to order two bicycles to start an agency. He ordered the two, and I imagine the company has been waiting ever since for the second order. That is the way of Wilbur. Everywhere he bought for wholesale if legitimately possible.

We embarked at Quebec third class on the *Empress of Ireland*. For twenty-seven dollars we had the passage, including meals, and, without extra cost, a railroad ticket from Liverpool to Glasgow after we arrived. Our first pilgrimage upon reaching Britain was cycling through the "Lady of the Lake" country of Scotland, then through the English Lake Country, then cross-country through the heart of England: Chester, Coventry, Stratford-on-Avon, Oxford, Henly, Winsor and Longdon.

There is something about seeing a country on a bicycle that one never can get in a railroad train, nor even in an automobile. One gets the *feel* of the country in one's bones and in one's muscles, in one's lungs and in one's blood. The cool wind upon one's cheek, the sun upon one's back, the ruts and bumps of the road upon one's pounding legs, enable him to carry away a portion of every land he travels through. Every man we met passed the time of day with us; every landscape we passed left its indelible imprint upon our memory.

A little framework built upon our bicycles carried a tiny case with night things, a change of socks and one pair of long trousers. Our other luggage we sent ahead by parcel post. Reaching a city at sundown, we changed our knickerbockers and stockings for more gentlemanly attire and spent the evening at theaters or art galleries. Only the young can see so much in so short a time. Like a pair of sponges we mopped up all the Europe we saw.

In every city we found our guardian angel in the form of John, the policeman. Unlike our American variety, he seemed to have no idea whatever of arresting anybody; his sole purpose in life seemed to be to serve. Not only would he show us the way to travel, the place to shop and the sights to see, but he might even walk a block out of his beat to give more exact directions.

In every hotel or rooming house we found Beelzebub and Mrs. Lucifer in the form of the regular platoon of uniformed servants. Whenever we were discovered paying our bill to the proprietor a great commotion occurred: bells were rung, maids came running from kitchen, dining room and bedroom, bootblacks and bellboys sprang up from nowhere, and a line formed on the right with outstretched palms. Behind this seemingly trivial comment lies a great underlying truth in regard to the character of the Europe of that time that may help us interpret conditions in Europe today. The state-owned and state-operated activities of Europe were handled with efficiency and with a sort of selfless consideration for others, a paternal consideration for all the needs of the individual. The privately owned and operated activities were handled with obsequiousness or rudeness, dependent upon the size of the gratuity in the offing. The symbol of monarchy or state ownership was that of a courteous *helper*, of democracy was that of an obsequious or an officious *beggar*.

We noted the smooth-running, government trains in contrast, at that time, to the outrageous graft in our own railroads with their watered stock and their insidious control over state legislatures. We especially admired the city governments, apparently functioning without a suspicion of graft in contrast to our own city governments which at that time were smelling to high heaven. When our own nation, trained in democracy for a century, was making such a wretched and scandalous showing, I can see how Europe, completely untrained in democracy but adjusted to government controls, looks askance at our democratic processes in times of serious readjustments. .

Paris may be France, but London is not England. One doesn't know England till he has wheeled along the ribbon-white roads, skirting beautiful hedges and stone fences, and has slept in the coffee houses and talked with yeomen along the way. In England the roads between cities were kept up in remarkable style but the side roads were neglected; the great estates were handed down intact to eldest sons, the younger sons were neglected. In those days the younger sons sought careers in South Africa, India or Australia. Half of them became failures, the other half ruled England.

At the Tower of London an old guard who looked exactly like John Bull himself asked if we were from America. When we replied in the affirmative he asked when we would have a war with Japan.

"It is coming sooner or later," he said; "why don't you jump in now and smash the little devils?" This was thirty-five years before Pearl Harbor. Then he gave quite a dissertation on the Anglo-Saxon race. He said, "We are the greatest land-grabbers the world has ever seen. No, don't debate the question. Look at your wars with Mexico and Spain. No, don't apologize. Be proud of it. The Israelites started the land-grabbing. They grabbed the Promised Land. Yes, all the great races are great land-grabbers!"

On the boat to Germany we were all entertained by a German and Englishman debating the subject, Could Germany land an army in England? They couldn't do it, the Englishman said, but if they did, they could conquer England in one week, he admitted.

In Italy I obtained a copy of Ruskin's *Stones of Venice* and read his descriptions right in the very cathedrals and before the very pictures he described. In Florence I basked in the atmosphere of Michelangelo and da Vinci. But the two memory pictures of Europe that stand out most vividly are, first, my arrival in Strassburg, where everyone looked French, wore French styles, had French noses and eyebrows, and talked French. Presently I rode by a great citadel and line of barracks where fifteen thousand German soldiers, almost half as many as our entire standing army at that time, were constantly encamped. Old women in the yards were busy cleaning muskets, dingy soldiers in fatigue uniforms were hard at work, cannons were arranged in rows mounted on carts and ready to be hauled at once to the frontier. Further on I was passed by a detail of German infantry going to relieve the pickets. In a narrow street I had to dismount to let a cavalcade of cavalry trot by. Germany was jealously on guard all those years. My last memory of that city was that of a statue of a German poet, and inscribed upon it his ominous words, "The Rhine, Germany's river, not Germany's boundary."

The other picture that will stay with me was in Hamburg, at the vast playground of German children. Boys of eight to twelve and even younger were finding their chief joy in playing soldier, marching, drilling in earnest fashion. And above them stood a gigantic statue of Bismarck leaning on a mammoth sword, his bulldog jaws set and an ominous leer in his heavy eye gazing off toward France. These little boys of ten were boys of seventeen when the war of 1914-18 broke out. I can hear the footsteps of them now, marching into Belgium. How many of those boys died under the gunfire of the Marne! And how many of *their* boys died before General Patton's guns?

En route to Europe I had let my beard grow. When I left the *Empress of Ireland* at Liverpool I looked like the Russian nihilists who had ridden in the same steerage. But when I had it trimmed in the style of each country into which I entered I found that if I kept my mouth shut I was taken for a native. By letting Wilbur Schilling, who had grown a Kaiser Wilhelm mustache, do all the talking in English or in German, the prospective landlords took him for the valet of one of their own native sons and we escaped the extra "tariff" usually visited upon "rich" Americans.

Later, upon my arrival at Harvard I decided to keep the beard for the sojourn there. This had one beneficial result: at the graduate students' meetings which were usually attended by members of the faculty, I was easily distinguished from the rest and often sought out by the faculty men as one of the "more mature" students. I treasure the informal conversations with President Eliot, Professor Palmer and Professor William James above everything else. Professor James loved to talk with me about my Grinnell teacher in psychology, John Elof Boodin, who had been a favorite pupil of his. William James' unique message to me was, "To know a thing is only half of the qualification of a genius. The bigger half is the power to get it across to others. There are no dumb Miltons. If they are dumb they are not Miltons. I think every candidate for a doctor's degree should be required to write his doctor's thesis in such popular language that all could understand it."

Professor Palmer told me one day, "I had a classmate who was very dear to me but we two specialized in far different fields. I took a narrow field of philosophy and he a still narrower field in science. Every step we took carried us farther and farther away from each other. But finally there came a time when our specializations had carried us so far that they lay bare to us the basic truth at the center and core of all fields, and then, behold, we found that our very specializations had brought us together again. Therefore I would advise you, young man, that it doesn't matter so much what field you go into, provided you are willing to go all the way."

I have often recalled that conversation as I watch the scientists today carry us through their tunnel of science to molecules, then to atoms, then to electrons, then to basic energy, and finally to the thought behind the energy, ending at the place where only God can stand. And then I turn to watch the theologians coming to us through their ponderous tunnel of ecclesiasticism and dogma, sometimes reaching the center only to find that the scientists have arrived there before them.

When I discovered that to get a doctor's degree in English at Harvard I would have to waste one full year in the study of Old

French, Anglo-Saxon and Old English, and most of another full year in writing a thesis about some old data that other writers in the dim past had plowed over, I completely gave up intentions in that direction. Instead, I determined I would be satisfied with earning an M.A. at Harvard and an honorary degree someday in writing, God willing, some new literature of my own worth the reading. In dear old Dean Briggs' writing class I tried my best to get a novel started, but nothing worthwhile came forth. The whole atmosphere of Harvard University was not conducive to writing novels, not to one fresh from the warmer atmosphere of Sunnyside and Grinnell.

My chief pals were Russell Story and Ralph Chase, both majoring in history. In my own department I grew to know Ray Nichols, William Beeheimer and Rodger Williams. I carried away very few friendships from that immense university. One can make more friends in one year at a small college than he can in four in a great university. In a university a boy can go through more college; but in a small school more college goes through the boy. My faith still rests in the small college.

My teachers were Bliss Perry in Tennyson, George Kittredge in Shakespeare, William Allen Nielson in Chaucer and Dean Briggs in composition. I admired them all, but Kittredge furnished the glamour. All of us who went out teaching after sitting under Kittredge became little facsimiles of him—until the first month was over. Only Kittredge could get away with Kittredge. For instance, he got his regular morning constitutional and setting-up exercises in our class by walking like a caged lion to and fro across the ample platform as he lectured. Occasionally he would pause in this three-mile walk and turn his white sideburns and glowing eyes straight upon us, then swing around and dash off a word on the blackboard, and without deigning to glance back, he would toss the chalk nonchalantly toward the blackboard, and it would *always* land in the chalk rail.

My first year of teaching Shakespeare I also strolled back and forth, to the mystification of my pupils, and I, too, nonchalantly tossed the chalk toward the blackboard. But alas, my chalk always bounced against the wall and fell crashing and splintering upon the floor. After a debonair fortnight of being Professor Kittredge I humbly turned to being Professor Clark.

BOOK FOUR

Responsibilities Begin

CHAPTER XII

William and Vashti

IN THE closing days of my Harvard year I began corresponding with various schools regarding possible openings in the English departments. I was in correspondence with Whitman and Beloit, when out of a clear sky came a definite call to head the English department and be director of athletics at William and Vashti College, Aledo, Illinois. What was this college? What was this town?

It was a brand new college starting on its maiden voyage. Would it be a flashing meteor or a planet destined to long life? Did it have a future? The president would not say. He would answer no questions. Sufficient that it had a present. I could write my own ticket, chart my own course. I could build from the foundation up. The president continued to bombard me with telegrams, "ANSWER IMMEDIATELY."

Dean Briggs urged me to accept. He said the independence I could have intrigued him. I wired my acceptance. And then began an experience unique in the annals of teaching.

President T. J. Davis had gathered around him a very efficient faculty, a freshman class of unusual quality, and an academy to serve as feeder for the future college. The plant consisted of a beautiful college building and a very adequate boys' dormitory, a gymnasium built entirely for basketball and a president's mansion. An old farmer, William Drury, had left four hundred thousand dollars to establish a college. As there was already a Drury College, the first names of himself and his wife became the title.

So here was my chance both to teach and to coach without concern as to what the alumni would think and say. I proceeded at once to build up a great Shakespeare course, a la Professor Kittredge, a novel course a la Seldon Whitcomb, and a creative writing course that was entirely the product of Glenn Clark. It was at this college the following year that I created my course in world masterpieces.

But it was in athletics that freedom from alumni control enabled me to give free play to all my original ideas. My football candidates were a bunch of farmer boys, fairly husky and strong, most of whom had never had a football suit on in their lives. The forward pass had just come in the year before and I had witnessed the famous Carlisle Indians under the tutelage of Pop Warner play rings around Harvard. By combining my own high school plays with a modification of the Warner strategy I worked out a system of plays that would warm the heart of any coach. I took those boys and built Homeric epics out of them that made that little section of Illinois open its eyes and gasp.

Among other things, I taught my signal caller to start calling signals while the players were still on the ground from the previous play. Into this signal was woven the formation call, so that the boys instead of first lining up and then shifting into a formation actually went to the shifted formation *as they lined up*. Moreover, because we called signals so rapidly, even before the previous play was finished, the other team was often taken off guard. In fact, we outdid the "hurry up Yost" system which was known as "a play a minute" team. We were halfway down the field finishing perhaps five plays in the time that it takes a modern team to get out of its first huddle.

Out of this little college of thirty-eight students I got together a football squad of eleven men. As we might need replacements, two diminutive rah-rah boys, good in the cheering section but of doubtful value on the football fields, donned suits for the sake of Alma Mater and offered themselves as substitutes. Fortunately, we had to use only one of these boys and for only one game.

How to hold a team in such perfect condition that it could come through a grueling season with no injuries was the biggest part of my problem. Game after game, year after year, eleven "iron men" started the game and the same eleven ended it. Here is where the training of old Jack Watson served me in amazing ways. "Little and often," said Jack regarding training, and in good old Greek style added, "In nothing too much."

We had passes, double passes, lateral passes and long and short forward passes. I trained every man on the team to be a passer and when our diminutive squad of eleven men spread out over the field to warm up before a game, sending a battery of balls flying through the air to all corners of the field, we were the admiration and wonder of every school we played. Even in their defeat the opposing colleges felt they had received their money's worth in watching our boys demonstrate the "new game" just then coming into fashion. Iowa Wesleyan, the oldest college in the Middle West, when defeated by us, the youngest college, begged us to come back for their Thanksgiving Day game, claiming that they could get out an immense crowd to see our team play. The Galesburg papers were filled with stories of our razzle-dazzle exhibit when we played Knox.

I should like to write a page about each one of those splendid lads: Martin Justice, our triple-threat player whose play in football and basketball was poetry in motion; Robert McCord, the best tackle for his weight I ever saw; McCleary, Lee, McCaw, Shakleford, Harding, McLaughlin and the brilliant Clark brothers, one of whom, "Potsy" Clark, became nationally famous.

The college was too young to have a college song, but they improvised a song to their coach instead; whatever it lacked in rhyme it made up in spirit. I blush even now to think how that song rolled across the field to the tune of "There's a Grand Old Flag":

> He's a grand old Clark–
> And he is in our hearts,
> And his worth we will show you today;
> He's the idol of the teams we love,
> That fight for the red and the gray, rah, rah!
> And we'll fight for him, though we lose or we win,
> For we know that he does his part,

Though other coaches may be good,
Take your hat off to old man Clark.

The acclaim I never received as a player I received far beyond my deserts as a coach.

When spring came I relived with the boys the romance of King Arthur's knights on field and track. With Paul Blazer, son of the Aledo *Times-Record* editor, able to outsprint and outjump any man in the state, and with McCleary to throw the weights and Diefendort and Thompson and Corey in the middle distances, I knew I would have a team equal to any in Illinois, if I only had a hurdler. Then one day a long-legged farmer lad, Rollie Dunn, amused the team by the way he could wrap his long legs around his neck.

"Grand!" I said. "Cut out your fooling and do that split act over these ten hurdles." He and his brother Forest soon became the hurdle champions of the state.

Four years of idyllic college life in classroom and on the athletic field were the years at William and Vashti.

CHAPTER XIII

Marriage

RIDING on the train toward my wedding day, I was not riding alone. It seemed that all the unseen forces of the universe were riding with me. All my past was riding with me. All my future was riding with me. With this sense of converging forces focusing upon me, I wondered if I could ever go through with the event. I found myself almost atremble in the littleness that was "me" before the awful bigness that marriage represented.

It was while I was in this state that Mr. Fiebeger entered the car. Down the aisle he came, tall, white-haired, with a faraway look in his eye, as though his mind was not concerned with the little journey being made by these bodies slumped down in their seats. When he reached my seat he paused as though he had in some extrasensory way perceived that I, too, was at that moment not of this world.

I have described that meeting in more detail in *I Will Lift Up Mine Eyes*, in which I took the liberty of slightly foreshortening the preceding events. The outer preliminary events, however, were hardly needed to deepen the intensity of the inner significance of that meeting.

"Pardon me," said Mr. Fiebeger, "but would you mind if I sat down in the seat beside you for a while?"

"Certainly not," I replied. As soon as he was seated he turned to me.

"You are engaged in religious work of some kind, are you not?" he asked.

"Oh, no!" I answered, laughing. "I am merely a teacher of literature and a coach of athletics."

He hesitated for just a moment.

"But you have a spiritual influence upon the young men you associate with, do you not?"

I hesitated. "Well, perhaps I do."

"I am in a business," he began, "that carries me to all parts of the country. On every journey I find myself led to tell my story to one person. God always directs me to the person to whom I am to tell it, and now I find myself led to tell it to you."

"I shall be glad to hear your story," I replied.

"It happened to me in this wise. I had come to Akron, Ohio, as a young man of energy and promise. I threw myself headlong into my business and it began to thrive beyond all expectations. I was soon head of the firm. Not satisfied with being president of one concern, I organized another, and then became director of others. I was making money hand over fist. All I thought about, morning, noon and night, was money, money, money. And then something happened. It always happens when you burn the candle at both ends and leave God out of the picture, doesn't it? I had a breakdown.

"Well, the doctor said I was done for, that my working days were over, my only hope lay in making some drastic changes in my life. He told me to go to a lake and recuperate, doing nothing but rest for months and months. Then he would see if I could do any work again.

"I went to Isle Royal in Lake Superior. As my strength gradually returned I would go out in a rowboat and idle about for hours. Something about the wide expanse of water beneath a summer sky rested me; it was doing something to me inside and outside. A new peace began to enter into me. And then the great experience happened.

"I had gone out in a boat, near sunset. I was rather drowsy and before I knew it I had fallen asleep. When I awoke hours later the boat was out of sight of land, and there was no way for me to determine whether I was north, south or east of the island. Knowing how quickly a squall can arise on Lake Superior and how easily a boat is overturned, also how drowned bodies never come to the surface in this coldest of all northern waters, I was filled with a panic of fear. I started to pray, and then found that I couldn't. And why? Simply because I wasn't worthy to pray. My whole past came up before me. What would be the value of saving a man like me, a man who did nothing but accumulate money for himself? What would the world lose if I should never return?

"And then I made a promise to God. I promised Him that if He would save me, I would devote half of my time henceforth to His work, to helping mankind, especially young people. And then the answer came."

At this point the old gentleman fumbled in his pocket and brought forth a picture postal card. It looked exactly like a photograph. It was a pictorial arrangement of a man alone in a rowboat on a lake, and above his head were the moon and stars, and among the stars one immense star about ten times the size of the other stars and about one-fourth the size of the moon. I wondered if the Star of Bethlehem could have looked like that.

"This star suddenly appeared in the sky," he said, pointing to the large star in the picture. "It was an immense star, such as I had never seen before. I was overwhelmed with the mystery and wonder of it, but taking it as a sign I fixed my eyes upon it, and keeping it at the tail of my boat, I rowed and rowed without looking around for hours and hours. When I finally did look around, I was going straight up to the landing pier whence I had started.

"That is all of my story," he ended abruptly, starting to rise. "Keep it in your mind and plant it in your heart, and someday it may bear fruit in your life. How and when I know not, but this I know: what comes from God is eternal. What God has not planted will be rooted up; but what God has planted will bear fruit one-hundred-fold."

"Please wait a minute," I said. "What happened to you afterwards?"

"I merely took an elevator and went up to another floor. My life, the regular business and church life I had been living, went on as usual, but in an entirely different world. I found myself living thenceforth in a heavenly world where love and peace and happiness were everywhere about me including my business associates and even the chance acquaintances I meet upon my travels." And he smiled at me.

"But how did you get up to that higher level?" I asked.

"It is a secret," he replied, "a great and wonderful secret. But if you really must know the secret, here it is: 'HE MAKETH MY FEET LIKE HINDS' FEET AND SETTETH ME UPON MY HIGH PLACES.'"

It was not until years later that the significance of these words "hinds' feet" dawned upon me.

Could his description be a premonition of my own future life? Was I going to have, not a nervous breakdown, but a state of nervous and mental exhaustion and ennui over burning my candles too long, over monotonous, mundane pursuits? Was I to take a period to rest and find myself, in which I would discover a star likened unto the Star of Bethlehem, which would guide my course straight to the Port which God had destined for me?

When I got off the train I was as a man in a daze. It seemed that I remained in that daze more or less up to and through my wedding, and that I never *completely* awoke from it until many years later when I finally discovered the meaning of making one's feet like "hinds' feet" and mounting to one's "high places." But that time was still afar off.

On December 29, 1909, in George and Flora Miles' home at 1018 Park Street, Grinnell, Iowa, I was married to their youngest daughter, Louise. The wedding was very simple as the Miles family always liked to do things with no ostentation of any kind. Saintly old Doctor Parker, emeritus professor of history of Grinnell College, performed the ceremony, Raymond Chittick and Morton Macartney sang, and it was over. Dear old Doctor Parker must have been psychic, because he drew me aside and said, "Wives may know that their husbands love them, but they like to be reminded of it occasionally by their husbands' telling them so."

Of all undemonstrative persons I think I have been the limit. When I returned from my year's absence in Europe and at Harvard my sisters exclaimed that they were very highly honored because that was the first time I ever kissed them.

Upon returning to Aledo with my bride we found an immense rambling house we could rent while the owners went south for the next few months. The first thing I did was to hurry to the basement to start the fire. And there over the furnace door was a name plate bearing the title, the Fiebeger-Akron Furnace Company; and so the unknown friend who had been my guardian angel on the train warmed our house as his words have all the years since warmed my heart and the hearts of thousands who read my books.

My yearning for immortality was a very real yearning. Having assembled my ancestors I felt it my duty to assemble my posterity. I wanted children sent from God. I wanted children of my own blood. I also wanted children of my own soul. I wanted the children of my blood to be also children of my soul. But I didn't want my soul children to be limited to my blood children. Denied the privilege granted to Abraham that my children would be like the sands of the sea, I asked for soul children that would people the earth. .

God heard my prayer and granted it in His own way. Without haste, without waste, in His own leisurely, efficient, unhurried way, He brought me the children I asked for from the womb of heaven.

We waited seven years.

"Give me children!" I cried to heaven.

"Not now," said God. "You shall have no children until the Jacob in you is turned to Israel and the Leah in Louise is turned to Rachel. If you want your children sent from heaven you must wait until heaven is born in *you.*"

When the seven years were up, Rachel was born in my wife, Jacob was transformed to Israel in me. I did not go to a physician; I went to a man of God.

"Pray for me," I said, "that I may have children." Then he said one strange and startling thing:

"I will, provided you will no longer believe that your mind is confined to this little prison house called the brain. Your mind is confined in nothing and to nothing. It fills the universe; for you and the Father are One. You are part of the Universal Mind and that Mind will solve your problem for you. Go home now and I will pray for you."

I went home, but did not dare tell my wife of this unusual conversation. But at suppertime I had to tell her. For as I sat at the table that evening, suddenly the walls fell away and my mind flowed out and filled the entire universe. The entire universe entered into that room and filled me. Israel that moment was born in me. I knew my time was come. Nor did the feeling of it and the wonder of it cease when my wife's voice began speaking.

"What is the matter with you?" she was saying. "You are so silent." And I found her looking at me with awe.

"The answer to our prayer has come," I said. "The Lord will send children."

One day we were alone on Wapagassett Island in northern Wisconsin. Lovely Miriam Wallace had asked us to share her family's cabin so she could be on the island when her family was away. How we enjoyed that island! Miriam was a wood nymph herself, a child of nature, the embodiment of the spirit of that perfect island. The God of nature spoke to us from every stick and stone. Miriam left us one day and we were all alone with nature and God. Just as the Holy Spirit drew near and enveloped Mary, so we felt the Spirit of Heaven draw near and enfold us in its wings.

"I guess you are right, Glenn," Louise said. "Our children had to be born first in heaven before God would give them permission to be born on earth. Let us hope they bring part of heaven with them."

Nine months from that day Helen May arrived. The wonder of that arriving is past belief. Only parents who wait long and who yearn know the full glory of their children's coming.

CHAPTER XIV

Creating a Home

A FEW months after my marriage I came to my twenty-eighth birthday. It had become my custom on my birthdays to sit down and meditate on the series of "seven-year plans" that God had given me. From fourteen to twenty-one I was to develop my inner resources, or, in the new psychological lingo becoming popular at that time, I was to be an introvert. This I had certainly been through my high school days and the opening years of college, a shy, introspective boy.

From twenty-one to twenty-eight I was to mix and mingle with the world and adjust myself to others, and become an extrovert. That, too, I had done. Now at twenty-eight I was to start the interweaving of the inner and outer threads in preparation for my life-work. There was discipline in those seven years. I had been brought up in a home where every desire of childhood had found wholesome and joyous expression. Now I was married to a sweet, high-minded girl of strong Puritan ancestry. I touched through her all the negatives of the world. Not the evils, for, through her, evils were canceled out. But in canceling out the evils through the doctrine of the Puritans, some of the negatives, as far as I was concerned, were canceled in. In Louise's home it had been considered wicked to play cards or dance. Since she was frail during all her childhood she had never learned to swim, play tennis or skate. Her shy, proud, perfectionist nature led her to shrink from doing anything she could not do well. Consequently, she had

121

never made speeches, or taken part in a play, or written poetry, and last but not least, she had never sung, even in congregational singing. She had never taken lessons in playing the piano or painting or in any other art.

One who is not a participant in life becomes a critic of life. Louise was not a criticizer but she was an analyzer. My thought-life was given over entirely to synthesis and when synthesis runs head-on into analysis the result is paralysis. At least, the result is paralysis when the ego takes control. But—and this thrilled us when we discovered it—this union of analysis with synthesis could become a kind of genius when the soul takes control. The seven years from twenty-eight to thirty-five were a winnowing out of the ego in both of us and the discovery of our souls.

When an irresistible force meets an immovable body something occurs. When all the positive forces of the universe meet all the negative forces, something dies or something is born. An interlude now occurred, an interlude that was as filled with suspense as life and death. This interlude lasted fourteen years; the first seven saw something die in me, for there was plenty that needed to be sloughed away; the last seven saw something born in me, so precious that I would have gladly endured unlimited sojourn in the farthest wilderness to have found it.

During this period there was no lack of love in our home, but there was much hard schooling. Marriage is not an easy thing; no one should enter into it lightly. It is the hardest of schools—even though it may be at the very same time the highest of heavens. In every home each must *give* something as well as *receive* something. A pet idiosyncrasy must be given up here and another pet idiosyncrasy accepted there. Such mutual adjustment is acceptable and accepted. But when all one's trend of life comes smack up against all of another's trend of life, heaven and earth seem shaken by the impact. The meeting of these two forces, the resolving of them into victory through the adjusting of our lives to higher forces, is in itself enough to write this book about.

Louise had had scarlet fever in her childhood, rheumatic fever in her youth, and when we first moved to St. Paul she lay in the hospital for nine weeks hovering between life and death with typhoid fever. These three fevers would have been enough to kill an ordinary person.

They left Louise with a leakage of the heart so that doctors forbade her doing the washing and ironing and other heavy work. After lunch she always took an hour's rest and I did the dishes. There was a man across the alley who often helped his wife and scandalized me by wearing a *lace* apron when he dumped the coffee grounds in the back yard. My brother who was an architect sent me a carpenter's apron which I wore at my kitchen tasks, and knowing that the grocery delivery man was likely to come bursting into the kitchen at any moment I kept a saw and hammer handy. When his steps came pounding up the back porch I hastily wiped my hand and grabbed my carpenter tools.

"Doing a little carpentering, eh?" he would ask.

"Oh, just a little puttering around."

After supper I often wiped the dishes while Louise washed them, a system I would commend to any husband as the ideal arrangement for free and happy conversation. Occasionally our conversations took on the proverbial debate between the optimist and the pessimist, where one sees a difficulty in every opportunity and the other sees an opportunity in every difficulty. Knowing that the best definition of a pessimist is "one who has to live with an optimist" I found myself taking more and more an apologetic tone for my optimism. The beginning of victory for both of us came one day when I threw all my conciliatory and sympathetic methods aside and became for once a cave man.

Louise was expressing her deep concern about our financial condition, as she had been doing off and on for months.

"I am not trained for anything, Glenn, and haven't enough strength to take in washing. If anything happened to you what would happen to the family?" And she paused a moment to rinse the plates for me. Then, as she plunged her hands back into the sudsy dishpan, "You had only one hundred dollars saved up when we were married. Here five years after we are still paying for this house—"

At this point I interrupted her by blandly and deliberately breaking a cup on the kitchen draining board. She screamed. Very deliberately I continued to break the cup into small fragments, picking up one piece after another until all were smashed on the sink.

"What are you doing, Glenn?" she demanded, aghast. "I am just showing you how opulent we are. We shall always have all we need.

To prove how we are rolling in abundance, I shall always break a cup whenever you worry about money."

Not a peep after that for a week. Then the old pessimism again spoke forth. Again I picked up a cup and strode toward the draining board. She saw me in time.

"I'll be good, I'll be good!" And thus at the cost of one five-cent cup I broke my wife of a habit pattern that all my arguments and pleading had failed to accomplish. Years later Louise said to me one day, "You should have been a cave man long before, Glenn. It surely worked! I have hardly worried since."

Which all goes to show that five cents' worth of action is better than a thousand dollars' worth of argument.

Louise loved travel and took great joy in tracing the journeys of our relatives in our giant atlas whenever they went on trips. She loved studying house plans and planning houses, although her family had always lived in "bought houses." The acme of her delight, her great dream, came true when we purchased a lot and the architects said that the plans which she drew were so accurate they didn't need to change a line.

A garden was made for Louise, also a miniature orchard. I had three apple trees and one plum tree set out in our back yard. Living there thirty years, we enjoyed the fruit. I planted currants and rhubarb, and she planted flowers, the names of which I never learned.

We played games occasionally. Louise laboriously learned five hundred and whist. But I found now that they bored me as much as they bored her. We went occasionally to movies. But above all she loved to go to people, especially old people or people in trouble. I recommend to all my friends a book entitled *The Secret Garden*, by Francis Hodgson Burnett. One would not need to read that book if he knew Louise. Her sunshine and cheer emanating from her own Secret Garden was more wonderful than a mere book could give.

CHAPTER XV

Macalester College

AFTER four years at William and Vashti I felt that it was time for me to "graduate." I enrolled in the Clark Teachers' Agency and they immediately put me in touch with a college president who refused to reveal his own name and the name of his college until he was sure that I was exactly the man he wanted. All the correspondence between us was carried on through the agency as the go-between. Never had I been in a transaction so shrouded in mystery.

The suspense continued to grow until on my thirtieth birthday a letter came. And there at last was the name of the president and the name of the college. He wanted me, badly. He had chosen me from among scores of prospects and he was sure I was just the man for the job.

I hate to admit it but I had never heard of this college before. And when we finally did arrive there, the first view of the school was not especially encouraging.

As a matter of fact, the first things I saw when I came to this college were streetcars running by its campus, and a barbed wire fence stretched around it to keep out the people and to keep in the cows that were pastured there to nip the long grass. In the hard times of the late nineties and the decade that followed, the college could not afford to have the grass cut. Shortly after my coming I was influential in having that fence removed and in having lawn mowers installed to perform the service which the cows had performed more thriftily before. In fact, I early set my heart on changing many of the more unprepossessing features of the college which had irritated my outward sight when I first arrived. But once I was inside the college, I wasn't so sure anything needed reforming.

Probably there comes a day in the life of almost every professor when he finds himself inside his college. That day I found myself inside, I went under the porte-cochere entryway as usual and climbed the steps to the old chapel and noticed that the stairs were all worn in little hollows that told the story of hundreds of feet running, bounding, trudging, lagging, up to the third story chapel. I went into the classroom that was my classroom and I got the chalk and blackboard smells that are as dear to the confirmed college professor as the scent of battle is to the war horse. A college has its own fragrance; call it musty or musky, and try as you will to break it down into its component odors of laboratories, books, radiators, lounges, landings, boys and girls—there is still something about it as elusive as sunlight through tall murky windows and as intoxicating as memory. I stood in my room, looking down at the initials carved on the old armed chairs in front of me, and suddenly I saw invisible hands coming out of the past to welcome me. I began to feel the beating of the heart of the old college. Since that day I have not bothered much to tell people of its location or how to spell its name. One can waste hours of time trying to tell people things they can never understand until they share an experience.

A college itself is often an elongated shadow of its faculty, so I was curious to meet the teachers I was destined to associate with. First and foremost I must tell of my "long-lost cousin." I always knew I had a long-lost cousin waiting for me somewhere in space. We all do, you know, but few are given the privilege of finding him. It was my father who calmly said to me when I was leaving my old home for this new land of total strangers, "I think you have a long-lost relative up there, a man whose name is John Porter Hall."

A cousin on my mother's side cautioned, "But be very, very careful to examine him well before you claim him. I once moved to a new town where I had a long-lost relative. I invited him over and he came at once, unwashed, unshaved, and smelling of gin. So look before you leap."

I asked my father, "But what if I want to claim him? What password can I use to verify my claim?"

"'Aunt Jane Courtney' is the password," said my father without a moment's hesitation. "Everyone back in Indiana among all my relatives on his side of the family would know of Aunt Jane Courtney. She was the life of every party."

So the first day on my new location I asked a boy to tell me about the faculty. Without a moment's hesitation he replied, "John Porter takes the cake among the boys. He's a prince and a wow."

"That will do," I said. "Thanks." I didn't know what might come after the "wow."

Then I met John. He was a teacher of Greek and registrar of the college, a rare combination of classicism and realism, of dreams and common sense. He gave expression to his bent for romanticism on the athletic field and in the glee club. But my initial contact with him was as registrar. Here he was all realism, brief, terse, business-like and making no effort to capture the affections of the new English teacher. I wrote my cousin on my mother's side and said, "The question is not, Do I like Cousin John, but, Will he like me?" After many days' casual attempts to win his interest on my own merits, I felt at last ready to try out the password.

The occasion was the opening reception where all the students and faculty came together to write names on one another's cards and to get acquainted. Cousin John, who was not married and who was as popular with the girls as with the boys, was surrounded by a bevy of coeds in the front hall when I arrived. He caught my eye and nodded to me. Before I knew what I was saying, the secret blurted out, "What would Aunt Jane Courtney think of all this carrying on?"

I shall never forget how his expression changed from surprise, unbelief, curiosity, to recognition and amazement. "What—what do you mean?" he stammered. "Where—where did you ever hear of that name?"

"Oh, I was just referring to a great-aunt of mine."

"She—she was my grandmother!" he stuttered.

"Well, well," I exclaimed. "Then we are long-lost cousins, aren't we?"

Almost before the words were out of my mouth he had vanished in the throng. "Now I have done it," I thought to myself. But a few minutes later when my wife joined me—she had been delayed as all wives are when they take off their wraps before a mirror—I saw him coming toward us, pushing his sister ahead of him.

"Meet our long-lost cousin, Abbie," he said. And from that time forth it was always Cousin John and Cousin Abbie and Cousin Glenn and Cousin Louise.

Thus began one of the subtlest and strongest friendships that I have ever known. Never was there a friendship that was more completely relied upon and yet less employed, more constant and yet less talked about or flaunted. There were basic similarities and contrasts between John and myself. We both loved sports and the boys that were associated with them, but he coached baseball and I coached track. He edited the catalogue; I was adviser for the *Gateway* magazine. He led the Glee Club; I sponsored the Quill Club. John never wrote; I never sang. He taught ancient Greek but in a modern way; I taught modern English but in an old-fashioned way. With both of us the students always came first, the subject matter second. Perhaps neither of us was a scholar in the commonly accepted use of the term but like Mark Hopkins we tried our best to know the boy on the other end of the log.

Another man I loved was Newton Kingery. His face was rugged, open; he was ever masking his kindliness under a cloak of brusqueness.

"Add a foot to your stature," I said to Newton one day, "and you would be a perfect replica of Abraham Lincoln."

"I didn't know I was quite as homely as all that." He had an art of deflecting even would-be compliments. Indeed, he converted a compliment almost before it was out of your mouth into something derogatory. But within every slam that he ever cast against any other living soul—and he cast many—was a golden lining of appreciation.

Then there was Dr. George Davis, teacher of political science, who brought with him the culture of England, strongly flavored with the rugged tang of the dunes of Devon. He loved words, did Doctor George; more, he revered them as living things. When he cut a word it would bleed. Every word was measured, weighed, and delicately fitted to its task like a mosaic window; moreover, each word was articulated, modulated, and blessed as it left his lips. He was especially in demand for speaking on occasions that required great delicacy and appropriate phrasing. I shall never forget when he conducted the funeral of a colleague, Professor David McRae. The service was held in the large Central Presbyterian Church. Below the platform on which the Doctor stood rested the casket containing the body of his friend. Toward the close of his brief tribute he stepped forward, and looking down into the other's face, he said, "Brother," and addressed the remainder of his obituary to his silent friend. Such sudden flashes of audacity were rare, but always they were master strokes both of propriety and of taste, and the effect, as in this case, was always tremendous.

Richard Uriah Jones was a scientist with emotions, a scientist with faith in God. From the chapel platform he spoke like Jeremiah, the pessimist, and in the laboratory he laughed with his whole soul over a good joke. Welsh through and through, he loved music, but none so much as the music which came from reading a Psalm or offering a prayer.

Out of the past looms Professor Henry Daniel Funk, of German extraction. He died in his prime. Not by bullet, not by poison gas, but of a broken heart—another casualty of the Great War. A strong, vital man, he loved passionately—both Germans and Americans—but he loved God most of all.

Looming like a flashing Elijah, invoking fire from heaven upon all the evils of society, was our dear old Dr. James Wallace, father of Miriam Wallace and of De Witt Wallace. Doctor Jimmy had distinguished mustaches, softened by sideburns; all his hair having migrated to the underside of his head, his polished cranium rose out of this foliage like a cathedral set among pines. One night during World War I when great speakers from all over the wide nation had come to give our city a feast of oratory, our Doctor Jimmy came out and stole the show. The hour was late when his turn came but when he began in cadence reminiscent of old Scripture prophets, he swept the entire audience to heights of enthusiasm such as our city had rarely experienced.

One day in chapel when he finished a tirade against the willful bloc of Senators who were opposing President Wilson's dream of entering the League of Nations, he ended by branding them as "those picayune, pygmy-minded, peanut politicians." Leaving chapel he overheard a student swearing at a companion and he rebuked the young culprit for his profanity. The boy grinned and replied, "If I could handle the English language as you can, Professor, I wouldn't need to swear."

The sufferings and trials of the early college years had left scars on Doctor Jimmy, but he bore them hardily and, approaching ninety, he still remained as sprightly and keen-minded as most men of fifty—wearing well the title of "the Grand Old Man" of the college.

One of my favorite places to drop in for a moment's chat was the classroom of my colleague in the English department, Mother Jay. Her students never got over calling Julia M. Johnson by this affectionate title. Her gift was to make her students love literature.

Professor Hugh Alexander was our honest Cato. He was rigidly honest in every statement he made in a teachers' meeting, in every grade he handed in to the registrar, in every fact he presented to a class. And he demanded the same rigid honesty from his pupils; deep was their respect for him.

Professor Andy Anderson was a teacher of the old school. Next to Doctor Jimmy in years of service in both church and college, he was on the board of elders for fifty years, clerk of session for thirty-one years, secretary of the faculty for fifteen, and like Registrar John, the chief repository of old reminiscences of early times of the college.

Then there was Grace Bee Whitridge of the drama department, who taught beauty. While all the world might be a stage, her particular place on that stage was always *behind the scenes*. She was genuine, with a kind of abrupt naturalness that took boys and girls as they came to her from farm or city and created living dramas.

There had been no addition to the faculty for about ten years until I came. Then almost another ten years elapsed before there were any other newcomers. Like all Gaul, the faculty seemed to be divided into three parts—the old veterans, the new recruits and myself. At times I was a bit lonely out there in no man's land, between the old and the new. Fortunately those closest after me in point of time were four who were also close to me in spirit. There were honest, puritanical Otto Walter, and handsome, debonair Clarence Ficken. There was also Margaret

Doty, our spontaneous, effective dean of women. And then there was Grace May–cheery and approachable, the quintessence of kindness.

Every morning at ten o'clock in those early days I climbed up the three flights of worn steps to the chapel. The little dents in the stairs worn by countless hundreds before me made me aware that I was a part of a cosmic procession. Ardent loves, creative thoughts, little despairs, high aspirations, harbored cynicisms, spontaneous humor–all had trod those stairs together. And as the years rolled by, I learned to look at the eager, passionate faces moving by me in the hallways, as so many living narratives whose stories, if told, would surpass all the novels on our library shelves.

In the autumn I could see from my window the battle-clad boys on the gridiron, struggling together. In the winter I could see gliding, whirling hockey players. In the spring I could see runners and jumpers, and throwers of javelin and discus. I saw Baldwin coming down the track, leading the way. Now it was Hauser, now Cochrane, now Westrell. Their feet crunched through the cinders, breaking records.

And then there were my writers. For them literature did not begin with the classicists of Greece nor end with Pope and Dryden, nor even with Whitman, Hawthorne and Poe. Literature is an upspringing thing, bursting through the sod of young minds. This is a beautiful world, I would tell my students, but much of the beauty escapes us. Dig as hard as we wish, seek as hard as we can, we are sure to miss most of the gold. Let us sit down together once in a while and share our visions. Let us gather around the fireplace, throw on an extra log and sit far into the night, telling the tales that the minstrels once told in the nighttime under the moon. Let us sing ballads–not the ones that were written for ancient folks in ancient days, but new songs that well up in our own hearts. Let us make our minds and souls porous to beauty and gather it like the dew that falls in the morning. Let us be still and listen to our own and our brother's expression of goodness and of truth. What matter if it comes out of the same reservoir whence all legends and tales of all ages came? Who can hinder us from the joyous experience of dipping in a spoon where Ben Jonson stuck in his trowel and where Will Shakespeare stuck in his spade?

Some of my students' dreams have been recorded in books, some have been built into institutions, more have taken expression in actions and achievements of many kinds. Some of these dreamers have been brought back for commencement from time to time to make speeches to us and to receive honorary degrees. I had the privilege of presenting one of them, named George Rowland Collins, dean of New York University, to the trustees for a doctor's degree. My throat choked a little as I did it, but not any more than his did when he stood before us to receive the degree.

Every true teacher gets greater happiness from honoring his students than from being honored himself. For the object and the aim of every true teacher is to produce someday a scholar who can outstrip him. But whether my students succeed or fail, I have reserved a place in my heart where all of them shall succeed—where nobody shall ever fail—and there, at least, I shall honor them whether they know it or not—whether the world knows it and acclaims it or not.

CHAPTER XVI

Adjustments

THE life of a college professor is not all roses. If there had been discipline in my home life, there was discipline in my college life as well. The adjusting of the inner desires of one's soul to the outer requirements of one's profession is not an easy thing. I had prepared myself to teach Shakespeare and the novel. With the exception of those four years at William and Vashti, I never again had an opportunity to teach either subject. At Macalester my senior colleague taught all the literature and left me to teach all the composition. She covered the entire field of literature for this small college by offering different courses in alternate years, and saw no reason why I should encroach on her field. The constant correcting of papers–"washing my pupils' dirty linen"–began to affect my nerves. To have no outlet through the open window of Shakespeare or Carlyle or Browning was stifling. The frustration actually manifested in my body in the form of palpitation of the heart.

Finally I began to compensate by making short-story writing as fascinating and intriguing as I could, to myself as well as to my students. The inevitable result of this effort was that my classroom activities finally splashed over into a couple of textbooks–one of which, *The Manual of the Short Story Art*, has persisted as a text over quite a long period of time. Indeed, its sales in 1949 were larger than in 1923. Personally, I preferred my other book, *Personality in Essay*

Writing, but the publishers of that book failed and I have never taken time to get it on the market again.

Eventually I obtained permission from my colleague to give a course in literature and took the opportunity to work up a field that was entirely new to me, the field of world masterpieces. We hear much talk about the values of college education, the rewards of culture, the opportunity to know the world's greatest writers, such as Homer, Aeschylus, Sophocles, Dante, Shakespeare and Goethe. But before the recent revival of general education, these literary giants were little more than a name to most students.

For a score of years, while I taught this course, I lived with Homer, Dante, Shakespeare and the Book of Job. Their spirit got into my blood. Out of the years of comradeship with these literary masters grew a book of my own, an allegorical novel in which I attempted to weave the theme of all the world masterpieces. The book was called *Water of Life*, and its theme will be just as appropriate for 1982 as for today; indeed, the key incident which gave the book its title probably will not occur until 1982.

The college in St. Paul had no newspaper. I started one, the *Mac Weekly*. It had no literary magazine. Out of my class in advanced writing the *Gateway Magazine* was established. The college had no track team. I not only organized and coached one, but organized the first Minnesota Intercollegiate State Track Meet.

When the president first wanted to make me dean of the college, I refused, since I was the youngest and newest member of the faculty. But the next year when he insisted, I consented to be called "acting dean." The following year the trustees elected me full dean without asking my consent.

As dean I had to pass on every student who applied for admission. The high school credits were handed to me as a boy or girl came in. It irked me that I had to look at a sheet of paper instead of at the boy. I didn't give a snap of my fingers whether he came from an accredited high school or not. What I wanted to know was whether he was an *accredited boy*. What I wanted to ask the boys and girls was: Are you accredited in habits of industry, do you have an enthusiasm for learning, do you possess a capacity for creative stillness? Do you know how to think straight in at least one field, can you express yourself effectively either in writing or speaking, have you done some wide reading? If I could have established the set of standards that Page and I had worked out in our boyhood, what a grand college we could have had!

Many things had to be done at this college to bring up the academic standards. I attended conferences of educators, studied curriculums of the leading colleges, wrote long reports and scholarly papers on what things should be done, and, what was more, undertook the arduous work of seeing that they were done. When the president resigned, I finally retired from the deanship, feeling that that phase of my lifework was over. The time I had been giving to the writing of reports on curriculum I could now give to the writing of books in the fields I loved. But I am getting ahead of my story.

I felt it was the duty of an institution of this kind that looked to the high schools for its student material to render service and inspiration to those students while they were still in high school. So I published each year as one issue of our *Gateway Magazine*, an anthology of the best writings of the Minnesota high school pupils for the year. I also established a State High School Discussion League and a League in Extemporaneous Speaking where winners of the various district contests would gather at Macalester for the finals.

The Discussion League differed from debate leagues in that pupils could take whichever side of the subject they believed in, give a seven-minute constructive talk, and then later have a three-minute rebuttal in which they could defend their viewpoint against all comers. Seven or eight schools could thus be represented at one contest, one speaker for each school, and no restrictions were placed upon them as to which side they should take. Often there would be five on one side and three on the other, but it did not matter. William Jennings Bryan, then Secretary of State, sent me a letter of congratulation on starting a type of contest in which the chief emphasis was upon conviction of the speakers and not merely upon the winning the debate.

The strain of doing all these things under my own power, plus all of the adjustments in my own life that I have mentioned, was taking a toll. The palpitation that had come upon me like a wild tiger in the dark of the moon was now almost a nightly affair.

And then I had three dreams in succession. At the time we had just entered World War I. My cousin Clifford was dead of the flu. Casualties were coming in. And my three dreams were the symbolical kind that spoke the one word, Death. Death to me!

I recalled the three dreams I had had of Page and the way in which seven years later, he had left us. Would I be leaving this good earth seven years from now? How old would I be? Just forty-two! That fact startled me. Age forty-two was the year beyond which everything was shrouded in mists when the vision of my Life Plan had come to me. Everything in the Plan had stopped abruptly at forty-two. One night my concern grew so great that I sat down and wrestled with it in hope of finding some peace.

Then it was that a great revelation came to me: We are in God's world. All things work together for good for those who love the Lord and strive according to His purpose, even the seemingly bad things. By a simple turn of a screw, as it were, premonitions of evil can be turned into premonitions of good. Why not? When one is traveling through space and a foreview comes to him of a bridge that has broken down, he does not necessarily have to go down with the broken bridge. He can make a detour to a better bridge farther down the river. Then why need one who is traveling through time go down with a bridge he has not yet reached? Why cannot he, too, make a detour around it? Thereupon, while that revelation was still fresh upon me, I sat down and said to God:

"Lord, if it is in the Divine Plan for me to step into the Kingdom of Heaven when I reach the age of forty-two, then, Lord, if it is not asking too much, could You grant me the unspeakable privilege of stepping into the Kingdom of Heaven right here on earth? Your only begotten Son came to this earth to tell us all about the Kingdom. He said to seek it first and that it was right here within us. We don't have to die in our physical selves to start living in it. But Jesus did make it clear that we *must* die to our egotistical selves. So I am asking You, Father, to help me so to die to my little, selfish self in the next seven years that when the time comes for You to take me, You can take me so completely, so utterly, so wholly, right here on this earth, that I shall start actually living in the heaven here and now. In Jesus' Name, Amen."

I don't know when I have ever offered a more sincere prayer, a more heartfelt prayer, and a more *believing* prayer. And this I can say without hesitation or equivocation, without compromise or doubt—never have I prayed a prayer that has borne such a precious harvest of fruit as this one has. My prayer right now is that every reader of this book when he reaches this page will pause for a moment and then reread the prayer and make it his own, that he, too, may share the unspeakable privilege of living in the Kingdom here and now. I have a strong feeling that if a million people started living in the Kingdom today with all their strength and with all their minds and with all their hearts and with all their souls, that the millennium would begin tomorrow. Maybe a few less than a million would suffice.

BOOK FIVE

Revelation Begins

CHAPTER XVII

The Brother of the Carpenter

IT WAS my sabbatical year. The only sabbatical year I had ever taken. And it was only a half year at that. The shouts and huzzas of the 11th of November, 1918, had hardly died away when my wife and I began preparations for our journey into the Golden West. A new era had dawned for the world. And without our knowing it, a new era was about to dawn for us.

As men had been going down to their death, my family of children was coming into life. It was as though the same power which was pressing souls out into the vast unknown was pressing other souls into the known. The world was big with vast, indescribable forces.

"Where shall you go for your sabbatical leave?" I was asked.

"To La Jolla, California. It will be my last chance to fellowship with my father on this earth, and my first opportunity in a long time to swap yarns with my younger brother who is a carpenter in La Jolla."

Little did I realize when I got on the train that I was starting on a journey that was destined to bring me into a fuller companionship not only with my earthly father but also with my Heavenly Father and not only with my younger brother, the carpenter of La Jolla, but with my Elder Brother, the carpenter of Nazareth.

We went into a little home my brother, the carpenter, had built and remained there seven months. I had gone to meditate and think and learn how to pray. Our daughters, two-and-a-half years, and seven-months, could get the sunlight and the sea breezes. My tired wife could build up and recuperate.

But as we crossed the continent we could hear all along the way the sound of the galloping Four Horsemen. One horseman had left a great harvest of woe behind him, the one who carried the sword of war. The one who carried the insignia of famine was on ahead in Russia and India. But one kept pace with us all the way with his red, reeking hand of pestilence. The flu was sweeping across the continent and we were sweeping on with it. Every letter, every newspaper told of friends falling by the wayside like locusts. The horseman of war had reaped ten million lives; the horseman of pestilence was not to halt until he had reaped twenty million.

"When, oh when, will the tide turn, O Jehovah?" This was the question in my heart some weeks later as I sat on Mount Soldad, with a golf club in my hand and my father at my side, looking out over the wide Pacific. "How long must the world know war and woe, O Lord? When, oh when will the Pacific, not only in name but in spirit, become the center of the world's heart and being? When that time comes, the sword will at last be ground into pruning hooks, and the nations shall not know war any more."

A Jewish rabbi happened to come up and stand at my side, and as we talked he pointed his hand across the great expanse of sea.

"Over yonder is Asia," he said. "Out of Asia came all the world's great religions. I am a son of Israel but I admire your Master as I admire no other one. He was also of my people. He came out of the Orient. Over yonder also is India, whose psychology is as far ahead of our psychology as college is ahead of kindergarten."

As he spoke it seemed the ocean showed a change. The tide was commencing to come in.

"Have you heard of Einstein," he asked, "and of the fourth dimension?"

"Of Einstein, yes; of the fourth dimension, no," I replied.

Then as he talked the tide rose to its height, I with it. For I suddenly stood in a world without time or tide. I stood in a universe with no Past and no Future. All that I had ever known or had ever experienced stood before me in the Now.

When I returned, my wife asked, "Were you with your father on the mountain today?"

"Yes, I was with my *Father* on the mountain today," I told her.

So it was that I came out of the house which my brother the carpenter had built for my father, and which my father in his kindness had lent to me; and with my little family and with my Elder Brother, the Carpenter of Nazareth, now abiding in my heart, I boarded the train for St. Paul. Obviously, my journey was now taking me in a direction totally opposite from that which I had traveled when I came West. Not only was the geography different, but the cosmos was different. It seemed as I traveled that all the forces of the universe—at least the forces as they focused within my own soul—were also traveling with me in a direction opposite to the one in which they had been moving during the previous four dark years. In my heart I knew that for me the tide had truly turned.

When we returned to St. Paul my wife was carrying back within the folds of her being a son. I was carrying back also as yet unborn, an Idea which was bigger than any idea I had ever before found. In fact, it was not an idea but rather the *power to produce ideas*. It was not a new power but one as old as the earth was old. It was the Power which created all that was created. "In the beginning was the Word, and the Word was with God and the Word was God. . . and without the Word was nothing made which was made." The Word had come also to dwell within me, a Word which, like a child in the womb, was biding its time to be born and made flesh.

But how could the word become flesh? I became for a season like the haunted soul in Coleridge's epic who could find no rest on sea or land till he could discover a means of speaking the Word. I tried this and I tried that, and finally I tried prayer. Somehow I sensed that only through prayer would I find peace. But prayer, as I then knew prayer, was too tiny a channel, too clogged with its little, external rites and rituals.

I was still heavy with this potential Thing when I reached St. Paul; this Thing that I could not bring forth. I could not analyze it; I could not classify it. I seemed to be seeking something which had to be "found" rather than something which was to be "thought out."

Moreover, I had to find it whole—otherwise it was not to be found at all; indeed, otherwise it did not exist. But everywhere I went my questing was futile.

The difficulty in the situation was that the Thing was inside of me, within me, rather than outside. If it were a Thing I could reach out and touch with my hand, or see with my eye, if it were something I could find in a book, in a city, in a house, it would be easy. But it was something that had to be—what was the word I was trying to find to explain it?—it was something that had to be *born*. That was the word! *Born!*

While I was still seeking, a new experience came to our home in the birth of a son. It was a wonderful experience to me, and weeks elapsed while I forgot altogether my own search for the birth of an Idea.

Just a month later a telegram came announcing the serious illness of my father, asking me to take the next train. As I walked the length of the station to the Pullman car, the same lightsome feeling came over me that had come as I went to the hospital to sit beside my wife while she brought to birth a child. It came to me with a clear, deep realization that the process of death was exactly the same as the process of birth, the freeing of a being from a small, limited prison house of flesh to a larger freedom of infinite growth. I had just experienced the release of seeing my own son set free in this world. I was now to sit beside my father while his real Self was set free in a higher world.

Arriving at the city where he had been stricken, I sat at his bedside and held his hand as his spirit took flight, even as I had foreseen I was going to do. And the sensation of release I had was the same sensation I had experienced while witnessing the birth of my child. Then I realized with a deep, incontrovertible realization that only as I gave myself to the Spirit of God and was reborn as a Son of God could I bring into birth a Truth of God. So I stopped my little brain from thinking and let the Holy Spirit rise within me, overshadowing me.

Riding home on the train from my father's funeral, my mind ran back over the years to that other train ride when a white haired gentleman had sat down beside me and talked of "hinds' feet." From there my mind ran back to my sojourn on a Wyoming ranch when I was given the privilege of riding the fastest horse on the range, a horse that was imperfect in only one particular. Its rear feet did not hit the identical tracks his front feet made. This lack of perfect tracking might seem a small thing in itself, but it was sufficient to make climbing up steep mountainsides unsafe, because a misstep of a few inches on a slippery crag might lead to a fatal fall.

Then there dawned on me the tremendous meaning hidden in this subtle passage of scripture: "He maketh my feet like hinds'[1] feet; and setteth me upon my high places." As the rear feet of the hind are to the front feet, so is the subconscious mind of man to the conscious mind. And as the creature which has the most perfect correlation between its front and rear feet is most certain to reach the mountaintop in safety, so the person who has the most perfect correlation between his conscious mind and his subconscious mind is most certain to reach the heights in life.

I now knew what Jesus meant when he said, "Have faith in God. For verily I say unto you, That whosoever shall say unto this mountain, Be thou removed and be thou cast into the sea; and shall not doubt in his heart, but shall believe that those things which he saith shall come to pass; he shall have whatsoever he saith." "If ye have faith as a grain of mustard seed... and nothing shall be impossible unto you." Our lips speak the thoughts of our conscious mind, but only the heart speaks the thoughts of our subconscious mind. "As [a man] thinketh in his heart, so is he." "Out of the heart are the issues of life." And when the lips and the heart are in alignment, when they track together with the absolute certainty that the rear feet of the deer track together with the front feet, then nothing is impossible, whether it be the climbing of mountains or the casting of mountains into the seas. The wonder of this burst upon me with such force that I could hardly wait until I could get back to my work and put my new discovery to the test.

Now I saw that I had been missing the greatest blessings of life—and merely by inches. But in these seemingly trivial inches lay the secret of the supreme power and security of the seers and the saints and the prophets who lived in the mountains.

The secret of the mighty works of Jesus lay in the fact that he

---

[1] deer

gave himself in totality and entirety to the Father—his front mind, his subconscious mind, his unconscious mind, his entire mind. He gave his love to the Father with the same entirety, with all his soul, and all his heart and all his mind and all his strength. He told us that if we give ourselves in the same way, "greater works than I have done ye shall do because I go to the Father."

All this raised tremendous questions: Where did my conscious and subconscious mind track together? How many things had I done with "all four feet"? I had filled many students' outer minds with learning; how many inner souls had I inspired? I had filled my own mind with information about things; did I know any more about the stars than my ancestors knew? I had accepted all the promises of Jesus with my conscious mind; how many of them did I accept with absolute unquestioning faith with my subconscious mind?

Ah, there was the secret. Once achieve that perfect integration of the conscious and subconscious, once achieve that totality of surrender of all of myself to God, once step with all of my being into the presence of the Father, and whatsoever I shall ask I shall receive.

"Where two or three agree together asking anything," yes, where two or three parts of the same mind agree together, asking anything, it will be given. When all of a seed, not just the outer shell of it, is placed in the ground, it grows into a tree and the birds rest in the branches thereof.

At last the great Truth that had been pounding upon my heart and brain had been born. And in accepting it, I found that I myself had become reborn.

CHAPTER XVIII

I Make My Feet "Hinds' Feet"

WHEN one is born again he has to learn how to walk all over again. Now that this Thing was born I would have first to learn the art of making my feet hinds' feet so that I could mount to my high places. To this end I began to read voraciously and my reading fell into three lines.

The first was the teachings of Jesus—everything in the New Testament. This was also the first time I had given Paul a fair show, but he still failed to do for me what the simple Gospels did. Jesus' outright promise, repeated seven times, "Whatsoever ye ask in my name that will I do" challenged me. Not to accept the promise (after its seventh repetition) was, I saw for the first time, actually and literally to brand Jesus as a mere teller of tales. I stood convicted as one who had done exactly that. All at once I felt challenged to lay aside all inhibitions and step out completely upon the Truth of his Word.

My second line of reading was the mystic line: Rufus Jones' *Mysticism* and Emma Herman's *Creative Prayer*, and all of Evelyn Underhill's books that I could lay my hands on. I especially liked her definition of mysticism: "Union with Reality." I loved the covert way this same truth was brought to me in Brother Lawrence's *The Practice of the Presence of God*. These books I lived with.

The third line of reading was in such books as Ouspensky's *Tertium Organum* and Bragdon's *Fourth Dimensional Vistas*, and all

147

the scientific literature that I could lay my hands on that opened new dimensions of thinking. Nothing widened the borders of my tent more completely than pushing back the curtains of this little three-dimensional world and stepping out into new areas where Infinity was flowing through every blade of grass, and Eternity was flowing through every minute of time. I began to live in a world where all past and all future converged into the immediate Now. I felt especially drawn to F. L. Rawson's *Life Understood*, whose abstract principles balanced the concrete simplicities of Brother Lawrence. F. L. Rawson was a British physicist who believed one's prayers could be just as scientifically infallible as the laws of physics and chemistry. He believed that merely to deny the existence of any evil would make it vanish away, and to affirm the opposite reality would make it appear.

Using Christ as my center, and putting my hand in my Saviour's as my guide and my friend, letting my whole being become released and expanded in this new dimension of heaven on earth, I trained myself in Rawson's denials and affirmations, and things began to happen.

I went to hear Rawson when he spoke in the Twin Cities and through a conversation with him discovered that he had never read a novel or a poem in his life, was purely scientific and used his imagination hardly at all. His power as well as his limitations lay in his capacity to accept Truth as simply as a little child, without looking to right or left. He was a foundation-layer but he lacked the imagination for converting his *science* of prayer into an *art*. I determined then and there not to be a mere follower of his, but to begin where he left off.

A little group representing many churches and almost all denominations met once a week in Minneapolis to study Rawson's book. It reminded me of the group of engineers representing all the airplane companies who gathered in Washington at the invitation of the Government during World War I. They were locked in a hotel room until they consented to pool all their secrets and their patents. The result was the Liberty Motor.

We pooled all our secrets about prayer and the result was a new liberty and a new motivation in our communion with God. We discovered that heaven is actually all around us here and now if we can only blow away the fogs of self and the mists of matter sufficiently to see all as God has actually created it. We perceived that petitionary prayer is a weak instrument in most of our hands because of the selfish motives that are usually associated with it, and the weak and flabby faith with which it is usually uttered. To lift our faith from a state of mere believing to a state of actual *knowing*–that was our problem.

When our little group convened we would step into a Quaker silence and drop our tensions, our prejudices, our fears and our worries, and try to feel the presence of God. The leader would read a list of names of people we were to pray for and we would try to "deny away" some of their troubles. We found that all mankind was One and if we cleared *our own* mind, the trouble of *the one we prayed for* would disappear. One strong denial and a number of positive affirmations seemed to be the most effective way to clear our minds. Dwelling too long on the negatives, we found, did more harm than good. The first real discovery we made was that we did not need to try to send telepathic messages to the person involved; all we needed to do was to lift our own consciousness to a state of positive assurance that all was well.

I was a mere silent listener in this group, a Presbyterian elder quietly seeking to learn to climb with hinds' feet. I rarely raised my voice to make a suggestion. We were all members of orthodox churches with the exception of two: one was active in New Thought and another was a teacher of Christian Science practitioners. The latter was just as silent as I was; she and I were both hoping to pick up some crumbs that we could carry back to our very widely contrasted creeds. One day, after I had been absent for several meetings, she turned to me and said in a chiding tone of voice, "Why is it that when you are present our prayers are answered so much more effectively than when you are away? Tell us what it is that you do."

"I don't do anything," I replied; "I merely pray for each name as it is read off."

"In what way do you pray?"

"I just love them," I replied.

If I had dropped a bombshell into their midst I couldn't have startled them more.

"I never thought of that!" exclaimed one.

"I just do some mental work," another said.

"I concentrate on our ringing affirmations," said a third.

We had already discovered that the first ingredient necessary for all true prayer was a Faith that amounted to an absolute Knowing, a Faith so complete that it filled our entire being; and now we were led to our second great discovery, and that was that Love is the most powerful of all ingredients in all true prayer.

It was a long way from St. Paul to Minneapolis for one who was so busily engaged in college teaching and athletic coaching as I was, so after a year and a half of meeting with this group I invited some friends to my home and started a prayer group of my own. I discovered that the Shepherd Psalm was a perfect model of Rawson's denial and affirmation method. I found Carlyle's "Everlasting No and Everlasting Yea" a thrilling dramatization of what Rawson gave, and in a less metaphysical sounding form. More and more I found right in the Bible and in the teachings of Jesus all the materials which were necessary to build my own cosmology of prayer.

At times I was a little annoyed by a young lady named Elsa Johnson, who arrived at these meetings so bubbling over with lightness and fun that it sometimes delayed our getting down to the serious business of prayer. But to my surprise it was on the days when Elsa was present that the power of the prayer was always greatest. So one day I asked her point-blank what it was that she did when we prayed. Instantly she replied, "I put a lot of Joy into it."

"Do you mean that you put Joy into it when we prayed for the one-legged popcorn man and for the poor old lady who had cancer?"

"Sure. It thrilled me to think how happy they would be when they got cured."

So that was our third great discovery. Next to a positive *Faith* and sincere *Love*, radiant *Joy* seems to be the chief ingredient necessary for prevailing prayer. Paul knew what he was talking about when he said, "Now abideth faith, hope (he could have called it joy) and love, these three." Indeed, Paul wrote again and again about this wonderful ingredient of joy. To the Corinthians he wrote, "We are helpers of your joy." To the church in Rome he wrote, "Now the God of hope fill you with all joy and peace." To the Galatians he wrote, "The fruit of the spirit is love, joy and peace."

Radar was not discovered at that time, but another thing we discovered is that there is such a thing as radar of the spirit.

There was one woman at these gatherings who was probably the least spiritual and the least effective in prayer of the entire group, but who was what one might term "very psychic." She would get "pictures" of what was transpiring in the one we were praying for. When we were praying for the popcorn man she said, "I see a burning red, like fire." I asked what that meant. One of the metaphysical-minded said, "That means that there is chemicalization going on."

Afterward I went around to the popcorn man and asked him how he felt at four o'clock that afternoon.

"I felt just like there was a burning fire in me," he said. "But it seems to have burned away the infection and I've felt a lot better ever since."

A year or two later I discovered that chemicalization is never necessary, that prayer can accomplish the cure just as effectively and yet perfectly painlessly whenever there is love enough in the prayer. I was the only one in our group that knew this man and I guess my job of loving wasn't quite big enough that day.

No pioneer of our West was ever more elated over his discoveries than I was in those first days of prospecting in this new frontier of the spirit. My wife, who was naturally as conservative as I was adventurous, was a little disturbed at times lest this new interest would absorb too much time from my regular work. She was conventionally more religious than I was, and naturally didn't want me to become a fanatic.

Students who heard of my new explorations in prayer asked if I could meet with a little group of them to share some of my discoveries. On Friday afternoons after all classes were over for the week they gathered in my room at college. I also announced that the second semester I would try to apply these principles in my essay writing class. When word was spread around, the registrations for the class trebled in number. Once a week I would lecture on the Seven Laws of Life and on the Seven Arts of Life, revealing ways by which one could put inspiration into ones' writing; and the other day of the week the students would bring their essays thus inspired. The quality of writing improved so greatly that the head of the English composition department of the University of Minnesota invited me to come to see him, and asked me point-blank how it was that the literary magazine in our little college was so much better than the literary magazine of his great university, then the largest university in the world outside the State of California. When I tried to explain, I found that I was using a foreign language as far as he was concerned.

One day when I was walking home from college with one of my boys, named George Todd, he turned to me and asked, "How do you pray? Won't you put it into writing sometime?" This was the first time anyone had asked me this question. I went home and got out a white piece of paper and started to answer his request. To my amazement the words simply poured out. Apparently the sincerity of his question had created a vortex that pulled out of me the exact answer, and to my amazement drew it forth in sequence, beauty and power. The next afternoon George Todd gathered some of his friends together to hear me read my answer to his question. Some of those who came to the prayer group in our home also came. When I finished reading it one of them exclaimed, "That is too good just for us! Why don't you send it to *The Atlantic Monthly?*"

Now I had already spent twelve summers writing and rewriting and polishing an article for the *Atlantic* which they had declined and which *Harper's* and *Scribner's* had also declined. I had learned that the Atlantic only accepts about one article out of each thousand that comes to it, and I knew they weren't inclined at that time to accept articles on religion. However, I obeyed my friend's suggestion and mailed my observations on prayer to Ellery Sedgwick. He replied that they had just received an article by Kirsopp Lake, professor of ecclesiastical history in the Harvard Theological School, on the subject of prayer, in which he maintained that prayer never accomplished anything except the satisfaction of communion with the Lord. The editors were hoping that they could find an article that would take the opposite side, but they did not want a mere trite, conventional treatment; they wanted something that came from authentic spiritual experience. Even while they were asking the question my article arrived.

The article was to come out in the August, 1924, issue. I had taken my family to Los Angeles for the summer and we were guests of my wife's parents. On July 27, when the August *Atlantic* appeared on the California newsstands, I purchased a copy at the corner drugstore and brought it home to my wife. It was a happy moment for both of us. The most cherished desire of every college professor of English in America is someday to become a contributor to *The Atlantic Monthly*.

"Why didn't you get two more copies to give to our mothers?" asked Louise.

"I will get a couple tomorrow," I replied.

But on the morrow the drugstore was sold out of the *Atlantic*. I went to another drugstore. All gone. I went from newsstand to newsstand and the story was the same.

"I can't account for it," said one proprietor. "The *Atlantic* is usually a drug on the market. It always moves slowly compared with the detective magazines, true story magazines and motion picture magazines, which go like hot cakes."

Then Mr. Sedgwick wrote, "Your article sold out the entire issue immediately and we have received hundreds of requests to reprint it."

"Let us hope that this interest will encourage magazines to print more religious articles," Louise said. Her hope was fulfilled at last with the *Atlantic*. For years after that they made it their policy to have one religious article in every issue.

That fall I felt inspired to write another article entitled "The Lost Art of Jesus." As I began the writing of this article there came upon me the overpowering revelation that a mystery lay hidden in the fact that Jesus always talked in parables after his initial statement of principles in the Sermon on the Mount. If I could find the correct definition of a parable all I would need to do would be to expand that definition and the article would "write itself." I turned to my rows of books, looking for my large dictionary which I always kept at hand. I couldn't find it. On the lowest shelf among my cast-off high school books was a little abridged dictionary that defined every word in a single word or at most in one short sentence—the poorest excuse for a dictionary that anyone could have devised. I went over the rows of books a second time, examining each book carefully as I came to it. No dictionary. Set on fire as I was by the visitation of this revelation I could not tarry long enough to run to the college library so I seized the little dictionary, opened it up and found my eyes fixed upon the following definition: "A parable is an allegorical relation of something real."

Had an angel come down from heaven and pronounced these words I could not have felt more inspired. The essay that followed carried me to the heights as I wrote it. When the last word was written and the last comma and period were placed I lifted my eyes to the row of books and there stood my large dictionary, smiling down upon me. I took it down, turned to the definition of a parable and discovered several scholarly disquisitions, not a one of which had any power to transform or inspire. I got down on my knees and said, "Thank You, God!" Yes, whenever the Lord slams a door in one's face He points to a better door on ahead.

When I sent this to Mr. Sedgwick it so excited the *Atlantic* staff "both because of its literary and psychological values," as they put it, that in the last days of December Ellery Sedgwick asked me to expand these two articles into a book and get the manuscript to them by the first week in January so they could bring it out in a special Easter edition. This would mean that I, an amateur in the field of writing, would be required to write an entire book in a little more than a week's time, something that would require a professional writer three months to accomplish. If I took out Christmas and New Year's and the two Sundays I would have exactly eight days, which would mean that I would have to write about one chapter a day. Then followed one of the most exciting experiences of my life.

I felt that God, rather than I, had written the first two articles. Therefore, if this book was to be completed as it was started I felt that I must put my complete dependence upon Him.

"Now, Lord," I said, "You have placed a task upon me that is far too great for my little power to fulfill. If You want this done You will have to do it. Use me as Your humble instrument. That is all I can hope to be. Amen."

Fortunately I had a running start. The first two chapters were already done and had met with the approval of the editors, and it was easy to complete the third chapter because "The Lost Art" had flowed over into the beginning of it. But it was as hard as pulling teeth to write the fourth and fifth chapters because I tried to put into them all the knowledge that I had accumulated about prayer in the last two years. And when I started the sixth chapter I didn't know what I should write about. That forced me completely to *let go* and let God do all the writing of that chapter. I was more amazed at what came forth than any of my readers have ever been. There are some parts of that sixth chapter that I never quite understood myself until years had elapsed. When the final day arrived I was ready to start the last chapter. Now I gave a sigh of relief. In this chapter I would simply include all the little Psalm-Prayers that I had been using for my own spiritual Quiet Hour.

One of the chief problems of my Quiet Hour had been how to shut out the sounds and sights and interruptions of the outer world that were entering through all my five senses. The best method of shutting these senses out, I discovered, was to concentrate my entire being, my mind, my will and even all of my senses upon God and heaven. I know it sounds paradoxical to take the five senses, which are geared only to the outer world, and use them as aids to contact the inner world. Here is where the sacramentalists are ahead of the rest of us, and I am not naturally a sacramentalist. But I had originated a little "sacrament" of my own that proved very effective. Having written down a number of Psalm-Prayers on the themes of Faith, Love, Joy, Gratitude and similar topics I adopted the following routine for my daily morning meditation, a routine devised to engage my senses so completely that they would be utterly impervious to the sensations of the outer world.

I held the sheet of paper in my hands, thus employing the sense of touch, looked at the words with my eyes, thus exercising the sense of sight, read the words out loud with my lips, thus utilizing the sense of taste, heard the words with my ears, thus using the sense of hearing, and if I had only burned a little incense as true sacramentalists might have done I would have been using every sense I had.

Unfortunately, these Psalm-Prayers had been written for my own private benefit and not for publication, and so there were only two of them that were really "literary enough" for this chapter. However, I was as limp as a rag, completely spent, and my intention was to turn these Psalm-Prayers just as they were over to the copyist, regardless of whether they were good enough, and send them right in. I had done the best I could and the Lord couldn't expect more.

But when I reached for them I could not find them! That was strange, for I always kept them conveniently at hand in my top drawer. Then it came to me what the Lord was trying to do to me. He was insisting in no uncertain terms that He was not going to accept any second-class, cast-off material for this book. Whereupon I sat down and proceeded to use the accumulated inspiration that the writing of the sixth chapter had brought me, and wrote from that inspiration a brand new set of devotionals.

"But Lord," I said, "the Psalm-Prayer on Love and the one on Inspiration *were* inspired and I feel it would be impossible for me to improve upon them."

"All right," I could almost hear His voice saying, "when you have rewritten all the rest I will reveal the hiding place of those two."

When I had completed the rest I looked again at that top drawer. Suddenly, without knowing why, I pulled out the entire drawer and reached my arm back as far as it would go, and there behind the drawer I felt a pile of papers. When I pulled them out, there were all the truant Psalm-Prayers, the one on Love and Inspiration among them. I had never in my life done that with any drawer before. Twenty-five years have elapsed since then and I have never pulled a drawer completely out and made a similar search since. "God moves in a mysterious way His wonders to perform."

After the little book's publication the letters that began to pour in to me, most of them addressed to *The Atlantic Monthly* and forwarded, almost overwhelmed me. I tried meticulously to answer them all, but I soon saw that with my teaching responsibilities I could not keep this up and ever hope to find time for writing again.

Lawrence Gould, second in command of the first Byrd expedition, wrote how he had carried my book lashed to his dog sledge[1], and how it helped the explorers through many perils. William Anderson, Senior Bishop of the Methodist Church, wrote how it had been a light on his path through the hardest year of his life. A woman in South Carolina wrote how it was sustaining her and her husband since the doctors

---

[1] toboggan

pronounced her baby boy incurably blind. Months later she wrote that the boy could now see, due to our prayers, but the most wonderful thing that had happened was the transformation all this had brought to her husband and herself.

One thing that surprised me was the way all creeds claimed me. A priest of Notre Dame University wrote a review of *The Soul's Sincere Desire* for a leading Catholic magazine: "While the author is one of our estranged brethren," he wrote, "there is nothing in this book that will hurt a good Catholic to read. It breathes the spirit of Brother Lawrence and Saint Francis." Quakers claimed me; Christian Science and New Thought joined the chorus. The Swedenborgian magazine wrote, "Glenn Clark may never have read Swedenborg but he states his law of correspondences better than any of our writers have done."

A letter from New England said, "I know you are a Bahai." I wrote a puzzled letter asking what a Bahai was. At that time I was shamefully ignorant of all these various sects. A woman wrote, "I have just finished reading *More Twice Born Men* by Harold Begbie, and I *know* that you are the mysterious man he refers to as F. B." A president of a great seminary came to see me. "You are the man who could unite the fundamentalists and the modernists. You go even farther than the fundamentalists in relying on the promises of God to see actual miracles happen in saving souls and saving lives, and yet you outdo the modernists in resting every deduction upon the scientific laws of the universe. You are the natural leader for bringing these opposing groups together."

"I am not a leader," I protested. "I would love to act as leaven, but I would never work with an organization such as you suggest. All I could work with is an *organism*. Would that help?"

"No," he replied, "it would require an organization headed by a leader, and inspired by a slogan and a shibboleth."

"That kind of outfit would be like Saul's armor to me," was my final word. "All I have is my little slingshot of prayer and five smooth stones of Faith, Hope, Love, Humility and Gratitude. Let me keep shooting these sentiments out into the hearts of people. If an organization is required, you or someone else lead the army of unification."

Most of the letters were calls for prayer. And to my consternation, most were for prayers of healing. I was not a "healer" and had no desire to be one. My wife and I both suffered from the common misconception that any group that attempted to apply what Jesus taught and demonstrated regarding healing would be branded as a "cult." But when calls continued to come from people in real need, what could a person do but comply and pray the best he could.

I felt as Jonah must have felt when commissioned to a task he didn't relish, and I found myself looking around for a whale to jump into. Whales were not abroad in Minnesota that year but the flu was. My subconscious wish to escape may have been responsible for the fact that I found myself coming down with the flu time after time that year, usually when calls for healing prayers came the thickest. One day I heard the front doorbell ring and my six-year-old boy opened the door.

"Hello, my little man. Does the Mr. Glenn Clark live here who wrote *The Soul's Sincere Desire?*"

"Yes, sir."

"Well, my boy, I want him to pray for my rheumatism. I wonder if he will be willing to see me?"

"Sure, sure! Daddy is sick in bed but you can go right upstairs and he will pray for you."

It didn't take me long to see the absurdity of this procedure. So I asked the Lord what was His "big idea" in putting me in bed in this way. If the Lord has a sense of humor He must certainly have enjoyed a laugh that day.

"What are you trying to teach me?" I asked. And then, almost as clearly as if it had been in words, came the answer,

"After a week in bed don't you realize that you rise very much stronger spiritually than when you went to bed, because you had twenty-four hours a day to turn to Me? Can't you see what I am trying to tell you?"

"Thanks, Lord," I exclaimed. "I catch the hint and will try to find time to turn to You without causing You—as well as me—all this trouble."

After that I took an entire hour each morning for meditation and prayer—*and the flu stayed away.* After a year I found I could "step into the Kingdom," as I called it, whenever I wished. But to secure the necessary morning time for this withdrawal I ceased taking the morning paper and did not resume it again for twelve years.

Louise was more troubled than I by all this publicity. "I thought I had married a college professor. I never dreamed I had married an author. I certainly never wanted fame to come to our door."

I never knew a family more completely free of all vanity than the family of Louise B. Miles. All of them were completely devoid of any desire for personal fame or glory. This was a great asset to me in my work. A "social climber" would have been a great detriment to me in the service that I desired to render.

I prayed that my children would inherit this sweet quality of modesty of their mother and to my joy this prayer was answered. I prayed that my books would draw people to God and not to me, and by the very nature of those books this prayer, too, was answered. True, when I go to a city there is often a small group of readers who come to meet with me, but the gratitude in their hearts is for the One who did the writing through me. I have often thought how actually terrifying it must be for a writer of a popular novel—a brilliant best-seller—to find himself met at every station by vast mobs of admirers all wanting an autograph or a handclasp that they might boast about to their grandchildren someday.

One day I noticed that The Atlantic Monthly Company, publisher of *The Soul's Sincere Desire*, put on the inside flap of the jacket this statement: "It is the personal record of a man who has learned to pray as naturally as to breathe, and whose every prayer is answered." Knowing how Louise disliked publicity and positively abhorred ballyhoo, shrinking from even the merest hint of an overstatement, I showed it to her and said, "I think I should write to the publishers to take that out. I don't know how they ever came to put anything like that in."

The next minute I received one of the greatest surprises of my life.

"No, Glenn," she replied simply, "I don't think you should bother to write the publishers. For I have noticed that ever since your mother died three years ago all your prayers have been answered."

This set me to thinking in a new field, from which I soon emerged with another of the greatest discoveries of my life. The next day I brought it to Louise.

"Mother had great wishes for me, but while she was on earth her wishes and prayers were circumscribed and limited by the tensions of a physical body and the inhibitions of a human mind. But the moment she stepped into heaven her wishes for me became multiplied in power by infinity and her dreams are beginning to come true!"

Immediately following this discovery I found myself impatiently awaiting the time when I too should die and *my* wishes (and such big wishes they were, for my children, my friends, my country and my world) would also be multiplied by infinity and my highest dreams come true.

But *is* it necessary to die in the *flesh* to accomplish this? Didn't Paul say, "I am crucified with Christ, nevertheless I live; yet not I, but Christ liveth in me"? Is it not possible to take a great big eraser and erase out the little, personal self so completely that only the higher Self can work through us? That very moment and that very hour I made that text my passionate appeal to God. "Erase the little self completely, O Father," I cried. "Let only Thy will henceforth take complete charge of every area of my life. And let Thy plan come into manifestation in Thine own time and in Thine own way!"

It was years later that I realized with an overwhelming sense of destiny that Page had stepped into heaven when I was fourteen, mother had stepped into heaven just before I was forty-two. Page had ushered in the first cycle of my life, and now I felt that mother was ushering in the second. With such partners on the other side I was as one living in the very foothills of heaven.

CHAPTER XIX

Athletes of the Spirit

NEITHER Louise nor I was carried away by these external "answers to prayer." What thrilled us was the inner *illumination* that was coming to people. The outer results were the mere by-product of the *real* answer to prayer which was the development of the character and the enrichment of the soul. My next step, therefore, was to put this newborn discovery into practice in the training of my boys and girls at Macalester College.

The lethargy of humankind is so great that people rarely exert themselves sufficiently to draw upon all their resources unless they have to. William James says that men use only one-fourth of their powers, leaving three-fourths untapped except in times of crisis. I have verified in my own experience all that William James has said and can add this observation besides: when it comes to spiritual powers the average man rarely uses even 10 percent and then only in times of trouble. That is one of the reasons—indeed, the only reason as far as I can see—that God permits trouble to come into the world. "Trouble," I wrote in *The Soul's Sincere Desire*, "is the most valuable thing that can come to you next to God Himself, provided it turns you to God."

Fortunately, there is another road to God which, if one takes it, enables one to bypass the road of trouble, and that is the road of High Endeavor. By that I mean, undertaking something that requires not only *all* your powers, but demands more power than at present you think you possess. As a matter of fact, this latter road can become a road of trouble if you *don't* turn to God, but it gives the traveler an opportunity to turn to God *before* the trouble comes.

Now it so happens that there are at least two activities that require capacities greater than the average human possesses, two activities that demand more strenuous endeavor than most people normally are capable of giving, and those two are: (1) Creative writing, and (2) Competitive athletics. As these were my two special fields of work at Macalester College the opportunity for putting my philosophy into action was all made to order. I first turned to the field of athletics. From that moment the athletic field was to be my outdoor meeting house for developing character in the boys. An athletic coach has more influence over the lives and characters of his boys than has the president of the college. "Dad" Eliot, the famous Y.M.C.A. secretary, said, "I have rarely found the spiritual level of any college rise any higher than the spiritual level of the football team."

When I established the track team at the college there were only three men capable of winning any points: Virgil Guthrie, Harold Baldwin and Sam Schiek. The first one has now gone on into the unobstructed universe, victim of World War I. The other two are ministers of the gospel. Those three men helped me set the standards and create the spirit which have become the permanent possession of all the Mac track teams that followed.

In my booklet, *Power in Athletics*, I elaborate on the disciplines to which the track athlete has to submit, disciplines which are tough enough to put any church member to shame. What power we would have in our churches today, for instance, if every church member gave himself one hour's training in spiritual culture every day, if he kept up the training until he could do one thing well, and if he would eschew all excesses of all kind, obey the rules of his code, treasure above all things the *esprit de corps* of his team, and give all his strength and skill and devotion to the cause for which he was trained!

There is a discipline required on our athletic field that is very easy to turn into spiritual discipline. To begin with, no smoking or drinking or late hours are allowed. To those rules I added, "No profanity." Knowing that an athlete's character is molded by a coach not so much by the rules he lays down as by the way they are laid down, and that any attempt to develop character in a college man by the "goody-goody" method is doomed to failure before it begins, I accomplished my purpose by telling the story of Farmer Burns, who was the world champion middleweight wrestler until he retired just this side of sixty years of age. When he had finished a match he always made a speech. "Boys, the reason that I can throw any man of my weight in the world is because I don't drink, I don't smoke, and I don't swear. Did you ever hear a man swear when he was walking down the street, master of all he surveyed? No, but if he stepped on a banana peeling and went down in the gutter you might hear him swear. In other words, a man swears only when he is down. Now, boys, if you swear before you start a match you are down already. Mark my words, boys, true winners never swear."

The besetting sin of adolescent years is selfishness, usually expressed in the form of a deep self-centeredness. The moment a boy removes his center of reference from self to others or to God, something happens within him that blesses him the rest of his life.

I had one boy named Bob Moran, a fine chap, very desirous to prove himself worthy of the team, but whose work all the season had been only mediocre. One day during a meet in which he was running last in nearly all his races, I saw him sitting apart, morose and unhappy, blaming himself bitterly. Several days later just before the next meet I took him aside and asked him what was the matter. He said he was disgusted with himself, and had come to the conclusion he was never going to amount to a row of pins in track. I said I thought he was taking himself far too seriously. "You act as though you think the fate of the entire team depended upon your own individual running. It certainly doesn't. We can get along without your running if you find you can't run. But we can't get along without your spirit of enthusiasm and good will. Now forget yourself entirely in the meet tomorrow. Go around and pat the other fellows on the back. Spread encouragement to all. And when time for your race comes, get down on your marks with a feeling of sheer joy in your heart for the opportunity of self-expression it gives you. Run for the joy of it, dash down the stretch for the love of it. Don't give a hang about winning."

I shall never forget the 220 the next day. It had to be run around a curve and the track was in poor condition. Moreover, the runners had to face a stiff wind blowing up the straightaway. But there came Bob around the bend twenty yards ahead of his nearest competitor, his face raised with a glorified expression upon it. When the time was announced, revealing that he had broken all local records, and had run the course at least two full seconds faster than he had done the week before, he could hardly believe what he heard. "But it's a curved track," he protested, "and the wind was against me."

"Never mind," I said, "three stop watches caught you. They ought to know."

Time after time when my boys began slumping until they ceased to have any hope of winning for themselves and finally decided to keep on with the squad merely out of desire to help the morale of the team by not quitting, I found that they began to win races. Conversely, when honors and plaudits began to come to men until the steady stream of adulation made them conceited or self-conscious, they were almost invariably in danger. In other words, the more unself-conscious and unself-seeking my athletes were, the clearer channels they became for the great inner powers of the creative spirit to flow through them.

I rarely found it necessary to speak to the boys of the existence of a God and the value of faith and prayer; nearly all of them consciously or unconsciously took all this for granted. But I found it very worth while to help them discover the necessity of banishing self thoughts, anger thoughts and fear thoughts which serve to block the channel for the clear expression of their own natural simple faith. Some of my boys discovered also, that when a man is "in tune" he can trust the natural, instinctive impulses that well up within him.

For instance, my half-miler, Wesley Tennis, the president of the college Y.M.C.A., told me that whenever he entered a race with love and joy in his heart, and without thinking of winning, he always found himself starting his sprint at exactly the right time and in the right way to win the race. Strange to say, this impulse to sprint often came at times which were quite contrary to the orthodox time for starting a sprint. But regardless of the orthodox technique, whenever he let himself be governed by this inner direction no matter whether he passed his opponent on the curve or on the straightaway he invariably won his race. Once at a state meet when he found himself about to sprint thus, he let his little calculating self-thought enter in and checkmate the impulse, thinking that in so important a race he should let the orthodox standards of racing govern him. The result was he lost first place by about six inches which could easily have been overcome if he had started his sprint when his inner impulse commanded him.

I am aware that athletes from time immemorial have felt these impulses and all agree that they come only when they are "in tune." The result is that nearly all athletes are either very superstitious or very religious. Athletes—as well as other folks—are superstitious if they stress the results; they are religious if they stress the "getting in tune."

I have found that athletes do not have to be urged to trust to the Unseen; they have to be urged, rather, to carry this trust far enough. I have no use for what are commonly called "taboos" and "hunches," which are the mere surface waters of the psychic realm, but what I do respect are the profound inner inspirations which take their rise from the deep artesian well of the Spirit. So I take my stand like Paul on Mars Hill and try to convert superstition into true religion by discouraging the tendency to look for signs and hunches, and in its place encouraging "getting in tune." And the best way to get in tune is to "do justly and to love mercy, and walk humbly with thy God."

Twenty years have gone by and Bob Moran, a salesman, still looks out for the welfare of others, and Wesley Tennis, a minister, still looks to God for his guidance and inspiration.

But sometimes something more complicated is required than merely looking out at one's associates or looking up to God. Sometimes there is something down deep inside that must first be removed. I called that process "throwing out the ballast."

One day a boy named Ray came into my office and said, "There is something wrong with my life. I always thought an athlete had to be tough, and the tougher he was the better the athlete. But I find that the best athletes on your team are the finest boys in college. I asked the captain what was the big idea. He replied, 'We have found here that if you want to travel far and fast you must travel light. In other words, you must throw out the ballast.' That set me to thinking. I know that I can't do my best until I get right inside."

"So there is something you want to get rid of—some ballast?"

"Exactly. That is it."

"Well," I said slowly, "I wonder if you realize that most of what is bad in this world is only something good in the wrong place?"

"I don't understand," he replied. "Take the garbage they feed to chickens and pigs. Garbage is all right in the garbage can, better still in the trough where the pigs and chickens can eat it. But it is in the wrong place if you keep it in the kitchen."

"That's true," the boy said.

"Suppose a selfish woman is so jealous of her neighbors who own the pigs that she won't put the garbage in the trough where they can get it, and so she conceals it in a big can in the kitchen. Pretty soon that can is filled and she has to buy another, and then another and another, till the whole kitchen is filled with garbage cans. Pretty bad state, isn't it?"

"You're sure telling me!" the boy exclaimed.

"In the same way suppose you have a lot of energy and you keep it shut in for your own selfish uses; it becomes cruelty, doesn't it? And thrift shut in for your own self becomes miserliness; love used for selfish gratification becomes lust; self-confidence that eats in on itself becomes arrogance, and so on. Do you get me?"

"I sure do. But how can a fellow get rid of some of those things? How can he empty out the garbage?"

"I'll tell you," I said, rising. "To make the thing very simple, suppose you hand me these things you have shut up in yourself right now, and let me toss them out the window."

"I'll be only too glad to." It was like a sigh.

"Sweep the old barn debris out into the garden," I said as I threw wide the window, and let the Good Gardener convert it all to His use and service." I paused and then added, "There, it is all gone," and I slammed down the window.

"I am not sure whether you caught all I was driving at," I remarked as I turned to the lad.

He seized my hand and said with feeling, "I am sure that I did, coach. Thanks an awful lot." And he vanished down the hall.

That evening I said to my wife, "I am going to see our basketball team play. We have lost all our games and we shall probably lose 50 to 10 tonight, but we are going to play the champions of the state, and there are two all-state players to watch, which is worth the price of admission."

Sure enough, those all-state players came dashing down the court with such skill and teamwork that nothing seemed able to stop them. Then it was that I saw the boy that I had talked with that afternoon standing under our basket. Suddenly he shot between the two all-state players, intercepted the ball, and dribbled down the court and made a basket. When the game ended that evening the championship team had made twenty-one points and Ray single-handed had made twenty-three.

When I took my track team to Grand Forks that spring to engage North Dakota University I overheard one of my boys say to some others, "I never saw anyone change in three months as Ray has." He became the champion all-round track athlete that spring and made the all-state football team that fall. But the outstanding thing about him was the way boys and girls said that all they needed to do was to look into Ray's face as they walked through the halls and their whole day was set straight. The Y.M.C.A. elected him their president and he made one of the best presidents they ever had.

Out of these incidents which centered around Ray there followed a series of chain reactions which prove that goodness is more contagious than badness and love is more penetrating than atomic bombs.

A very irreligious chap who had lost his temper many times in athletic contests came to my office one day and said, "Ray told me to come here and see if I could get the freedom that he has." So some more ballast went out the window. Indeed, so much ballast went out that window that the angel Michael or whoever is delegated to destroy such garbage must have been kept busy shoveling for years to come.

At the Lake Geneva College Men's Conference that summer, Wesley Hager, a Hamline University boy, came to all my talks and followed me wherever I went. He even sat down by my cot one night after I had retired and asked for a special prayer. He said, "I want to get what Ray has if it takes all summer." Two years later I addressed a

Minnesota State Y.M. and Y.W. conference, and a Hamline girl came to me when I had finished and said, "There is a boy at Hamline who fits your description of Ray. It's a common saying that if you can look into his face as he goes through the hall, your whole day will be *all right*."

"Is his name Wesley?" I exclaimed.

"Yes, how did you know?"

The following year I was invited to the University of Wisconsin to talk to the track team. The boys came in their track suits to the new field house where the talk was to be given. I didn't talk about winning meets. I told the story of Ray and how to cast out the ballast. When I had finished, a handsome chap, slightly bow-legged, came up, grasped my hand and said, "I want to get like that." A few weeks later I read in the morning paper that the Big Ten Indoor Field Meet would be held the next day and that the championship lay between Ohio, Illinois and Iowa. The next morning the paper read, "The surprise of the meet was the way Wisconsin ran away with the meet, led by a little bow-legged chap they couldn't stop."

One day a lad named Bert Boerner, a cowboy from the West and another all-state football player, came to see me.

"If the boys at the dorm got wind of what I want to talk about they would certainly climb my frame! I want to talk religion."

"What is wrong about that?" I asked. "Go ahead."

"Well, when I came here as a freshman there was an upperclassman named Ray Cochran. When I went out for the freshman team he came through the line on the first play and bowled me over. He came over to me while we were lining up for the next play and asked if I had been hurt on the play. Somehow I got a tremendous admiration for that man and all he represented. It's made me want to make my life count for something in the world. If I were a speaker I might even want to go into the ministry. But anyway, I want your help in finding my lifework."

My guidance was to introduce him to Mrs. Vandervaart who had spent her life in social service and for half a century had been head of a social settlement in Chicago that ran parallel with, and almost equaled, the famous Hull House of Jane Addams. When she retired from active service at the age of seventy-five she prayed to the Lord to make her last years creative for good. As a "direct answer" as she put it, she was led to read *The Soul's Sincere Desire*, then one day to hear me talk at the First Presbyterian Church in Chicago. The next year she packed up her things and came to St. Paul, rented a "little house by the side of the road" on the Lincoln Avenue that I traversed every day on my way to college, and for seven years was a saint and an inspiration to all my boys and girls, who grew to love her like a mother.

After his first interview, Bert Boerner became definitely one of her "boys." Through Mrs. Vandervaart's influence Jane Addams accepted Bert as one of her helpers in the boys' work at Hull House and the second year he was made head of all the boys' work, with seven full-time workers and twenty-three part-time workers under him.

Bert Boerner found that Hull House at that time was a frequent meeting place for Capone and his gang. The youngsters were largely the sons of these gangsters and Bert was never sure when he started for home in the evening whether or not he would get there because these youngsters with their slingshots and B.B. guns liked to take pot shots at their leaders as part of their practice in preparation to become gunmen themselves one day.

Up until the time Bert came to Hull House, the one department which had seemed to fail was the boys' work. The youngsters were almost out of control. In the boys' quarters, as fast as curtains or pictures were hung, they were torn down. No one as yet had found a way of coping with these young vandals.

Then one day Bert completely reversed his tactics. Instead of hanging the pictures and curtains he got there before the boys and *took them all down*—at least what was left of them.

When the boys discovered their bare walls they exclaimed, "What's the big idea?"

"The big idea," said Bert, "is that from now on you can have things just the way you want them. These are your quarters. If you don't want decorations you don't need to have them. If you want them you'll have to make them yourselves."

"Make them ourselves?"

"Yes. There are art classes here. Most of you boys are Italians, descendants of Titian, Michelangelo and Raphael, and here is a chance to prove your ability, your ingenuity and your initiative. I suggest that if you do fix up these quarters, that you appoint one of your own members to be sergeant at arms and guard the place against any rascals that might want to tear things down."

As a result of this move the boys entered into a period of unusual creative activity. They decorated the place, elected the toughest member of their gang to be sergeant at arms, and the boys' work, instead of being a blot on the work of Hull House, became one of its outstanding successes. Moreover, a way was found to ban the Capone gang from the place and Capone's chief lieutenant was won over to a new life and became Bert's leading helper.

Now if anyone thinks that this message of the power of the Spirit on the athletic field was used as a means only, in order to win victories over rivals, I can easily dismiss this misconception at once. Not only I, but my boys also, spread this philosophy among our rival schools. I gave a talk to the Augsburg basketball team at the request of their coach and the next week they defeated our team.

One of the best examples of the contagion of a big idea is the story of Bill Rose of Hamline. Bill ran the two-mile on their track team and usually came in near the last in all the dual meets. Then one day in the state meet he astounded everyone by the way he romped in ahead of all the boys including the Mac boys who had previously and consistently defeated him. At a gathering where he was called upon to speak this is the story that he told:

"It was in my sophomore year at Hamline University that my mother gave me a little pocket-sized book about *Power in Athletics* written by Dr. Glenn Clark of Macalester, Hamline's ancient rival.

"Much to my surprise the help and advice I found in this book did not tell me how to get a longer stride, what diet to follow, or suggest a training schedule. It told how to change my attitude toward others through love and prayer.

"This little book told me to get rid of any ballast I might be carrying, not material ballast but ballast in the form of hate, jealousy, fear and the desire to be a hero. My job was to learn to work for team spirit, to be good friends with everybody, and to realize that victory didn't depend on me.

"I kept this book near my bed so I could read it every night. As I began to absorb and practice some of its contents, I began to do something I hadn't done for a long time—and that was pray. I prayed not that I would win but that I would do my best.

"In my next meet it took me eleven minutes and four seconds to run the two-mile which I had chosen as my specialty. I had improved fifteen seconds over the year before. Besides, I had won the race. As the season progressed I won only two races while losing two. Although I had continued to improve, my biggest test was yet to come—the state meet at Macalester. My coach thought I might be able to place fourth. I was meeting four men who had better times than I had and one of these men hadn't been beaten in three years. He and his teammate were favored to win first and second as they had done in years previous.

"I arrived at the Mac gym about 3:20, changed clothes and proceeded to warm up for my race. I returned to the locker room and after sitting awhile I got down on my knees and prayed. I told Him He wouldn't need to worry about the first six laps but on the last two I'd need plenty of help. Then through the stillness of the room I heard the coach's voice, 'First call for the two-mile.'

"If I ever felt good before a race, it was that day. I was entering with everything to gain because no one was counting on me to win anything. 'Last call for the two-mile.' The long-awaited moment had arrived.

"Next thing, the starter was barking his orders. 'Runners to your marks. Get set.' Then followed three seconds that seemed like minutes before the crack of his pistol sent us on our way.

"The first lap I was tenth. The second lap I moved up to fifth and then something happened. Some men from the sidelines were picking up the champion and favorite from the track with a badly aching side and stomach.

"The fourth and fifth laps found me in third place. On the sixth I passed a man from Macalester for second. The man still ahead was the fellow who had won second for two years. But as I watched him bound along I noticed he was feeling the effect of not having his running mate, the champion, pacing him. As we started the seventh lap I told God I needed help. He didn't send it then. He waited awhile. On the back stretch of this lap I made two attempts to move into first but couldn't quite make it. Just before we passed the judges for the last lap, two things happened. First I remembered how Gregg Rice and Walter Mehl had raced the last quarter in the NCAA meet the year before. The second thing was the surging through me of the strength I had asked God for. That was all I needed. I raced my opponent to the corner and beat him. From that point to the finish line I increased my lead to twenty yards. Victory was mine but another surprise still remained. I had run the race thirty-nine seconds faster than the year before and twenty-three seconds faster than my first race of the season.

"As I stood under a shower rubbing my tired muscles, three thoughts came to my mind. There underneath a shower I thanked God for helping me, my mother for giving me Glenn Clark's book, and my parents for their faith in me."

CHAPTER XX

Student Conventions

ONE day Jeanne Hugo, our college's representative on the State Christian Association Planning Committee, brought me word that the Y secretary, Hugo Thompson, and the other state officers wanted me to be a speaker at the State Convention at Northfield, Minnesota. I went but I had a previous engagement that prevented my arriving until the convention had been going for two days.

Immediately after I gave my first address, which happened to be on "Overcoming Anger and Fear," all the leaders descended upon me en masse. The spokesman said, "We have a problem we want to lay before you. One of our discussion groups, the one on Men's and Women's Relationships, has gotten off on the wrong foot. In fact, if something is not done quickly it may wreck our entire conference. We want your help on it."

As I looked around I saw an excellent group of leaders: Kirby Page, Conrad Hoffman, Miss Eleanor Loucks (now Mrs. Harrison Elliott), "Dad" Eliot, and Pitt Van Dusen, who was once described by Sherwood Eddy as the greatest discussion group leader in the world. What could I an amateur do among them? I finally stammered, "I don't know how to solve this problem, but do–do you mean you want me to pray?"

"Yes, that seems to be the only way out."

I silently asked for God's guidance and finally said something like this:

"When a drop of water in a mud puddle asks to be free from all the impurity around it, to press the mud down will only stir it up worse. To pour in antiseptics would merely exchange one impurity for another impurity. But there is *one* thing that we *can* do. We can tell the little drop of water to give itself to the drawing power of the sun's rays, and immediately it will be drawn into perfect purity and harmony. Let us all agree together to give this group completely and utterly to the drawing power of the Son of God." Then I offered a little prayer, a prayer that took less time to give than it had taken to relate the parable preceding it.

Two days later when I got on a bus to go home a radiant little college girl was seated beside me. Suddenly she turned to me and said impulsively, "Wasn't our convention just wonderful!"

"Very fine, indeed," I replied. And my mind ran over that remarkable group of leaders. "By the way, which one of the platform speakers did you get the most from?"

"Oh, I didn't get so much from the platform speakers"—I smiled at her candor for I myself was one of the platform speakers—"I got my big inspiration from the discussion group meetings."

"Which group did you belong to?" "I belonged to the one on Men's and Women's Relationships. The first day it was just terrible—perhaps I should say awful. And then something changed. None of us could explain it. But it became the most inspiring gathering that I ever was in. It seemed as though we were just lifted up into another world."

The rest of the journey my heart was singing a silent song of gratitude to the God of Love who never forsakes a sincere cry in time of need.

I had another unusual experience at this convention that I believe is worth recording. The night before I left, I awoke with a severe case of palpitation of the heart, an affliction from which I had been suffering for years. The only way I could bring my heart back to its normal rate was to establish peace of mind and the only way I could do that was to turn to God and send out love to others, taking my mind completely off myself. I accepted this attack that night as a God-appointed opportunity to pray for all the other leaders. I proceeded to take them up one at a time, the entire group of grand men and women.

The only one I had never before heard of was Conrad Hoffman. At the time he was not well and the only address he gave after I arrived was at the end of a long evening's program, following two other speakers. We were all exhausted by the time he began and he must have been more exhausted than we were. Consequently, his address fell on heavy ears. I wondered why they had brought such a dull speaker there when they had plenty of leaders without him.

But when I came to pray for him that night my prayer went straight up to heaven. I had never found anyone so easy to pray for. It was like a door to a bird cage flying open at a touch, letting the bird go soaring unobstructed into the skies.

Just as I was hurrying from the hall the next afternoon to catch the bus I happened to pass Conrad Hoffman at the door. He looked tired and depressed. All the compassion in my heart welled up within me. With a spontaneous movement I seized his hand and blurted out, "During my prayers last night the Lord told me that I could pray for you with special power."

His response almost overwhelmed me. Seizing my hand in both of his he exclaimed, "You don't know what that means to me! I can never, never find words to express my gratitude for what you have just said!" His radiant face I carried with me all the way back to St. Paul.

The following week Miss Quail, an international Y.W.C.A. secretary from Europe, addressed our college chapel gathering and immediately afterward asked for an interview with me.

"I came here ostensibly to address the college," she began, "but the real reason was to see you. For several years I have been assisting Conrad Hoffman in his work among the indigent students in war-torn Europe. Thousands have found in him their only hope. To me he seems the most Christlike man in Europe today. Right now he is in America trying to raise funds to help thousands of worthy students continue their education. Last month when I was talking with Margaret Sangster and Dean Bosworth at Oberlin of the magnitude of the task, Miss Sangster said, 'Have you tried prayer?' Then Dean Bosworth said, 'Why don't you go and see Glenn Clark?' So here I am."

"Dean Bosworth," I replied, "was my inspiration when as a college boy I went to Lake Geneva, twenty-five years ago. I have never seen him since. But it heartens me beyond words that he sent you to me. And now may I ask you, has Conrad Hoffman seen you since the Northfield Conference?"

"No, why?" "Because just as I was leaving it I was prompted to tell him that God had told me that I could pray for him with special power."

"What!" she exclaimed. "God surely does work in mysterious ways, His wonders to perform. Before one asks He will answer!"

Since that meeting twenty years ago I have met and prayed with Conrad Hoffman many times on his brief trips to this country. And I have never once lost contact with him in the realm of the Spirit.

Before I left Northfield, Miss Loucks asked me to be a leader at the Women's Geneva Conference the following summer and "Dad" Eliot asked me to come to the Men's Conference at Lake Geneva. These conferences turned out to be very inspiring. There was an army of leaders there from whom I derived great inspiration.

However, my effectiveness as a person and certainly my peace of mind were limited at that time by severe palpitation of the heart that continued to seize me every night. One day a call came to me to speak for a week to the Rocky Mountain College Y.M. and Y.W.C.A. Conference at Estes Park, Colorado, 8,000 feet above sea level. Heretofore I had carefully declined any calls to high altitudes. I had spent three days in Denver once and my heart had palpitated with the speed of an engine with its governor belt off. Because I knew that my family needed me and because there surely must be important work for me to do in the world, I felt that I had no right to risk my life. So the invitation was declined. "Dad" Eliot, who had heard me decline the invitation, said to me, "I don't see how you have a moral right to decline any sincere, earnest call to speak at camps like this when God has given you such an authentic and special message to speak to your fellow men."

That remark remained with me, and would not let me rest. A month went by. Finally I sat down and wrote the Rocky Mountain Conference secretaries that I would come. I went in the same spirit that a soldier would volunteer to lead the "forlorn hope" across no man's land to rout out a machine-gun nest in the face of a withering shower of lead. When I said goodbye to my wife and children my eyes lingered long on their faces.

I went because I felt that God, speaking through the Rocky Mountain secretaries, was asking it. I went because God, speaking through "Dad" Eliot, was commanding it. Whether my family needed me or whether I had more work to do for the world, that was not for me but for God to decide. If He snatched me away before His work was done, that would be God's hard luck, not mine. I did not belong to myself, I belonged to God and His Kingdom, and if He needed me He was capable of taking care of His own.

In that spirit I went and in that spirit I led the prayer hour before breakfast each morning. As the sun came over the mountain peaks I threw back my head and looked into the sky, realizing as never before how God speaks to us through His handiwork. Words were not really needed in those hours; they seemed trivial intrusions upon the mighty silences of God. After a few days God began to speak through me with a hint of the same power that He was using to speak through the mountains. People asked me the secret of the power. The secret of it was this: those mornings of transfiguration were but the fruitage of the nights of Gethsemane that preceded them.

The very first night that I reached Estes Park palpitation seized me as usual about two in the morning. I looked about the strange room and then remembered–I was up on a high mountain. The words of my hostess returned to me, "We have given you a room away from the other leaders, so you won't be disturbed." How kind it was of her to place me where I could not even knock on the wall and call a companion to come if I should need help! The Lord certainly had "placed me far out on a limb." To God and God alone I could turn in my hours of need.

I looked out the open window. Outside, the moon made everything as bright as day. Framed in the window sash was a view of a high mountain, remote, snow-capped and gleaming in the moonlight.

"I will lift up mine eyes unto the hills," I said slowly, "from whence cometh my help. My help cometh from the Lord who made heaven and earth. You made me, Father. I am more wonderfully made than any mountains. If You want to take me–take me. If You want to preserve me You can easily preserve me. I leave it entirely to You, O Lord. You decide it. I am Your man."

Night after night, instead of getting worse, my heart was eased. When I returned from Estes Park the palpitation and even the tendency toward it had gone. I was as one liberated from a sentence of death. And so I found that the way to save one's life is not to run away from death but to face death fearlessly. Jesus was right; he that giveth up his life shall find it!

After this string of conferences, Eleanor Loucks and Pitt Van Dusen came to me with a cordial invitation to lead the prayer discussion groups at the contemplated national conference of all the college Y.M. and Y.W.C.A.'s in America, to be held in Milwaukee the following winter. This was the first national conference of its kind ever held in the nation. Three thousand students came to it. Every college in the country was represented.

I was to address whatever students had a major interest in learning more about prayer. The committee had assigned me to a room that would hold fifty. Seven hundred came. I never saw a group of students so hungry to learn how to pray. We were moved to the large auditorium and for the following days a room was reserved for us that was large enough to hold all who came.

Bruce Curry had the platform the first night and President Coffin the second. Next night there was a speaker whose address split the group into heated discussions. Thursday some speaker got the throng still more divided. Instead of the spirit of unity, and harmony, we were moving toward chaos. Studdert-Kennedy set a high spiritual note in his early morning devotions before the entire group, but as the conference drew toward a close it began to grow clear to the spiritual barometers of those who were especially sensitive to spiritual weather that the conference would end with hopes unfulfilled. "The mistake," President Coffin said to me years afterwards, "was that we had our 'satisfactions' at the start and our 'altercations' at the end. It should have been reversed."

Then came Friday morning. I was breakfasting with Charles Corbet, a member of the committee on program. "Dr. Hamilton can't come for tonight and we are puzzled whom we should ask," and one by one he named men, all of whom I knew would increase the tension and dissatisfaction. Suddenly every bone and cell and nerve in my being cried out, "Drop all your false modesty, Glenn Clark, and tell him honestly and impersonally that God had withheld the speaker for tonight so that you or Studdert-Kennedy could fill the gap that he has left. The boys and girls at this conference are hungering and thirsting not for more controversy but for an authentic experience of God—not for eloquence but for manna."

Divine Selflessness said speak, but human modesty held fast my tongue. I had never had an experience just like this before. I felt as a man might feel to whom swimming was as natural as walking, who found himself standing in a crowd on a pier when a child fell into deep water. He would love to leap in and save the child but he sees Andrew Carnegie standing by so he refrains lest people might think his motive was to get a Carnegie medal. So he prefers to remain modest and watch the child drown.

It was with real agony that I watched the convention "drown" in altercations and controversies the last two days without being able to do a thing about it except to salvage those I could in my prayer group hour. I am not implying that I could have done the job that evening, but nevertheless, I felt partly responsible for the failure of the conference because I had not obeyed the inner voice. What I am sure of is that if Stanley Jones had been there the conference would have ended in a blaze of glory.

At this conference I met two remarkable young men who were destined to lead dedicated lives of great service, Glenn Harding and Paul Sanders. One day a group came to me and asked if I could meet with a special fellowship of which these two men were the leaders at a late hour following the regular evening meeting.

"I certainly can and will," I replied. I was getting very curious to meet these two young men whom I had heard so much about but had never seen.

I never met with a circle of more responsive folk. They were great seekers, and plied me with questions. One young man who appeared to be the very youngest of them all and yet their leader, said, "You remind me of Bill Simpson. Both of you tell us to go all the way out with God, but while you show us how to do it better than he did, he radiated more joy than you do."

"That is interesting," I replied. "I never met Bill Simpson, but what you say I accept as a challenge, and hope someday to radiate more joy. You yourself seem to have that gift. May I ask you your name, young man?"

"My name is Glenn Harding."

That was my introduction to a man who was destined to become closer to me than a brother—a friendship almost equal to that with my brother Page. He was to furnish for me and my friends that radiance which I myself do not always convey, my supplement and complement to whom I owe much of the permanent success of the Camps Farthest Out.

There followed many years when I was a regular leader at student conferences at Lake Geneva. When I stepped on the grounds of Lake Geneva and witnessed the loveliness of its landscape, its trees, its lake, an almost perfect replica, I am told, of the Lake of Galilee, I heard a voice deep down within me saying, "It is in places like these, and through gatherings like this, wherein rest the hope and promise of this republic."

Now at some of these conferences there was a vigorous battle for first place between the "psychologists" and the "evangelists." Sometimes these controversies waxed very bitter, poisoning the atmosphere of the entire gathering. I am all for honest debate as to ways and means if all can unite in their final purpose, but I never forget the words of Dr. Brougher, a great Baptist preacher, "My little boy said to me once, 'Mrs. Jones who leads the Ladies' Aid reminds me of a porcupine.' 'Why?' 'Oh, she has lots of good points but you can't get close to her.'" And then he added, "I would rather have a drunkard in my congregation than a troublemaker."

A political convention poisoned by alcohol is no worse off than a church convention poisoned by hate and controversy. In these student conferences very little of the intellectual power was lessened by this controversy but at least three-fourths of the spiritual power was destroyed.

The following year when called back to be a leader of the Midwest Y.W.C.A. Conference, I decided that my chief job was to pray, with special stress on the unity of spirit. If I could do nothing else but meet with its leaders each day and pray with them and then let them do all the leading and speaking while I faded into the background, I would be content. But the very moment that I relinquished any desire for prominence at this gathering something happened. That year there was a new face, Mrs. Katherine Willard Eddy, fresh from Japan. When the schedule of group meetings was announced Mrs. Eddy exclaimed, "This plan is very disappointing to me. I came especially to hear Glenn Clark and now the only time he speaks is at his daily prayer group that meets the same hour that all the rest of us meet with our discussion groups. Isn't there a time when he can give his message to all of us leaders?"

Her wish was seconded by others, so a special hour was set and all the leaders came to it. The effect of this gathering upon the entire conference was felt immediately, somewhat similar to the effect at Yale University when Walter Camp coached the football coaches. In those years Yale won the national championship every year. As soon as this leaders' meeting started, a similar power poured into our conference. The source of power did not come from the leader but rather from the complete orchestration in spirit that such a gathering produces. Jesus said, "Where two or three agree together" wonderful things will happen. And in that word "agree" was packed all the power that is found at its best in symphonies and orchestras. The following year this meeting of leaders was again adopted and these two years, according to Miss Gwinn and the other leaders, marked the high-water mark of spiritual camps at Lake Geneva.

That second summer before I left home for the College Men's Camp at Geneva my little son came down with a severe attack of what the doctor called glandular fever. His temperature was 105 the day I left, but I assured my wife that if I kept this spiritual appointment that God had laid on me, it would speed his recovery better than if I remained home. This little boy meant more to me than life itself, and I spent every minute on the train praying for him. Arriving at Geneva, I went straight to Vision Hill and spent more hours in prayer. Every cell and fiber of my being yearned for his recovery, and I held him in my heart until I could put him utterly into the great heart of God with such trust in His goodness that I could accept His verdict with the peace and the radiant acquiescence I had counseled all other parents to feel. Every night in my tent I prayed until midnight and awoke before dawn to kneel by my cot and pray again.

One day I noticed a newcomer in my group, a middle-aged man with lines of character in his face. Two days later he came to my tent and said, "I am Jesse Wilson, general secretary of the Student Volunteer Movement for Foreign Missions. I have been at many summer conferences but never felt such spiritual power on any grounds before, and it was not till I went to your group that I discovered where the power came from."

"If that is so," I replied, "the strength doesn't come through my strength but through my weakness. Because I have such a deep well of need, the vast ocean of God's love has had to pour in a whole gulf stream to fill it."

And that, I later learned, was perfectly true. Years when I went to conferences nonchalantly and casually, expecting to take them easily in my stride, I usually found heavy going after I got there; whereas, whenever anything in the way of sorrow or suffering was pressing upon me, the power rolling through the conference was tremendous. Having learned this lesson I made it a practice when called upon to undertake a difficult or important assignment anywhere, to do a lot of passionate praying *before* the assignment started, without waiting till suffering or trouble *forced* me to do it. It became very, very clear to me why Jesus went up into the mountain to pray the nights *before* he started on his speaking journeys.

CHAPTER XXI

The Camp Farthest Out

A T ALL these camps there was Light, but at some it was as fitful and sputtering as a faulty kerosene lamp; at others it was as brilliant and glorious as a cluster of electric light bulbs. What was the reason for this variation? Invariably the difference in intensity went back to one thing: the harmony or lack of harmony among the leaders. One year I found great jealousy among the leaders as to who would have the most platform speeches. That year the light was short-circuited as completely as if a hand had turned off the switch. Another year a professional psychologist present considered a professional evangelist a hopeless old fogey and the evangelist regarded the psychologist as antichrist himself. Instead of a spiritual powerhouse, the camp became a shambles.

At such camps every fiber in my being yearned to rush forth and start a camp of my own based upon Jesus' promise that "where two or three *agree* together I shall be in the midst of you." That word "agree" comes from the same Greek word that "symphony" comes from. How wonderful it would be to turn all these jarring notes into a symphony of the soul!

Another lack I found at these camps was the great emphasis they gave to lectures and discussions and the little emphasis they gave to prayer. All the leaders believed in prayer as a routine part of religious practice. A meal should begin with prayer and a church service should close with a benediction, but as to believing that prayer would actually accomplish things, that was ridiculous!

Since my particular function at these camps was to lead the group that wished to specialize in prayer, I frequently found the atmosphere I was trying to build up torn down by the different emphasis created by social action speakers who believed letters to congressmen the *only* way to reach the Government and by orthodox religionists who believed praying for the sick smacked of cultism. At such times another yearning pulled at all the fibers of my being to start a camp where *all* the leaders believed that prayer was the mightiest force in the world.

Another feature of the camps was the time taken up by many committees and discussion groups over matters pertaining to the peculiar needs of running an *organization*—the raising of money, the increasing of membership—time that I should like to have seen spent in training folks how to put God into their homes and classrooms, into their work and play. In short, I yearned to see a camp where people ceased merely talking *of* and *about* God and the Kingdom—prepositions that too often implied separation—and started immersing themselves in God and the Kingdom, in every area of their lives.

These student camps might be serving their purpose well but I wanted to go further. How did Edison lift us out of the era of candles and kerosene lamps into the "age of light"? It was by building a laboratory where he could experiment for years emptying all the air out of bulbs of glass so completely that the metal filaments were able to stand the heat generated by the mighty energy. Laboratory work was the secret. I must establish a laboratory and what would be a finer laboratory than a camp in God's beautiful outdoors—where folks could meet and learn how to empty themselves of self, and learn how to love God with all their strength, with all their mind, with all their heart and with all their soul.

This laboratory must not be merely a laboratory of ritual and doctrine, nor should it be a mere forum for debate. Not only must the mind and soul be rendered incandescent, but the heart and body also if we would obey Jesus' Great Commandment.

And so one year I started on a journey—a journey down through the heart of America—to find the laboratory, the seekers and the method by which we might help to usher in the Age of Light for this dark and weary world.

My first stopping place was Lake Geneva, where students from eight Midwestern states were gathering in an open air conference for building personality around the pattern of Christ. My task was to stress the need of making one's entire soul empty and incandescent and completely surrendered to God. I talked about spiritual orchestration. When I wasn't speaking I listened to other speakers on similar themes. But one afternoon I stumbled upon a little gathering in which Miss Ruth Raymond, a teacher of art appreciation, was leading a rather unusual group of young people in a rather unusual way.

"Erase your faces," she said. "Wipe out all your old preconceived actions and ideas and make your mind incandescent. Now—tune in to Beauty, Love and Joy." And as the hour went on, I realized that here was what I had been seeking for. One day she had them work out dramatic poses to illustrate different emotions. The next day, she took up color and told them to feel themselves as vapor drawn about by the colors of the rainbow while she explained the significance of the colors: red, signifying blood and excitement; blue, remoteness and loyalty, and so on through the spectrum. One day she had them read original poems or poems of others which were particular favorites of theirs and therefore, "belonged to them."

And then one day I drew her aside and told her of my dream of establishing an open air laboratory to help bring to pass the Age of Light. "In my spiritual orchestration hour," I said, "I am telling people about the divine laws of life as stated by Jesus, and how one can use them as shafts to tune right in to the infinite power of God. As one attains oneness with God, he turns on the Light in his own soul, and brings light to all who are in the house. Now I find you doing with art what I was trying to do in terms of religion."

She responded at once. "I believe that the arts may be our avenue for losing our self-consciousness in a sense of oneness with God. When we yield ourselves to the spell of the great artist, we 'lose ourselves' through our imagination in his creation; we are swept along with the movement of the music; we find repose in the spacious ease of the seated 'Fates' of the Parthenon, or draw deep breaths of courage with the 'Victory of Samothrace.' If the piece of beauty we contemplate is great art, it has elements of the Universal in it; through it we push out our horizons. It manifests Unity; through it we experience peace. For the moment of our contemplation we have lost that self-consciousness which insulates us from God. I believe through art we can turn our attention from our self-axis to our wider orbit, and through art link ourselves into the source of radiant energy and creative power, bringing ourselves into true relationship with the universe in which we live."

"Would you be willing to come to a camp next summer and put your philosophy into practice with a specially chosen group of people who are willing to give all they have to the releasing of themselves to your teachings and opening themselves up to God?"

"There is nothing in the world I would rather do. I would go to the ends of the earth to find such a group," she said.

My next stopping place was New York City, where I was to be the guest for several weeks of an efficiency expert, Oliver Lyford, whose family, by the way, brought Coué to America. The first thing I found awaiting me when I went to my guest room in their home was a letter from Gerald Stanley Lee, a gentleman I had met only once before in my life.

"Come out to my island as my guest for a week," he wrote, "and let me demonstrate my wonderful new discovery. I have found a way of making the body an instrument of prayer."

I accepted his invitation and there on the Island Farthest Out, off the coast of Maine, I studied this man who tried to make people as relaxed as the sea. And as I watched the great ocean move in its irresistible and ever relaxed way, I captured a little of the tremendous spirit of the sea in my own soul and knew from whence he had derived his secret. One day I asked him to put into words what he was doing.

"If you were to ask me to say in a single sentence what I am doing," he replied, "I would say I am teaching people how to pray—teaching a definite technique which a man can depend upon and use for praying with his body, a technique by which man makes himself sensitive, radio like, to the Unseen, by which he opens himself soul and body to God.

"Prayer in its fullness as a sense of communion has a technique for connecting a man with God which is as definite, to put it in a homely way, as turning on the light by putting the plug in its socket. Prayer in its fullest sense is the act of fitting one's soul into one's body, of lighting up one's body with God.

"I believe that until we provide people with a definite technique for praying with their bodies as well as with their souls, we are not going to be able to bring the world singing and crowding into our churches."

"Could you come to a camp next summer and teach a group of serious seekers how to do this?" I asked.

"I myself am fastened to this island," he replied, "part and parcel of this island as much as that old lighthouse is a part of it. But suppose you select one of your group, one of your finest seekers, to spend a month or two with me and my wife and learn my method and let him pass the technique on to the others."

Some time later when I returned to the home of the efficiency expert, he said. "Do you know I have been practicing your philosophy in my business and I find it works. Your idea is that if a thing is put into perfect balance it will work itself, the kinks and errors will fall off of their own weight, so to speak, isn't that it?"

"Something like that," I smiled.

"Well, when a great business fails and I am called in to put it on its feet, I invariably find that somewhere or other things are out of balance. And I find that the philosophy of looking for spiritual unbalance first is a good thing. Therefore, the first thing I look for is a man in the establishment who is what you would call 'in tune'; that is to say a man who is humble yet efficient and willing to do his best without regard for recompense or glory, but for the good of all. Sometimes this man is one of the undermanagers or a sub-foreman, but even if he were the office boy or janitor I think I would take him. This man I pick out and appoint as the head of the firm until conditions begin to improve. I tell the rest that he is the 'king' and they are to do exactly as he says."

That comment suggested another idea to carry to the camp: how a man can put his business into balance while he is putting his soul, mind and body into balance. So I decided then and there that we must have an open forum hour for businessmen and others to discuss spiritual life from this practical point of view. How glorious it is to think that one can become an office boy or janitor or under-manager for the

Lord! Sometimes I wonder if all the really successful men are not merely God's janitors and office boys in disguise! Daily it was growing clearer and clearer to me that this taking religion into all the affairs of life was not demeaning heaven to base ends, but rather was a lifting of the sodden affairs of earth heavenward. At this camp we must learn to put every phase of our life under the leadership and under the control of Christ. More and more I became thrilled with the conception of the wholeness of the spiritual life.

Years ago I had taken football teams down to a camp on the Mississippi River two weeks before college opened, for special training in the fundamentals of football. These camps were always thrilling affairs but not nearly so thrilling as this new kind of camp I was contemplating, a camp for training athletes of the spirit.

Then a set of problems began to arise.

These football camps were financed by an athletic board. How was this new kind of camp to be financed? We wanted to keep expense per person as low as possible. But there was going to be some expense that would not be small. For instance, we knew of no one in the Middle West who understood this new philosophy of physical coordination, so there remained nothing for us to do but send someone east to study for several weeks or months the system which had so intrigued me on my journey of discovery. Better omit the physical side, some of my friends said. Instantly I said, "No." Our camp must provide an adventure into the *wholeness* of the spiritual life or it would be nothing. Unless we could make an all-out attempt we would not even start. Otherwise ours would be just one more camp. So I selected one of the most spiritual young persons I knew, Vivian Combacker, and sent her east. We never regretted that investment. It has certainly borne fruit a hundredfold.

Then suddenly out of the blue sky without my soliciting it, twelve men in my Plymouth Bible Class came forward and offered to underwrite the camp to the extent of five hundred dollars. Moreover they paid the money down. I am glad to report that when the camp was over we were able to return to them two-thirds of what they had advanced.

Another thing to give concern—at least it gave my wife considerable concern—was the preparation of the messages for such an extended study of prayer as this one would be. "Do you realize that this is a three weeks' camp, and you are scheduled to speak morning and evening? I don't remember ever seeing you write down a speech in your life. Are you sure you could give forty-two talks?" Of course, this was the most sensible sort of advice. Fortunately, I was going to Lake Geneva again to give a series of nine or ten talks and I promised to take special pains in preparing them. But, alas, when I returned and with some elation started to produce my notebook with a dozen talks outlined to show my wife, I discovered that I had left the notebook on the train never to be seen again. I accepted the loss as God's leading that in this camp we must trust *all* to Him, and that He would say what should be said, through me or through others at the right time and in the right way. And God never failed us.

There remained one serious problem, now that the time for the first camp was rapidly drawing nigh. Would the right persons come to it? In fact, would any persons come to it?

The first letter of acceptance came from a young woman we had never heard of before—a Miss Sparrow. If the robin is the first forerunner of summer, that Sparrow was harbinger and forerunner of the Camp Farthest Out. For she wrote, "I am so thrilled with this idea of making ourselves complete channels for the Christ to work through us, that I am going to Lake Koronis two weeks before the camp begins, and be quiet there with God, and walk beside the still waters and look at the woods and hills and prepare my soul for the Divine Spirit to come down and bless us all."

"If they all come with her spirit," my wife said, "the camp will be a success."

And they did come with that spirit, from east and west, from north and south, until nineteen states were represented—seventy self-chosen souls, or perhaps I should say God-chosen souls, for no one who ever came to these camps seemed directed from any other source than God.

But how to amalgamate and blend together easily and quickly all of these people, from every walk of life, representing practically every profession, as well as all ages of men, women and children? How could we gather together the threads of these lives, the deep hidden consciousness of all these people, nearly all strangers to one another, and blend them together and make them one?

That question was answered the first night. Glenn Harding arose and led us in song. Strange we had not thought of having a song leader present! And Glenn was a revelation to us of what a true song leader "born of the spirit" could be. Of all the forms of spiritual and aesthetic coordination, this most wonderful means of all, the method of song, had been left out of the picture. The word "picture" fits well here because anyone who has ever seen Glenn lead singing at Koronis or the other camps, will never forget the picture of the way he leads and blends and sweeps us into that glorious oneness where soul meets soul while voice blends with voice out in the starlit night.

When calls began coming from other states begging me to start a Camp Farthest Out in their neighborhood I was surprised, for I considered myself the world's worst orator. When people explained that they didn't come for oratory, they came for manna, I began to comb the country over for men who could bring them manna in a better form than I. George Washington Carver and Rufus Jones were too old to embark upon a new adventure of this kind. Stanley Jones was busy with his own *ashrams*. Then one day I picked up a copy of *Love Can Open Prison Doors*. Here was the story of a man who after spending twenty-five years in the underworld had an experience of Christ comparable to the experience of Saul on the Damascus Road. I wrote him. He came to a camp. I looked into his face with the scars of suffering upon it, scars that vanished like shadows at midday when a beautiful smile spread over his face as he spoke of redemptive love. At last I had found a man who believed that the day of miracles was not over. This man was Starr Daily.

Then one day Frank Laubach on his way from the Philippines dropped into a camp and we begged him to tell of his game with minutes. Here was a modern Brother Lawrence practicing daily the Presence of God. Thus one by one the leadership of the camp grew.

A typical day at a camp begins with a meditation at seven o'clock led by Glenn Harding with inspirational readings strung like beautiful beads on a string of meditations and prayers. As we move from the chapel to the breakfast hall, Alice Kraft in ringing accents commands all to empty the trash out of their lungs and systems and with uplifted arms welcome the day in all its newness and freshness.

At nine o'clock Starr Daily addresses the group in accents reminiscent of Lincoln. "If you would have me give you a character analysis, a personality reading, I should ask but one question, 'What is it you adore?' Should you answer that question honestly, truthfully, I could then give you a general history of your life, past, present and future. If we adore gossip we shall, in all our characteristics, become like gossip. The timbre of our voice will betray us, the cast of our eyes, the set of our features, the tilt of our heads, our mannerisms, gestures, the way we sit, and the way we walk—all will proclaim to the world, 'Behold, the gossip!'

"We may choose what we wish to become in our hearts and minds. The difference between suffering and happiness, defeat and victory, resides in the self-advanced inquiry, 'What is it I adore?'"

And then for an hour he holds us transfixed as he talks of the Redemptive Love of Jesus.

Then, under the trees, follows an hour of worship led by Alice Kraft spreading blessings to the right and left and kneeling in reverence before the altars of God.

In the creative writing hour which follows, the teacher tells the group that each one there has access to the same three sources of originality that Wordsworth, Dickens and Shakespeare had access to: our reminiscences, prejudices and convictions. Be true to your own personality, dip into these three reservoirs honestly and sincerely, and you can't help being original. All you need then is to point your words and put rhythm into your sentences and you will have something worth while. The writing hour is one of the most inspiring hours at the camp.

In the afternoon after a rest and quiet time the class in art meets. Here Claire Boyer says, "When God created the earth, that was architecture. When He shaped its valleys and mountains, that was sculpture. When He tinted it with grass and flowers, that was painting. When He started the wind and the waves and the birds singing, that was music. When He hid infinite meanings in His nature-forms, that was poetry. When humanity began to react to nature, that was drama. When man moved in harmony with God's great eternal laws, that was the art of the dance! Thus the art world was created, good and true and beautiful and whole! Diversity in Unity, related and purposeful! That is the reason that art can integrate man—it calls to his spirit and spirit always responds in all its original wholeness."

After that the entire group is divided into a series of prayer sections meeting separately in different parts of the grounds. These groups remain intact for the duration of the camp, but the leaders rotate, thus spreading both contagion and technique for forming similar prayer groups when individuals return home. Many churches all over the nation have been revivified by folks who derived new inspiration from such groups.

Sometimes we have passed around an open Bible and asked each to lay his hand with his particular burden upon the great promises in this precious Book. Great answers have come. Sometimes we use petitionary prayer, sometimes a Quaker silence, and sometimes we broadcast the Love of God to all the world.

After supper we gather for the half hour of song before the Galilean Hour. People who have never sung before find music pouring from their throats.

"If you can't sing," cries Glenn Harding with the radiance that seems always shining from him, "just open your mouth and feel the music of the rest vibrating upon your vocal chords. When two pianos are in the same room all you need to do is play upon one and the corresponding chords in the other hum in response. Open your mouths and let the breath of God flow through, and all our aeolian harps will blend in one grand harmony."

Some songs preach and some songs teach, some songs pray. Glenn in his joyous, loving way makes every song period a complete religious experience in itself.

Then Frank Laubach rises to speak—the man who has been teaching the silent billion to read, and whose compassion goes out to all the benighted ones of the earth. It is an experience to hear this great man. Tonight it is half speech and half prayer.

Leaning intimately across the pulpit with hands folded, he speaks softly…"I've been hungry for the last few days to get with a small group like this that believes in prayer. Our Lord has so few to follow His thoughts through with Him. If we become more like Him, then the circle will reach around the world. The greatest failure of the Christian Church is that 'we try to save our own souls at all costs.' The further out the needs of Humanity are the less concerned we are! Make us bigger"–his discourse becomes prayer–"in the circle of our praying, love, interest and thought." Then he turns back to the listeners. "We have an ever-growing confidence through experience because prayer– when we are honest and willing to be used–is the mightiest power in the world. …If we follow through prayer with our lives, we are then irresistible. If we open up to Him, open the center of ourselves out to Him and if we open ourselves down and out to the world, then we let Him flow through. Then and then only do we become channels. Otherwise we are mere trickles of power of service."

It is good to be praying with a man like this. We watch him use the back of his large hand to wipe away his tears surreptitiously. He tries to talk; finds it laborious and just quits and begins to pray again. He makes this point that gives us pause for thinking–that if in prayer we ask for anything lower than God's Will, it will not be answered. If we ask up to His Will, then our prayer will be answered above what we ask.

And as the days go by, each one filling the cup of inspiration a little higher than the day before, we sometimes reach a saturation point where one drop more would cause an overflow. When that time comes we turn one entire evening over to lightsomeness and mirth–a "stunt night" where the students alternately lampoon the leaders or glorify their teachings in beautiful allegory and parable.

The relaxation and relief that only joy and pure fun can awaken in one prepare the group for the following night when is held an inspired broadcast of love and prayer to all the world, followed by an all-night of prayer, the climax and high point of the entire period.

BOOK SIX

A Wrestler for the Lord

CHAPTER XXII

Levers of Prayer

ONE day I was asked to speak on the subject of prayer at work in daily life to the athletes of Iowa State Agricultural College at Ames, Iowa, and in the group was the intercollegiate world champion wrestling team. I asked the captain to bring his heavyweight wrestler to the front of the room. There was a long table in the room and I asked one of the wrestlers to lie supine on the table. Then turning to the athletes in my audience I said,

"Some great philosopher once said that there were two things that differentiated a human being from an animal: his ability to use levers and his ability to use words.

"In Jesus' day the word was well-nigh perfect. The Greek language was adequate to clothe the greatest epics and dramas of all time; the Hebrew language portrayed the laws of God as no other language had ever done. What more need they ask? But in the field of the lever, about the only things the Greeks had were the slingshot and the battering ram.

"Today the word has lost much of its power, because it has become cheapened. We have too many words and they are too easily and too glibly used for us to respect them as we should. In ancient times a piece of paper with a word upon it was considered sacred. Today millions of them are ground out each few hours on our great metropolitan news presses; other millions of them are shouted over the radio. Books fill every library and home and so it goes.

"But as the word loses its power in our modern age the lever has risen in power. Since the childhood of the race, mankind has been haunted by the knowledge that around him were riches untold, if he could pull the right lever at the right time, and in the right way.

"Archimedes, the Greek scientist, said, 'Give me a lever that is big enough and a fulcrum to rest it on and I will move the world.' But it was not till three thousand years after the day of Archimedes when the great mechanical age dawned. Today the lever has come of age. If Christ should come to earth today, a gospel writer who attempted to give an adequate conception of this wonderful One might be tempted to begin his account as follows: 'In the beginning was the Lever, and the Lever was with God, and the Lever was God; and nothing that was done without the Leverage of God was done.'

"The simplest of all levers is the lever of the human body. Every one of you wrestlers know that or you would never have become the champions of America. Every one of you knows the name of Frank Gotch, the Iowa farm boy, who mastered just one leverage on the human body, but who mastered it so perfectly that he became the champion wrestler of the world. I am going to ask your wrestling captain to demonstrate Gotch's famous toe hold on the man on the table."

When the captain had completed his demonstrations to the profound interest of the audience, I continued, "After Gotch retired as the undefeated world champion, another farmer boy, Fred Stecher of Nebraska, mastered another leverage on the human body so perfectly that he, too, was able to throw any wrestler in the world and he became the world champion. Now I shall ask the lad on the table to demonstrate Stecher's famous scissors lock on the captain here."

After this had been done I went up to the captain and said, "I am now going to demonstrate a jujitsu hold which will enable a soft, elderly man like me to bow a world champion like you out of the room if I should so desire. What I shall show you will be of special value if a dangerous enemy should come into your room with a half-dozen revolvers in his pockets and a bowie knife in his teeth, intent on doing you serious bodily harm. Simply go up to him, reach out to shake hands with him thus, then slip your left arm under his arm and seize the lapel of his coat thus, and turn his arm ever so slightly so that the elbow joint is exposed helpless before the least crack you wish to give to his arm, and he is absolutely in your power. Then without letting go your grip politely bow him out of the room and request him not to bring quite so much artillery when he comes to see you again.

"Now would you like to have me show you men some levers on trouble and sin so you could cast them out the window?"

They all nodded assent. I never had a more rapt and responsive audience. Then I explained to them that every parable Jesus told was merely a lever for meeting some problem in life. With this introduction I gave them a talk on the parables of Jesus in language they could understand, ending with a number of applications to their own personal lives.

One day I received a letter from a man I had never met.

"Death has walked into my house. He has already taken our eldest daughter. He stands hovering over our little girl, our only remaining child. He has a grip on her that the doctor says nothing in medical science can make him shake off. I read something of yours which showed me you believe God can meet any situation. Will you come to my help? I trust all to your prayer."

Here was a task that would test any wrestler. Here was an adversary, Death. To meet him would require more careful preparation than I had ever made before.

Knowing how wrestlers strip themselves to the waist before going into action I began by stripping off my outer coat of self. I said, "Glenn, you must be very impersonal in this and think not at all of any personal glory you may derive from it." I next took off the waistcoat of covetousness, dropping any thought of reward of any kind. Then off came the necktie of fear that sometimes throttles the strongest man. In other words, a real wrestler for the Lord must make himself as positively and completely SELFLESS as he possibly can. I continued this process of throwing off all encumbering garments of the outer self until I was, figuratively speaking, stripped to the waist.

Then I went back to a practice of ancient days—a practice where each wrestler anointed himself with oil before a combat, so that the hands of his opponent could not get a firm grasp upon him. The oil I used was an ointment from heaven–the oil of Trust. It was the very Trust of the one who wrote me. I thought how amazing was Trust of a man who could put his problem so completely into my hands. Gradually all thought of him faded out of the picture and in his place I saw only Trust. It was such a perfect, such a marvelous Trust, deriving from the man who wrote that letter, that in its presence no destructive power of the visible or of the invisible world could take any grip whatever.

Then still thinking of the symbol of being anointed with oil, I remembered that not only does the Shepherd Psalm speak of anointing our heads with oil but also of our cup running over. The anointing with the oil of Trust prevents the adversary from getting a fatal grasp on *you* but the partaking of the cup of the Spirit gives you strength to get a grip on *him*. So I drank deep of the cup of the Love of God. The Love of God will not leave this house desolate, I thought, unless God has a greater blessing than life itself.

Instantly new strength entered my blood. I stepped forward and gave the little child right through the greedy hands of Death into the safekeeping hands of God Himself. "You, Father, are the God of Love," I said, "and we know that if this little one is to go from her present home it is because she will be more blessed in some other of Your mansions. But Father, so far as we can see, her work on earth is not done, and because of Your great Love for her and because of the great love of her family for each other, we have faith that You will let her stay right here safe and sound."

Even as I prayed I felt the adversary grow limp in my hands and with the slightest toss I threw him out the door. For here Love was complete, even as Trust had been complete. But note this carefully, had the parents of this child hated each other, the cup of Love would not have given me the power to defeat the foe.

A letter came in the next week's mail saying that the little girl had miraculously become perfectly well, and her recovery had begun during my hour of prayer.

About a year later the football team of my own college came into my office and the captain said, "We are to play a team tonight under the arc lights and the newspapers say we shall lose 40 to 0 and we have the jitters. We hope you can steady us."

I went to the wall and turned on the light.

"There was a break in the connection until I pressed the button," I explained. "The pressing of the button closed that break. Now, fellows, if there is anyone who holds a grudge against anyone else on the team, that grudge turns off the switch. If anyone is so egotistical that he wants to make all the touchdowns, his self-centeredness causes another break. If there are any such among you I won't bother to pray for you."

Immediately the captain exclaimed, "We are like the Three Musketeers—one for all and all for one."

They all joined hands in a circle and I stepped in the circle and offered a little prayer, not that they would win, not that they would do their best, but merely that God would use them in any way that He desired to use them—that He would have complete, full sway.

I doubt if any Macalester team ever played as that team played that night.

This technique of self-elimination and mutual good will was not new with me. My father started out as a lawyer, but a fire insurance company in which he had invested some of his savings was going downhill so rapidly, because of faulty management, that the director asked him if he would act as manager and see what he could do. His first act after taking control was to call in the agents from all over the state of Iowa.

"Above everything else we want a spirit of loyalty and good will," he told them. "If anyone has a grudge against anyone else, let us straighten it out now. If the company has ever been unfair to any of you let *me* straighten it out. We have to work together as a family, all working for the good of all."

They went out and doubled their business within a year. Many years later father was made director of agents of another company. He gave the same directions and they doubled their business within a year. He was made president of another company and their business doubled at once. If a thing happens once we can call it an accident, if it happens twice we can call it a coincidence, but if it happens the third time, we have no other alternative but to look at the possibility of its being a law.

One of the most remarkable illustrations of the working of this law was the experience of Eugene Briggs, president of Phillips University in Oklahoma. The summer of 1940 he came to the Camp Farthest Out at Lake Koronis, Minnesota, a very discouraged man. His university was badly in debt and his faculty, underpaid and for several months unpaid, was discontented and at times openly rebellious. Their spirit was far from the unity of the Three Musketeers. Four years went by and I found myself in Enid, Oklahoma, to give a series of addresses in the First Presbyterian Church in commemoration of its fiftieth anniversary. In the morning I was invited to give a series of chapel talks in the local university. Imagine my surprise to be greeted by Doctor Briggs, the president, but still greater was my surprise at his glowing, happy face, the perfect antithesis of that I had seen four years before. I never had a more responsive student audience, and at the close of my address, the faculty thronged around me with a warmth and cordiality I had rarely known.

When President Briggs had me alone in his office, he said, "Sit down. I have much to tell you. When I returned from Koronis I sat down for two hours with my faculty. I told them of your football team, I told them of your father's insurance companies, and I said that I wanted to be given a break. Let us try this *lever* of harmony and good will and put into operation Jesus' law of 'Where two or three *agree* together whatever you ask will be granted.' My faculty stepped into the plan heart and soul. As soon as this perfect harmony was attained, our prayers began to function. The $57,000 debt was paid off. Four new buildings came and they are all paid for. Four times I have been offered the presidency of the state university at almost double my salary and I have turned it down every time."

As I write this Doctor Briggs has become the international president of the Lions Club, the largest service club in the world.

Indeed, this making the circuit one of the most powerful of all levers is an instrument that I have used numberless times with marvelous results. I have seen business companies lifted from failure into success, churches changed from hovels of gossip and criticism into temples of glory, and colleges entering into their golden years by merely turning on the powers of heaven after the circuit was made whole and complete. Jesus proclaimed this law in one little sentence which is chock-full of spiritual dynamite: "If two of you shall agree on earth as touching anything that they shall ask, it shall be done for them of my Father which is in heaven."

From that time forth I became, in my own thought, a wrestler for the Lord. And why not? It might sound a little sacrilegious, but Jeremiah called himself a drunkard for the Lord. Saint Francis called himself a beggar for the Lord. Kagawa calls himself a gambler for the Lord. Many people call themselves soldiers of the Lord. And why should not someone be a wrestler for the Lord? At any rate my work was henceforth cut out for me. Here was a world full of adversaries. In every nation, in every city, in every home, if I looked hard enough, I was sure to find one.

CHAPTER XXIII

Levers of Power

LATE one Saturday afternoon as I was walking home from a football game which we had lost in the final minutes, I suddenly felt a great depression fall upon me. I am not moody or temperamental by nature. Things like this don't hit me without some very definite cause. Could it be the football game? Impossible. I was too seasoned a veteran in athletics to let one defeat get me down. To my surprise the depression stayed with me throughout the evening. I stayed up after all the family had retired, trying to get peace. But peace would not come.

I felt like a man wrestling with a phantom in the dark. I couldn't see him. I couldn't get hold of him. And I was all but done in by the incessant pummeling "he" was giving me. When I awoke in the morning the weight was still there, just a little abated. I again engaged my unseen adversary but the results were again very meager. That evening being Sunday, I gave a talk on prayer before a combined meeting of three Epworth Leagues. I closed my talk with a brief prayer laboratory, using the "lever" I had stumbled on at the Northfield Convention, of the drop of water in the mud puddle giving itself to the drawing power of the sun's rays.

Instantly my load was lifted. I felt light as a feather. At last I seemed to have obtained a half nelson on my unseen opponent and cast him forever out the window.

The following morning Ruth Gunderson, one of my students, came to my office and said, "Did you get my message Saturday night?"

"I certainly got somebody's message. What was it all about?" "I went to my home town for the weekend," she said. "My brother took me riding and we stopped at the home of a young couple we knew, and found that their little baby had double pneumonia and was not expected to live. I asked to be allowed to pray for her, and went into the room alone. When I lifted my eyes from my praying and looked at the little baby, it appeared so terribly sick that I became panic-stricken and cried out to you for help. I called your name aloud. It was five o'clock Saturday afternoon. Did you hear me?"

"Clear across the miles I heard you," I replied. "Don't ever shout so loud again!"

"I phoned our friends the next morning," she continued, "and the baby was slightly improved."

"Did you call them Sunday evening?"

"No, I left in the afternoon. Why?"

"If you had called them in the evening, you would have found the child completely out of danger."

"How do you know?"

"Because of the great peace that came to me."

And sure enough, the next morning a letter came, telling that the child had safely passed the crisis Sunday evening, and they had dismissed the trained nurse that very night.

A few months later I was in Detroit at the first national religious conference I ever attended. As I was walking to my hotel at the close of my last talk my thoughts traveled homeward. I could hardly wait to see my wife and three children. I was so glad the meetings were over. My reverie was broken by the raucous cries of a score of newsboys: "Extra! Extra! Russell Scott to be electrocuted at dawn tomorrow! Extra! Extra!"

I felt led to buy a paper and I read it as I approached my hotel. Scott, it seemed, was convicted of a murder he claimed that he did not commit. It was in Illinois, where death is the penalty for such crimes, and he was now in the deathhouse in Joliet, awaiting his execution.

In *I Will Lift Up Mine Eyes* I relate how I sat up that night till eleven, at which time peace came to me.

The next morning a reporter told me, "A news bulletin arrived in our office at exactly eleven o'clock, announcing that the Governor sent Scott a reprieve."

A few weeks later my wife and I invited some former college friends to dinner, among them the Boardmans. Mr. Boardman was principal of one of the Minneapolis high schools.

"You don't know what an honor Charles showed you, Louise, in accepting your invitation tonight," said Mrs. Boardman. "He has been turning down all invitations this year, right and left."

"Why does he do that?" my wife asked.

"Oh, he just sits home and works and worries."

"He ought to get Glenn's philosophy. Glenn believes in throwing all one's fears and worries out the window."

"My goodness!" exclaimed Charles. "You had better tell us your secret, Glenn."

"This is a party," I remonstrated; "it isn't a lecture."

But everyone present joined in the appeal and my wife abetted them. "It will be ten minutes before the roast is on the table, Glenn. You'd better tell them."

So I told them a little of what I had learned, and when dinner was served and we turned to a lighter vein I thought the subject was dropped. But when the guests were leaving, Charles drew me into a corner and pulled me into a chair beside him and said, "I am glad I came here for reasons besides good fellowship. I am in real need of help for my school."

"Did you know a group of us prayed for your school last year?"

"No, what about?"

"About the moral condition, which for years was the worst in the Twin Cities."

"You did!" he exclaimed.

"Yes, we had a prayer list and your school was one item on that list."

"Do you know, not a single lapse occurred last year except one and that was transferred from another school? Have you been praying for us this year?"

"No, we haven't."

"Well, you have my permission to."

"Well, Charles," I said, "what is your problem this year?"

"There are three problems," he said. "First, I am fighting against the parents who are trying to force fraternities and sororities into the school. Second, we are so overcrowded that some classes have to meet in the hallways with resultant confusion. And third, I am fed up on public school teaching and dream of getting into university work. With all these concerns pressing down on me what else can a fellow do than worry? What would you do?"

"I would pray," I replied simply.

"I don't know how," he replied.

"Then let me pray for you."

"I wish you would," he exclaimed.

When he stood in the doorway that evening saying farewell he said, "I feel that I have laid all my problems on your shoulders, Clark."

"Not on my shoulders," I shot back, "but on God's shoulders."

For a week I took great joy in praying for him. One day I told my wife, "Every time I turn to the problems of Charles I get the feel of one opening a cage and letting the bird fly straight into the sky, so easily do his problems vanish into thin air at the mere touch. I wonder why that is?"

My wife replied, "I think it is because of the great trust he has in your prayer."

But when the week was over I lost my prayer list and forgot him entirely. After two weeks my conscience troubled me. Why had I stopped praying for him? The answer came immediately from his wife.

"Just *one* week after you said you would pray for him, Charles received a letter from Dean Haggarty of the education department of the University of Minnesota, offering him the principalship of the University High School."

On another occasion a man came to my house and said, "A great enemy has come into our home and is beating us down. My wife's brother has become a hopeless drunkard. His mother and his sister and I are doing our best to help him fight this habit of drink but the monster is too big for us. He has such a grip on the lad that heaven knows what can break it. Can you help us?"

Such a request stirred all the wrestling blood in my veins.

"Let us get still awhile," I replied. And then in the stillness a great experience came to me. While my body sat relaxed in the chair the soul of me, like the boy David, went forth to fight this gigantic Philistine called Drink. I found myself moving around him in circles, seeking eagerly, hopefully, for a "hold." Finally I said aloud to my caller, "Does your wife and does his mother love the boy?"

"Indeed yes, their hearts are breaking, their love is so great."

This gave me just the hold I wanted on the huge sulking monster. But it was not enough. Such a giant fixation as this one only the Power of God can overcome. Suddenly I remembered the "grapevine trip" which my father, who was a great wrestler in his day, had taught me and which had given me as a boy a great advantage over my uninformed playmates. The underlying secret of the "grapevine" art was to utilize the very momentum and force of the opponent's attack to defeat him.

"The strength of Old Barley Corn," I spoke as one thinking aloud, "is derived from the power he has of making a person completely lose himself in a power greater than himself. It makes him drop his inhibitions, his self-consciousness, his little worries and fears. In other words, the way to get hold of this monster is not to fear him but to see the good thing at the heart of his power and use it to annihilate him. Instead of fighting Old Barley Corn with fear, let us welcome the germ of good in our adversary and by accepting it show him up for what he really is, a mere swindle and a sham. In other words, pray with me for the boy to lose himself as he wants so much to do, but lose himself in the *Holy* Spirit instead of in the *unholy* spirits; let him get drunk in the pentecostal way instead of in the barroom way. Now let us get still again."

My fear was gone. "Come on, old monster," I thought in the silence, "we accept any intoxication with Reality that you can give us. We want to lose ourselves completely in the Holy Spirit. Unafraid we welcome you. Come in full force with all the momentum you have. But we warn you, if you haven't Reality but are only the counterfeit of Reality, if the only spirits you can make us lose ourselves in contain within them a force that cancels out the good, then you will trip yourself up with your own deceptions." And in the silence I could see Old Barley Corn go sprawling out the window, thrown by the good old "grapevine trip."

Then I found myself led to say, "This is August. I know that when Thanksgiving comes you will have something to be thankful for. But let me give you fair warning—your brother's habit may appear much worse before he gets better." For deep down in my subconscious I had a premonition that Old John would put up a great struggle when he found himself in our power.

It was a year later that I met this man again.

"It turned out exactly as you foretold," he said. "The boy hasn't touched a drop since last October. But it did get so bad right after our prayer together that we almost lost hope. But when October came he quit completely."

From that time on this "hold" served me well in helping to heal many confirmed alcoholics.

A woman came to me with a goiter and a tumor and said, "I am in such a run-down condition the doctor says it might prove fatal to operate. All my hope lies in prayer." I sat quietly listening but my spirit was moving about the foe that she had brought into the room, looking for a chance for a jujitsu hold which I could use to cast him out of the room.

Then it came to me that when we desire, with an inordinate desire, something that does not belong in our life plan, we will get a physical fulfillment of our wish in the form of some physical growth in our body that does not belong there. If our desire is an innocent wish then the growth will be a tumor or a goiter. If resentment accompanies the wish it will manifest as a cancer. I explained this insight to the woman and when she agreed to relinquish her inordinate desire both her tumor and goiter simply *vanished* in the course of a few months and no operation was needed[1].

This experience led me, later on, to seek to find the psychosomatic causes behind every illness and see if it were not possible to prescribe a special lever for *every* ailment. The results of this quest I put into a book, How to Find Health Through Prayer. It was not until several

[1] This case is related in detail in How to Find Health Through Prayer (Harper), pp. 39-40.

years after these initial experiments that the magazines began to be filled with Dr. Helen Flanders Dunbar's discoveries along this line, which not only verified my discoveries but completed and rounded them out. Then it was that I recalled how twenty years before, when Helen Dunbar was a medical student, Mrs. John Sherman Hoyt had invited me to her Long Island home to pray with her that a young medical student named Helen Dunbar, whom she was sponsoring at the time, might someday become an instrument for bringing together the psychological and spiritual field with the purely medical field of healing.

But the lever that works most powerfully of all in the healing of loved ones is illustrated in the case which I have related in great detail on page forty-nine in *I Will Lift Up Mine Eyes*: A child had been given up to die by six physicians. It was a case of infantile paralysis. I simply asked the mother, Mrs. Lenore Klein, to relinquish her child completely into the hands of God with perfect trust that He would do what was best for the child either here or in heaven. She was a genuinely spiritual woman and her response was perfect. She said she was willing to accept with "radiant acquiescence" whatever the Father knew was best for the boy. The healing of this boy amazed the family, the physicians and the church to which he belonged.

I once had an auto accident and phoned to a repair garage to send me a repair man with a tire and a new nut and bolt. The man came and examined the car and then said, "What you need is a new axle. It would have saved us time and you money to have phoned for a high-ride car to convey your car right into our repair shop at once."

So I have learned not to ask the Father to send healing merely for this earache or for that arthritis. I give the situation *entirely* into the hands of the Father, giving Him full power to change an axle or a bolt, or if he sees best to keep the old car for good, to trade it in for a better and a newer model in the eternity that is before us. It may sound paradoxical, but ever since I have lost all my fear of death and have relinquished my sick friends completely into the Father's hands to keep or return as He sees fit, the healing power of God has often worked actual miracles through me.

The healing of the boy of infantile paralysis was followed by at least a score of calls to pray for little ones who were close to death's door. In every case where the mother was able to match her great desire for the child to live with an equally great capacity to relinquish the child, as Mrs. Klein had done, the child got well.

In several cases a great power was released through the use of another lever that can be summed up in the word "agree." Where a father and mother are at sword's points I insist that they drop all spirit of altercation and unite in complete harmony and love. Whenever love is assured results are greatly speeded and where this leverage is not available some tragic results occur.

There now remained only two ailments that I had never been able to meet; one was leukemia and one was insanity. To this date I have still been unable to find a lever for the first, but I know what the lever is because a dear friend, Mrs. Ruth Robison, has applied it. The leverage for this disease is joy but the power of the "opponent" is so strong that it requires an immeasurable burst of joy, tremendously greater, I guess, than anything I have as yet been able to muster. However, the little sister of leukemia, anemia, I have seen easily healed by the simple act of bringing in enough faith and joy, yes, and actual fun, so that all the unhappiness and frustrations were swept out in one vast sweep.

It was a secret wish of mine for a long time that no one would ask me to pray for an insanity case. But in a nation where over half the bed cases in hospitals are nervous and mental cases and where doctors predict that twelve million more cases will come as an aftermath of this war (the peak is predicted for 1956) this wish of mine was very shortly disregarded. God forced me into a situation where I learned what Jesus meant when he commissioned his disciples to cast out demons.

A mother called me to pray for her son who was pronounced hopelessly insane. For twelve years he had not left his room. After calling on him once a month for two years, I suddenly asked him what his conception was of the demons Jesus cast out. To my surprise he exclaimed, "To be possessed by a demon is to be obsessed with a half-truth. For instance, if a lion were caught in a butterfly net and thought he was a butterfly." That described his own situation so perfectly—a man imprisoned in a room he could easily walk out of—that I felt moved to give a silent command in the name of Jesus Christ for the demon to leave him. That very moment a transformation occurred and the next day he walked out of his room a well man. Ten years have elapsed and he is now one of the finest spiritual leaders and healers, as well as one of the most Christ-like men I have ever had the opportunity of knowing.[2]

---

[2] For fuller account of this see Recovery by Starr Daily (St. Paul:Macalester Park Publishing Co.), pp. 38 ff.

CHAPTER XXIV

The Cornucopia of God

A TALL man came into my office one day and said, "I would like your spiritual advice on a very serious problem. Last year I resigned as vice-president and stockholder in one of the largest companies in America. I took the savings of my lifetime and put them into a factory that I have been building for the production of a new product that is just being worked out. There remain only a few months before we start production on a big scale, and the word has just come to us that a rival company has obtained patents ahead of us on the very things we want to produce. A man whom we discharged from our laboratories has been working for them, and we think that he is responsible for the betrayal but we have no proof that would stand up in a court of law."

"Do you think this employee was fairly treated?" I asked.

"I looked into that," he replied, "and I'm not sure that he was."

"Then you will have to expect some grief."

"I am perfectly willing to accept anything that we deserve," he answered, "but I am just Scotch enough to believe that the fortune of a lifetime cannot be taken from a man who lawfully earned it. I put it into the hands of a Christian lawyer and we're not letting any resentment or antagonism enter into our approach in this matter."

"Then you need have no concern," I replied. "That which is your own cannot be taken from you. Here's a copy of John Burrough's poem, 'My Own Shall Come to Me.' Take it home and memorize the first, the third and the last stanzas. Now let us have a prayer for the situation right here and now."

Nothing can take from you that which is truly your own. This was a wrestling hold that I knew no opponent could break. A great peace came to me as we concluded the prayer. As I looked into the clear-cut, honest face before me and clasped the man's hand I said, "It comes to me that within a year's time this matter will be settled to the mutual satisfaction of all parties concerned."

A year after that this same man arrived two days late for the beginning of a camp I was starting at Lake Koronis, in Minnesota, bringing his wife and a moving-picture camera to record this first of all the Camps Farthest Out. Smilingly, he came in to report, "Things worked out exactly as you prophesied. This trip was delayed two days so that I could finish signing the papers by which the other firm grants us exclusive rights to produce the product in the United States and Europe, on payment of twenty-three thousand dollars."

I smiled and said, "It would take me an entire lifetime to save up twenty-three thousand dollars. Will your business be crippled?"

"The income for the first year will be one hundred and fifty thousand dollars," he replied.

A letter came through the mails, written by some woman from Chicago. "My husband is out of work," she said, "and I am studying in the Chicago Theological Seminary to prepare myself for work as a religious education director. Because of our need, would you be willing to send as a free gift to me and my husband copies of all the books you have written?"

I have some spiritual friends who are so sensitive that they can tell by the feel of a letter even before they open it what the spirit of the writer is. Occasionally I have that gift, and this particular time the feeling was not a good one. I said to my secretary, "If this is an unselfish, soul's sincere desire, I would be only too glad to grant it, but if it is a begging request of one who wants to exploit a temporary piece of hard luck to get something for nothing, I don't think I should gratify her. That would not be developing her strength but would be feeding her weakness. And that which we feed we perpetuate."

My secretary rather chided me for letting any doubts enter in, and so on a sudden impulse I said, "Well, here's the letter with the address in it, Tie up the bundle and send it to her."

At that time I had only a part-time secretary who took my letters and also mailed the book orders when they came in. The next day she reported that she had tied up the bundle, which totaled about six dollars' worth of books, but she added, "Did you give me the address?"

"Yes I did," I replied, "It was in the letter and it was on the envelope."

"That's what I thought," she replied, "but when I came back this afternoon I had mislaid the letter and try as I will I can't find it. I began to wonder if I had merely dreamed you had handed it to me,"

"It was no dream," I replied, "but if you can't find it, it means that God is intervening in this situation. Last evening I gave the problem completely to God to tell me whether I was right in sending the books. He has answered us today, and His answer is abrupt and final. He has withheld the address because the request that came to us was not in good faith."

A few months after that I was visiting my dear friends in Chicago, Glenn and Esther Harding.

"Thornton Wilder is a visiting professor at the University of Chicago this term," Glenn said, "and I should like to bring you two together. If we start right now we shall get there in time for his class."

Just then Esther interrupted us. "But don't you remember that I told Emma that she could see Glenn Clark this morning at ten o'clock?"

That being so, we had to forego the trip to see Thornton Wilder.

Twenty years have elapsed since then and I have never yet had the privilege of meeting him. But I did meet Emma! After a long history of her troubles she ended by saying, "The chief problem I want you to pray for is that my husband can find a job."

"I will gladly do that," I replied, "but prayer does not consist of words alone but also of attitudes and actions. I have a particular lever that I use in a case like this. I call it the leverage of the tides. As the tides go out they will come back; as one gives he shall receive. Tell your husband to find some people who need help, who can't do anything in return. For instance, are there any old ladies living near you whom he could help by shoveling the snow off their walks?"

"Yes," she replied, "but they would not be willing to pay him anything for it."

"If they paid him the lever wouldn't work," I replied. "If he did that service out of the goodness of his heart, without expectation of reward, the reward would come from some other direction in the form of work for which he would be paid."

"My husband wouldn't believe that. He doesn't take any stock in religion; in fact, he is very cynical about religion and religious men. He thinks they're all grafters, just in it for the money they can make. And now can you tell me," and her voice took on a querulous note, "why you didn't send those books I asked you for?"

"Goodness me!" I exclaimed, "Were *you* the person who asked me to send copies of all my books?"

"Yes," she replied. "'You just ask him,' my husband told me, 'and you will find that he is just as selfish as all the rest of them.'"

"See here," I said, "those books are all tied up, sitting in my office right this very moment, waiting for the address. But for some strange, unexplainable reason, that address simply vanished, something that has never happened before. Now I know why. Your husband's attitude erased that address just as definitely as if he had entered my office with an eraser. If your husband had unselfishly given of his time and energy to others, he would have created a vortex that would have drawn this package straight to him. In the same way, somewhere there is a good job waiting for him but his spirit is locking the very doors that could bring it to him."

In contrast with that episode where the doors of outgiving were closed is the following example of where they were thrown wide open. Bill Horne, who was something of an inventor, came to tell me in despair that he could not find work; his inventions didn't click and his family was hungry. He said, "If I could see you once a week during this hard period it would keep me from committing suicide." These weekly meetings continued for many months, during which time I discovered all his occupational abilities. Years before he had been a coach of debating teams. At the time of our meetings the depression of the early thirties was upon us. Our student body at the college had diminished and our income had dwindled. One day the president surprised me with the announcement that I would have to take over the coaching of the debate team in addition to my already heavy schedule. I turned to Bill and said, "I am going to ask a favor of you. Would you be willing to come to the college two evenings a week and coach the debate team gratis?"

"Would I!" he exclaimed. "I would consider that very small recompense for all that you have done for me."

He did the job so well that the president insisted on giving him a salary. Those two evenings a week released something in him that brought added creative powers to his morning work on his inventions, and they began to sell. He and his wife came to the faculty parties, the president discovered that the wife was talented and had once taught German. So when the German teacher broke her hip, the president asked Mrs. Horne to teach the German classes at a good salary. In this case the leverage of the tides proved its irresistible power. Because Bill was willing to serve others for nothing, abundance poured in.

One spring the president informed me that the college was cutting down its budget wherever possible and $250 was all that could be allotted for the track team that year. Five years before such an announcement would have floored me. "Only $250!" I might have exclaimed. "Other rival colleges of the state have at least $2,000 to provide for their athletic supplies, their trips and their general expenses." But now the announcement was merely a challenge to my new way of life. I welcomed it as an opportunity to demonstrate what God could do.

First of all, I decided to take *all* matters of finance into my own hands and out of the hands of the inexperienced student manager. I told him to organize volunteers among the boys to mend the broken hurdles, while I turned the laborious task of arranging the spring schedule over to my Senior Partner.

Immediately things began to happen. North Dakota University offered us a larger guarantee than we really needed for taking our little team to their city for a dual meet. Then, to my amazement, the Northern Pacific which was the railroad we always used made me a special offer that I had never dreamed possible. When I brought my team back from that trip I had $100 in my pocket. Another railroad company offered a special half-fare round-trip rate for a weekend meet with Gustavus Adolphus College. This time there was a surplus of $75. A similar saving was effected on two other trips, and then, to cap the climax, the track coach of the state university called me up.

"I am a close friend of the chief counsel of the Rock Island Railroad, and he has been chiding me for never using his train when we go to the Drake Relays in Des Moines. I told him the Rock Island took two hours longer to get there. So he has offered a special rate of $5.00 a man, round trip, if I will take a whole car. I still have room for eight men. I tried to get Carleton but their coach is sore with me and wouldn't take the call. Would you be thinking of taking two relay teams—"

I didn't give him time to finish his sentence. Would I! When the season had started with such a curtailed budget I had given up all hope of taking even one team to the Drake Relays, but now my dream could easily be fulfilled.

The season was a glorious success. We took more trips than any college in the state, won the majority of our meets, and everyone was happy. When the business office offered me the check for the promised $250 I said, "Divide it by ten and write $25 and you will cover our expenses for the year."

One summer I was visiting my mother in La Jolla, California, and found that my sister Helen, who had just married, wanted to sell her two little cottages so she and her husband could invest in a chicken ranch. They placed the cottages in the hands of a high-powered salesman who was doing his best to force two reluctant women to buy them. "All I require," said my sister, "is one thousand dollars down and still they won't buy."

"How do you know," I asked, "that they would be made happy by buying your property? If I were you I wouldn't trust to the salesman, I would trust to prayer."

"What!" exclaimed her husband, "ask God to harness His giant Niagara to our little pinwheels?"

"I know it may sound selfish to use prayer in a business matter," I replied. "But I didn't mean for you to pray selfishly. Pray to bring fulfillment to someone who could be made happy by these houses."

"This sounds interesting," my mother said. "Let's try it."

I went on to explain, "The physicists maintain that there is no negative pole in the universe but has its corresponding positive pole somewhere in infinite space, even if it be three thousand miles away, and that nothing in heaven or in earth can prevent their ultimately finding each other out. Is it not reasonable to believe that there is a similar law prevailing in the relations of man to man, and that when one has a useful thing to dispose of, another individual, somewhere, even though he be hundreds of miles away, can be made happy by that very thing? Couldn't it be that if we trust all to God, we might find that nothing on land or sea could prevent the supply and the need from finding each other?"

A few days later a friend of mine named Demaree Bess knocked on the door of my mother's cottage where I was staying. "I have two weeks' vacation from the *Minneapolis Tribune* where I am working," he said. "I heard you were out here and wondered if you would like to go swimming." On the way to the beach he said, "I love this climate here and if I could just get a job out here I'd never go back. But I imagine there is a long list of applicants for every job."

On our return from our swim he said, "If I could get a job out here the first thing I would do would be to buy a couple of little houses."

"Two little houses!" I exclaimed. "Yes. The only way a bachelor can ever expect to save is to have something that he has to put his money into."

The following evening he again knocked on our door.

"Rejoice with me!" he exclaimed. "I've spent the day down in San Diego, and I got a job on the *San Diego Union*. I can hardly wait until tomorrow when I can go around and look for houses. Say!" he stared at me. "Do you happen to know of any that are for sale?"

"Do I!" I exclaimed. "Just come with me."

When I showed him my sister's cottages he said, "These are exactly what I want, but the trouble is that I am only able to pay one thousand dollars down."

"That will be all right," I said.

Then when I brought him and my sister together I witnessed one of the most extraordinary business conferences ever held. He insisted that she wasn't asking enough and she insisted he was trying to pay too much. But as there was no agent or intermediary except myself, and as I refused to take a commission, both profited from the transaction. So this is the way that Demaree Bess, now one of the editors of The *Saturday Evening Post*, got his financial start in life.

Louise and I had been married ten years and had never had a car. One day I said to my wife, "While our children are small we should have a little car, but you say that with our rate of income we would find ourselves just one hundred dollars short when it came to making payments. I have been thinking of a wrestling hold that can help to clear our thought about this matter in the right way. When we were on the seashore this summer little Helen May dug a well in the seashore sand and waited patiently for the tides to come in and fill it. Let us think of our need for this car as that little well. If it is a real need the tides of God can easily fill it. If it is not a real need but just a shadow of a need, the tides will not bother to fill it. In that case we can continue to pull our little children along in wagons and baby carriages and still use the streetcars."

A few evenings later the doorbell rang and a young man said, "I represent a Ford sales agency and I understand you are thinking of buying a Ford touring car."

That is exactly what we had been praying for but we could not remember having told anyone except God. We told the agent frankly that unless we could see our way to add a hundred dollars to our budget we would not be able to buy a car. To this he replied, "You will have to let me know by a week from Monday or I cannot guarantee to get you the kind of car you want."

A week from Monday a letter came which, when opened, dropped at our feet a check for $108. The letter which accompanied it explained that William and Vashti College, where I had taught twelve years before and had contributed this amount to the endowment fund, was now becoming a junior college and they were returning the last hundred thousand dollars they had received toward their endowment. I have been connected with colleges all my professional life and the biggest miracle that I ever witnessed was a college returning some of its endowment fund!

It was right after that incident that my wife and I decided to tithe. Since our salary was less than twenty-five hundred dollars at the time we were not contributing a large amount into the Lord's coffers but the custom of tithing made a large difference in our lives. That was twenty-five years ago and from that moment we have never suffered lack of any kind. In fact, I cannot recall once since then of ever praying for financial help for ourselves.

But having discovered that there was such a thing as answered prayer in the meeting of financial needs, I found myself quite eager to use this "mightiest force in the universe" to help other worthy causes, and the first thing I thought of was the crying need for a gymnasium for our college. All the other colleges of the state had good gymnasiums. While their athletes were trotting around their indoor tracks in February and March my track team had to get its conditioning by wading through the deep snow and trotting up and down the boulevards of St. Paul in their winter garments.

"I do not believe that this need is only for the physical benefit of the boys and girls," I said to my wife. "I believe it will have a moral effect as well. A good gymnasium with a swimming pool will keep our boys away from the cheap billiard halls. A place for good, wholesome recreation and self-expression can have spiritual impact on the college as a whole. In other words, I believe this is a *real* well in the seashore sands. Let us ask the good Lord to let His tides flow in and fill it. If it's a mere shadow of a need He won't need to fill it."

When I pray with special earnestness about a thing, I like to have the cooperation, and if possible an "agreeing together," of those most closely associated with it. I asked my wife what would be the best way to approach the trustees in this matter. My wife was astounded at the mere thought of a college professor invading a trustees' meeting on a mission of this kind.

"That would be such an unusual thing to do, Glenn," she replied, "that I am sure they would not understand it. It would appear to them as very officious on your part, so please do not even think of it."

"But this is a great need," I protested. "If we get united prayer on this matter anything can happen."

But as I shared my wife's feelings in shrinking from doing anything that would appear egotistical or officious, her counsel won out. I must admit, however, that my refraining did not bring me a sense of virtue, but a sense of guilt. I felt like a coward retreating in the face of danger.

I asked John Hall of our faculty, who was close to the board of trustees, what he thought about my speaking to them on this matter, and he reminded me that we were in a depression and the trustees had voiced the opinion that it would be five or ten years before they could even consider starting a campaign for a gymnasium. I was not satisfied, however, until I talked the matter over with a very spiritual woman who had often presided at the meetings where I did my first exploring in the mysteries of prayer.

"No, you won't have to consult the trustees or anyone else," she replied. "You say that you and Mrs. Clark have done some praying about it? Well, as I sit here it comes to me almost like the Voice of God that that gymnasium is on the way, that it is coming faster than anyone expects. It is coming this year." She paused a moment and then suddenly exclaimed, "It is coming through some member of your writing class!"

I stared at her, but she was not looking at me. I didn't ask anything more, but hurried home and related this strange prophecy to my wife. We both smiled and proceeded to forget it, for we both rather prided ourselves on keeping our feet on the ground. We believed that with God all things are possible, but we didn't anticipate having Him tell us things too long in advance. However, we knew that the need was there and that the tides of God were always coming in.

It was in the middle of the winter when Lillian Le Ve Conte, a little sophomore girl in my writing class, came up to me after the class was over one day and asked to see me. I told her I had some very important people to see and that I would see her another day. When the class met two days later the little girl was standing in front of me when the class ended. I was standing beside my desk and did not bother to ask her to sit down as I anticipated that this interview would be very short.

"I worked for one of the trustees this summer," she began, "and I discovered what wonderful things the trustees have been doing for our college all these years. They work without a salary and they give generously of their time and thought. Every spring they help pay off the deficits out of their own pockets. Six of them have worked for the college twenty years and one has worked for us thirty-five years. In all that time the students have never done anything to show their appreciation. We honor our football team by cheering them and we give them sweaters in their honor. Why haven't we ever done anything like that for the trustees?"

"I never thought of that," I replied. "Well, I thought—maybe—it would be wonderful if the students, not the faculty but just the students, would give a party for the trustees."

Had a bolt from heaven struck me the effect would not have been any greater. My knees grew weak and I reached back for my chair. I could see a gymnasium floating right out of the sky.

"That is not your idea," I said.

"What do you mean?" she queried.

"It's God's idea."

She answered slowly, "I know what you mean. Ordinarily ideas come to me and I can put them aside, but this one comes to me at night and wrestles with me like Jacob's angel and won't let me go. But I wanted to get your thought about it before I said anything to anyone else."

My mind was now moving with inspired momentum.

"Let us select five of our students to present this idea before a convocation of the student body. Wesley Domes, captain of the football team, is a splendid speaker, and Jean McVeety, leader of the girls' debating team would have a popular appeal, and let us find out who is president of the freshman class."

She named two others. Then I added, "If the plan is accepted let us two get together immediately after the convocation and appoint another committee on arrangements."

"No, no!" she exclaimed. "There is only one request that I want to make, and that is that you don't tell any of the students that I had anything to do with this idea."

Then I *knew* that the gymnasium was coming! She was using, unconsciously, the greatest lever of all, and all the more powerful because she was using it spontaneously. Yes, the most powerful of all levers is the erasing of oneself completely out of the picture. She had done it so completely that where she was standing at that moment I didn't see her but only the Christ. The only name that was visible was Christ's name. "If two or three agree asking anything in my *name*..."

The convocation was held, the speeches were positively brilliant, and the plan for the party was unanimously accepted by the student body. Never in my life have I ever heard of any other college where the students, not the faculty but just the students, gave a party for the trustees! All the trustees came. All were thrilled at the honor bestowed upon them. Everyone present was happy. I went home that night walking on clouds of glory.

The next week the trustees held a meeting.

"That was a wonderful party!" one said.

"It is marvelous to think that we have such a splendid family of boys and girls belonging to us!"

"We should do something for them," said another.

"What do they need?" several asked.

"They need a gymnasium."

"Well, depression or no depression, let us give them a gymnasium!" And right then and there they laid two hundred thousand dollars on the table and in a few weeks the gymnasium began to go up.

St. Paul is a city of ice carnivals and skating tournaments but that winter turned out to be what is called an "open winter." Workmen could put a spade in the ground in February. The finest gymnasium of any college in the Middle West sprang up before the next school year rolled around.

My long-distance runner, Jimmie Dickson, who built up his strength running around that indoor track, found himself the next year falling in love with this little girl, Lillian. When they graduated they went to Formosa where they have become outstanding missionaries in that far-off land. During World War II they had to leave, spending the interim in British Guiana. As Lillian Dickson was passing through this country, in great demand for lectures, I was driving her one evening to a missionary meeting in the St. Paul Plymouth Church. She turned to me and said suddenly, "Do you remember, Prof, that you gave me a little bottle containing a portion of the first spadeful of earth dug up for that gymnasium? I have carried that bottle to Formosa and British Guiana, and I have it with me now."

"Always keep it," I replied. "It will be your permanent reminder that God's power is always available whenever you put yourself utterly and completely in His hands."

As I finish this chapter they are back in Formosa bringing thousands to Christ, the outstanding missionaries in that land.

BOOK SEVEN

Strength Through Christian Fellowship

CHAPTER XXV

The Fellowship of the Home

I DON'T understand all that your husband is talking about, but I hesitate to take his valuable time when he is so very busy. I wonder if you would be willing to explain some things to me?"

The answer to this question was always a very spontaneous laugh. "So you don't understand everything he says, either? It took me a good many years, myself. Come, let's go out in a boat."

And so, time after time, while the husband roamed the misty mountaintops, the loving, patient wife reached out her hand to stumbling, earnest souls at the mountain foot.

I do not know of any greater partnership between man and wife anywhere than the partnership that existed between Louise and me. Many scores of people who came for help from me at my home came afterwards to seek their help from her. For while I was seeking inspiration among the stars she was seeking it among the flowers. And more people feel at home in the garden than in the sky.

She loved flowers. Among her daily duties year in and year out was the caring for her flowers. But she loved people, too, especially humble people, and much of her life was spent bringing the water of life to them. Yet she did it quietly, unostentatiously, always drawing her simple illustrations from the garden, the kitchen, or above all from the absorbing experience of bringing up children. No matter how discouraged a person might be, she always could point out the silver lining of the darkest clouds. No matter how devastating one's past experience, she could always show how God's love could "restore the years that the locusts had eaten."

Tall, with an almost perfect figure, and always walking with easy, graceful rhythm, she gave the impression of splendid vitality. But actually she was always frail and needed carefully to husband all her strength. Loving action, it was one of her crosses that she had to sit by and watch much of the heavy work done when her own practical hands were aching to do it. She turned the enforced periods of rest each day to valuable account for building spiritual strength.

One day she said to me, "Glenn, I don't have that mystic sense of union with God anywhere nearly as completely as you do, but it occurred to me that you have some unseen assistance that I don't have. Your brother, Page, and your father and mother are free in the unrestricted universe opening the doorways for heavenly power to flow through. My father and mother and sister, and all my closest friends are still on this earth."

The very next year her father, who was eighty-two, passed away, and almost immediately a miraculous transformation came to Louise.

"Do you know what I am praying for, Glenn?" she asked me one day. "I wish the Women's Auxiliary of our Macalester Presbyterian Church would ask me to talk to them on prayer."

"What!" I was dumbfounded. Never before had she wanted to make a speech, partly because she was no "speech-maker" and partly because of her heart difficulty which made her feel out of breath merely at the thought of speaking. Then one day, the Auxiliary did ask her to speak to them, and I never saw anyone so happy as was Louise as she prepared her speech. She asked me if I wanted to hear it. The talk amazed me—to me it seemed equal to my mother's talk, on the ideal mother.

Later the women in a Merriam Park church heard of her splendid "address" and asked her to speak to them. "Good!" I said. "That talk was too helpful to confine to just one group. I hope you can give it to many groups."

"Oh, no, I won't give that talk over again, Glenn," she said. "It's too much fun working out new talks."

I stared in amazement. Here was a woman who had never made speeches in all her life, now so enthralled with the task that she couldn't give enough of them. She gave many talks after that.

"I feel that the windows of heaven are opening and *God* is writing these speeches through me. Isn't it wonderful! At last I understand what you have been doing all these years, Glenn."

This new closeness was the sweetest experience of all my life. Louise invited twelve genuinely spiritual women in the Macalester Presbyterian Church to meet once a week with her in a prayer group. This group continued without cessation for two years, and the pastor, Reverend Walker Vance, said everything about the church worked out wonderfully during the years they were meeting.

On May 9, 1934, I was returning home from Minneapolis after an all-day session of the Minnesota Sunday School Convention, when I decided to drop in at the George Johnsons' home for a ten-minute chat. Imagine my surprise when he asked how serious my wife's injuries were in the automobile accident.

"Accident!" I exclaimed.

"The paper tells all about it."

He handed me the latest edition which related how a car conveying five women from St. Paul had been turned completely upside down, and all the occupants had been taken to hospitals seriously injured.

I drove home as fast as the wheels would go. I rushed upstairs and to my intense relief was greeted by Louise's radiant face shining at me from the bed.

"I didn't go to the hospital," she said. "I didn't let them call you because your day was a day of prayer, anyway, and that was all that I really needed. I was the least hurt so you and I must pray for the others."

Louise had been at death's door many times. God could easily have taken her. Three severe illnesses, scarlet fever, inflammatory rheumatism and typhoid fever, which came upon her in childhood, girlhood and young womanhood had taken their toll and were responsible for her frail health in middle life. Now her last narrow escape was the automobile accident.

"When the Lord could have so easily taken me so many times

there must be some reason why He let me live," she often said. She was allowed to remain with us until her children were grown and ready to try their wings. She was ours until she had so built herself into her husband's spiritual life that no matter how far apart they might be in body, their souls would always be inseparable.

After that accident Louise kept a secret journal in her "quiet times." We discovered the journal five years later, after her death. Her own evaluation of the place of the Quiet Hour is pictured in this journal as follows:

"This summer I planted a little garden. Like my neighbors I put gunnysacking over most of the seeded ground and kept the place watered. In spite of heat and drought, at the end of six days the ground had produced such big plants that the gunnysacking was taken up and the garden prospered marvelously with average care and water.

"But the seeds that were not cared for in this way came up very sparsely, did not grow so well, and the miracle was not soon produced in them.

"It came to me that this is true of our spiritual life: as we begin to grow spiritually we should use the quiet, unseen method of being alone with God. Then we may weed and hoe out self and self-thoughts, water our delicate plant of spiritual growth with God's love, and in prayer and meditation give ourselves to the power of the Spirit working in us and through us, until we become so firmly rooted that we can stand the heat of life." [1]

She was deeply touched by the dedication of my book, *I Will Lift Up Mine Eyes:* To Louise, whose simple and beautiful life has made our home into a sanctuary where the sorrowing may find comfort, the erring may find forgiveness, and the lonely may find love."

She recovered completely from the accident and the next five years were the happiest and most fruitful years of her life. The last year was a paradox that even the physicians could not explain. Through prayer and right thinking she seemed to have overcome all her physical handicaps. Her blood pressure became normal. Her weak heart developed muscular compensation that promised almost normal

---

[1] *Stepping Heavenward*, Louise Miles Clark (Macalester Park Publishing Co.), p. 5 f.

living. And yet she said, in spite of seeming improvement, she knew that the least illness would sweep her away.

Three days before she left us, she began remarking about an unusual peace and happiness that was filling her from morning till night as never before. Each day it seemed to grow greater. The last day before I left for college I heard her reading to our son Miles a passage from *I Will Lift Up Mine Eyes*, after saying that for her it was one of the most beautiful things she knew.

"You do not take ruthlessly of your human love, but you give to it abundantly and abandon yourself to its will; then can you neither take nor command Divine Love, but must abide in its will and give yourself wholly to its beneficent power.

"So sure has become my faith in this love of God that I abide in it without question. When my human prayer is not answered in the way I would expect to have it, I am exalted, for I know that I have submitted to a will greater than my own and capable of infinitely more goodness.

"When a man is in love, he does not then exist alone. How much more is it true that if a man dwells in Divine Love he cannot exist alone, but is dependent and interdependent upon that love. I live upon it as I live upon air with as much faith, for I know it will keep me with life after the air of our earth has become nothing."

These were the last words that I ever heard from her lips. When I returned at noon that day I found her asleep. Detecting something irregular about her breathing, I called the doctor, who came at once. He explained that a stroke had come while she was napping and she never felt it. There was infinite peace written all over her face.

On October 8, 1939, at exactly nine o'clock in the evening, my dear partner of thirty years stepped from this little room of Time into the larger room of Eternity. That night between eight and nine the heavens were filled with the most glorious aurora borealis that we have ever seen in these northern skies. We would go out and witness this marvelous orchestration of the heavens and then return and sit at her bedside. It seemed that all the angels in Heaven were exulting. That night the leaves wore their customary late-summer drab brown. The next morning, as though a celestial painter had gone swinging through the treetops during the night, they burst forth in the most marvelous autumn colors that we have seen for years. A couple of days later, Helen May and Marion went with friends to Acacia Cemetery and found bluebirds where the interment was to be made, and they remembered that their mother always said that bluebirds stood for happiness. And so the skies, the trees, and the birds were all singing at what our dear old Doctor Wallace would have called "her graduation day."

The Catholic barber told us that his wife made a special trip to the cathedral with her beads that day to pray for a plenary indulgence for Louise. A mailman of ten years ago came out of his way to express his sorrow. The ashman[2], the delivery man and the milkman were among the mourners. A Negro woman who had worked for us broke down and sobbed that she had lost the only friend she had. The whole neighborhood was in grief and friends from everywhere came to our aid.

The services were held in the church which she loved so well. Professor Russell Hastings of Macalester played her favorite hymns on the organ, and her pastor, Dr. Walker Vance, read her favorite Bible verses. The ones she quoted most often to her children were, "Commit thy way unto the Lord; trust also in him; and he shall bring it to pass" (Psalm 37:5). "In all thy ways acknowledge him, and he shall direct thy paths" (Proverbs 3:6). "And ye shall seek me, and find me, when ye shall search for me with all your heart" (Jeremiah 29:13).

She was the most perfect example of the paradoxes described in Jesus' beatitudes that I ever knew. Physically frail but strong spiritually, with arteries too weak to hold the life, and a body too weak to hold her great love, the Soul broke forth from its casings and flew into its larger freedom. She is now awaiting us in the Kingdom Farthest Out.

The famous evangelist, Whitfield, ascribed the success of his great preaching tours to the prayers of a little lame man who always accompanied him but who rarely left the hotel room. I can ascribe any ability I may have to help people to the prayers of my "little bird with a broken wing" who rarely could accompany me on my journeys, but who always kept a light of prayer in her heart for me wherever I might be. And I feel that the light is burning for me far more powerfully

---

[2] the man who carried away the ashes from the coal furnace

and radiantly now than ever before. One friend said to me, "You have leaned upon her in so many ways; but where in the past she has been a crutch to you, she will now be wings."

After Louise's passing, my sister Helen, who had been a widow for twelve years, came to live with me and we turned our thought to the establishment of a magazine devoted to the life of the spirit, modeled on the plan of *The Reader's Digest*—a dream that we had shared for years. Ever since my high school days, my life had been singularly connected with magazines. In high school I had founded one; in college I had been editor of one; and as instructor at William and Vashti, I started *The Verdurette Magazine* and at Macalester College I started *The Gateway Magazine*.

Helen, who had been an associate editor with me both in high school and college, had done the preliminary work for establishing the magazine we had in mind by starting "Clear Horizons" in the form of a mimeographed magazine, "published" by hand, and distributed in love to all those who cared to receive it. In 1940, after Helen came to live with me, we launched our venture as a full-fledged printed magazine with five hundred subscribers. Just as an oak tree grows, it unfolded gradually until with the addition to its editorial staff of Frank Laubach, Starr Daily, Winfred Rhoades, Rufus Moseley, Albert Day, Ralph Cushman, Austin Pardue and Norman Vincent Peale it became what might be called the official organ for the Kingdom of God Movement in America—an undenominational spiritual magazine, controlled by no cult or creed, belonging only to all those who wish to go all the way out with Christ in absolute faith in prayer.

Five years later when the magazine was flourishing and well on its way, Helen stepped into heaven and I shall always be happy that she lived to see this desire of hers come true. My son-in-law, Norman Elliott, then stepped into her place as managing editor and within six months revealed talents in every phase of magazine editorship that rejoiced my heart. My other son-in-law, Kermit Olsen, found time above his ministerial duties to write the book I was looking for everywhere—the excellent book for beginners entitled *First Steps in Prayer* which Fleming H. Revell has given wide circulation. Then to complete the picture, my own son Miles came into our company as my assistant and chief adviser. With the continuous multiplying and spreading of the Camps Farthest Out and the ever-increasing influence of *Clear Horizons*, I would have little time for writing and lecturing if it were not for his timely aid. When he announced that he was going to marry Virginia Sanford, the charming and brilliant daughter of Edgar and Agnes Sanford (the latter the author of *The Healing Light*) my cup was running over. Meanwhile, my two daughters kept on aiding and abetting me with their love while their immediate attention was given to their little ones, who are to be our spiritual ambassadors to future generations. To have my entire family drawn into the very vortex and center of our common passion for a better world gives me abiding satisfaction.

I feel that Helen is still helping us with *Clear Horizons* and am so confident that Louise continues to help and bless all in our household that I frequently refer to her participation in the lightsome way that she herself would want us to refer to it. For instance, after waiting five years, the verdict seemed quite final that if Helen May and Kermit wanted a child they would have to adopt one. My youngest daughter Marion, who already had three children, was so confident that with prayer babies could come to Helen May, that she and I gave the matter to God in prayer. Presently word came that a baby was on the way. I said, "I can just see Louise saying to herself, 'They don't need to go around to orphan asylums looking for a baby to adopt. There is a far better assortment to choose from right here in Heaven. I will personally pick one out and send it down to them, immediately.'"

The baby was expected the middle of July, but mid-July arrived and day after day went by and still no baby. Louise's birthday was August 4, the day when the Camp Farthest Out at Koronis was to begin. I was starting for Koronis on the afternoon of August 4 when a wire came announcing LITTLE GLENN JUST ARRIVED. "Just like Louise," I said to those around me. "No doubt she arranged with the Lord to postpone the baby's coming till her own birthday so we would all know for sure that she had something to do with it." And then I recalled how often Louise used to repeat Wordsworth's lines:

> Our birth is but a sleep and a forgetting:
> The Soul that rises with us, our life's Star,

Hath had elsewhere its setting,
And cometh from afar:
Not in entire forgetfulness,
And not in utter nakedness,
But trailing clouds of glory do we come
From God, who is our home.

CHAPTER XXVI

The Discipline of Wistfulness

T HE way the gymnasium came into being through prayer naturally created in me the desire to use this prayer power to help the college in still larger ways. Edward Neill was its founder, the George Washington of its destiny. James Wallace was its savior, the Lincoln in its time of crisis. In the hard times of the nineties the college had used up its endowment and was deeply in debt, and the trustees announced they were going to close its doors and put it into the hands of a receiver. It was then that James Wallace had offered to shoulder its burdens and take upon himself the responsibility for its survival. With nothing but prayer and courage to build on, his faith was rewarded and the college lived. After the hard times were over he was made head of the Bible department and a younger and more "high-powered" money-raising type of executive was appointed president.

After the gymnasium came I gathered a little group of teachers and students who believed in prayer, to make it our special commission to pray for the college. When our group came together one day the conviction came to me with great force that the way to begin our vision of a perfect college was to see it as a whole, from its early past to its distant future—bringing its seed time and its harvest time together in their logical and irresistible sequence. Then it was that it came to me that just as the seeds of the Christian Church are the blood of its martyrs, so the seeds of Macalester College were the very wistfulness and yearnings and even the frustrations of Doctor Wallace and others like him who loved and believed in the college in its early days. Then I *knew* that those early prayers of James Wallace were going right on being answered.

I have often proclaimed before audiences that if I had the choice between having all the gold of the world or all its wistfulness, I would choose the latter. The asking, seeking and knocking at the gates of Heaven would bear results long after the wealth was all dissipated. And so as we prayed for Macalester College the figure and faith of old Doctor Wallace became the symbol of our prayer.

To trace the thread of all that happened after that would carry this researcher into realms where he has no right to tread. When I contemplate dear old Doctor Wallace's wistful hopes for three things that were dear to his heart, his children, his college and his world, I am in the realms of the intangibles and the imponderables. All I know is that all his dreams seemed to come into materialization. Without attempting to trace the steps of his wistfulness, from dream to destiny, I can sum them all up in these three simple words, *The Readers Digest*. In the original vision of this magazine in the mind of DeWitt Wallace, youngest son of Doctor Wallace, many of Doctor Jimmy's dreams came into fruition.

Exaltation is the offspring of success; wistfulness is the offspring of failure. In a previous chapter I referred with something like exaltation to the unfolding influence of a lad named Ray. I neglected to mention an earlier incident in his life that awakened in me a great wistfulness. When he had first presented himself as a candidate for my team—an unregenerate young lad who took pride in being called "tough"—my prayer for his regeneration lacked power. He had ridden "the rods" in a drizzling rain one night to Des Moines to watch the Drake Relays. When the meet was over and I had the team around me at the station in another drizzling rain, Ray came to me and asked if I could lend him money to buy a more comfortable passage home. When I found I didn't have a cent to spare, a great wistfulness went out from me for this lad who was doomed to ride another night in a chilling rain. In one night that wistfulness changed my sterile prayer into a creative prayer, and the great change that came to him, I have no doubt, was born that night.

As Stephen crumpled in death beneath the stones of his persecutors, he must have looked with wistful yearning at the young man Saul whom his teachings had utterly failed to reach. Can it not be that the wistfulness of Stephen in his dying moments contained the seed that brought the vast harvest of Pauline Epistles into being? Can it be possible that the wistfulness with which Jesus prayed on the Mount of Olives, "Let this cup pass from me," and on Golgotha, "Father, forgive them, for they know not what they do," released the cosmic power that created the great Christendom that followed? At any rate I do know this, that my own failures when coupled with wistfulness have borne greater fruit than all my successes.

I can illustrate the way this factor of wistfulness operates by an incident that happened on a journey to the Drake Relays which are held annually in Des Moines. On Friday the preliminary races are run and on Saturday the finals. One night after the first day of the races was over I tucked my boys in bed and went for a stroll into the section of the city where my boyhood days were spent. As I passed the Crocker School grounds where I had played tag, one-o'cat and blackman, wistful memories ran through my mind. I paused before the corner drugstore where I had often gone to buy the ice cream for Sunday dinner, or a bottle of castoria or a box of Smith Brothers cough drops. Old memories came back stronger and stronger, wave upon wave. When I saw the lights of the little cottage which was once my home, I was a boy again, going home to my father and mother, my brothers and sisters. I could see them all waiting for me around the evening lamp. As soon as I entered the cottage the reading would begin, or the game would start. With a beating heart I drew near the house. Through a window I could see the evening lamp upon the table, now burning electricity from the hills. I went up into the yard and peered through the window, and there I could see the old fireplace around which we had so often gathered. There was the old mantel to which we had fastened our stockings on Christmas Eve.

Almost unconsciously I started for the front porch. I wanted to burst in and tell father and mother how glad I was to get back, and then all of a sudden I came out of my dream. There I stood outside a door I had no right to open—a little boy who wanted to go home, suddenly discovering that his home was no more.

Homesickness flooded me, inundated me. I was well-nigh overcome, suffocated with nostalgia. Then I knew that all mankind and womankind suffer and will continue to suffer from homesickness. No matter how old, or how young we are, homesickness is the thing that grips us all. For as someone has said, "We are all born in the valley of the perfect, and we shall be homesick until we find our way back whence we came."

Since then when people come to me for help, I am not so zealous about probing into their troubles or sins trying to diagnose their symptoms in detail in order to find out the cause. I know their trouble before they start to tell me; I have already diagnosed the ailment and found the cause. It is always the same: homesickness. There is only one thing I need do for them—and that is to take them home. I must give them a vision of the ONE who makes all things perfect. If through anything I say, do, or am, I can arouse in them an urge, a desire, a supreme wistfulness to get to Him, then they are on their way home.

But how is the power in this wistfulness directed? How can we know it reaches its mark? The lever that directs it and releases it both at the transmitting end and the receiving end is Love. Antagonism or lack of love can ground it, shut off its power.

But even when its power is deflected from the point toward which it was directed, the power of wistfulness is never lost. The more barriers erected against it the higher its current rises until when it is lifted high enough it energizes the whole world.

When Jesus approached Lazarus' tomb, his wistfulness was so great that it burst forth into sobs, the only time we were told that Jesus wept. The hearts of Lazarus' sisters were responsive to this wistfulness and in consequence the door of the tomb gave forth its dead. But when Jesus was possessed with an even greater wistfulness for an entire city and cried out, "O Jerusalem, Jerusalem, how often would I have gathered thy children together, even as a hen gathereth her chickens under her wings, and ye would not!"—the door was closed against him and the city was destroyed. But the power generated by this wistfulness was not lost—it overflows even to this day, bringing blessing to cities that are open to receive him. Millions have been saved from sickness and sorrow and sin through what is called the redemptive love of Christ, which is another way of saying through his wistful love. Jesus described that love in his story of the frantic search of the woman for her lost coin, and the great rejoicing of the good shepherd over finding the one lost sheep. In the Gospels it is epitomized in John 3:16.

Of all my associates, the one who possesses this gift of wistfulness in greatest degree is Frank Laubach. Next to him I would place Kagawa. When Laubach gave his life to the Moros, Mohammedan head-hunters of Mindanao, in the Philippines, he was not permitted to teach them Christ. All he could do was to live among them and love them while a great wistfulness flowed out to them. He poured out his longing in personal letters to his father, now collected in *The Letters of a Modern Mystic*. Finally this wistfulness, dammed back for years, rose to such heights that it simply over-flowed the world. Therein lies the secret of the power that has enabled him to become the apostle of light to all the illiterates of the earth.

But while creating over a hundred new written languages in which he is bringing the story of Jesus to the illiterate, he is also discovering that we so-called literate nations, the center of a so-called Christian civilization, are the most spiritually illiterate people of all! Nine-tenths of the good, conventional church members know little or nothing of the marvelous languages by which we can carry on conversations with our Father in Heaven. I have often seen tears in the eyes of Frank Laubach, and heard his voice tremble as he pleaded with ministers and laymen to pray for world situations with the absolute faith that their prayer would be answered.

I hesitated a long time before writing these chapters that deal with answered prayer. But while I was hesitating, a letter came to me from Frank Laubach, right out of the heart of Africa where he was at that moment producing a score of new written languages where none had existed before. Here was a man whose phenomenal service to the world was entirely a result of prayer, as revealed in his book, *Prayer, the Mightiest Force in the World*. The tragedy today, he wrote, was the way Christian people everywhere were turning a deaf ear toward stories that dealt with the power of prayer. He begged me to set an army of researchers to work garnering all the authentic answers to prayer in my own life and the lives of others and spread far and wide the "good news" that God still hears prayer!

Agnes Sanford's book *The Healing Light* and Rufus Moseley's *Manifest Victory* are all part of the answer to this request of Frank Laubach. Another answer is *Recovery* by Starr Daily, telling the experiences of Pastor Brown. And finally this book that I am writing right now is my own feeble attempt to give to the world an authentic experience of answered prayer. The *only* excuse I have for writing the story of my life, the life of an ordinary college professor, is the service that such a story may render people in trouble, who may find in these particular chapters levers that will lift them from the dilemmas into which the world has thrown them.

If the reading of this book will turn people to the Scriptures I shall be glad. If these chapters will serve to validate the promises of the Bible something will be accomplished. But behind the promises of God lie the laws of God. Back of all these answers to prayer lie the disciplines. The reason I am giving these incidents in such detail is in order to make clear the disciplines. So I join my wistfulness to the wistfulness of Laubach and Kagawa for prayer to be accepted by the Christian Church everywhere as the mightiest force in the world. Only when that comes to pass do I see hope for the world in this age of need.

CHAPTER XXVII

Seed Sowers and Fruit Bearers

H ERE is what I call 'God's Little Workshop,' " Dr. George Washington Carver said as we had entered his place of miracles. "No books are ever brought in here," he went on, "and what is the need of books? Here I talk with the peanut firsthand and it reveals its secrets to me. I lean upon the twenty-ninth verse of the first chapter of Genesis, 'And God said, Behold, I have given you every herb bearing seed which is upon the face of all the earth, and every tree, in the which is the fruit of a tree yielding seed; to you it shall be for meat.'

"What other materials do we need than that promise? Here I talk to the peanut and the sweet potato and the clays of the hills, and they talk back to me. Here great wonders are brought forth." And he pointed to an array of bottles containing specimens which represented three hundred uses for the peanut—no, three hundred and one, for this morning he had discovered a new one.

"And up there along the walls are the clays," he added. "Again there is no need for books. Merely another promise in the Bible. 'I will lift up mine eyes unto the hills from whence cometh my help.' In my room I will show you a purple dye, the lost purple of Egypt. In only one other place in the world can they find that clay."

"How did you find it?" I asked.

"I talked with God one morning and he led me to it."

I stared at him, but he was feeling the clay tenderly as if it were a living organism.

"And when I brought my friends and we had dug up the clay, they wanted to dig farther, but I said, 'No need to dig farther. This is all there is. God told me.' And sure enough there was no more."

I watched this man whom I had come two thousand miles to see, and he told me of the miracles of the peanut and of the sweet potato. But far greater than any miracle he had produced was the miracle of himself.

"Could you describe your methods when you meet a problem?" I asked.

"I never grope for methods. The method is revealed the moment I am inspired to create something new. I live in the woods. I gather specimens and listen to what God has to say to me. After my morning's talk with God I go into my laboratory and begin to carry out his wishes for the day. It is not we little men that do the work, but our blessed Creator working through us."

"Why is it that so few people have this power?" I asked.

"They can have it." His voice rose to a sweet and almost piercing beauty. "They can, if they only believe." Then he laid his hand on the Bible beside him, "The secret all lies in here. Right in the promises of God. Those promises are real, they are true and practical, but so few people believe that they are real." Then he pounded his hand on the table. "They are as real, as solid, yes infinitely more solid and substantial than this table which the materialist so thoroughly believes in. If you would only believe, O ye of little faith."

Before we left God's Little Workshop he suggested that we have a little prayer together. I took his hand and, with heads bowed, we prayed.

This was the beginning of a spiritual partnership between us, for he made me feel that my part, however small, was important, too, in building the Kingdom. He, a black man from the deep South, I, a white man from the far North, loving and taking into our hearts all of our brothers, white and black, and giving them to the Father. He, approaching God from the realm of nature and science, I, from the realm of literature and the arts, neither of us a priest, and yet there was a power in our prayer that day that has gone with me ever since. Both of us believed utterly and completely in the Power of God to answer prayer and he took me into the very Presence.

Since then I have visited his workshop many times, and twice he has made the long journey to Minnesota to speak to groups I wanted him to meet. But the significant phase of this partnership was the power each of us felt when the other was holding him up in prayer. I feel blessed to have been of some small use to George Washington Carver.

Another man I made a pilgrimage to meet was Rufus Jones. I found him beside the lake at his homestead. His extreme simplicity, his complete relaxation of mind and body, his absolute naturalness, disarmed me. I had come rather tense and diffident, half-expecting him to make broad pronouncements about some world-wide spiritual movement. But I found that so far as he was concerned the state of the world was in the hands of God. For all his untiring effort in behalf of the American Friends Service Committee, he seemed neither ruffled nor perturbed. He had found a spiritual center.

The things which so impressed me was the tremendous equilibrium of the man, the perfect balance between idealism and realism, between high mysticism and deep practicality, a unique combination of profound love of God and intense affection for men. His was not the equilibrium of a wheel leaning against a fence, but of a wheel rolling down the road.

In the Christmas holidays of 1934 when the Quadrennial Student Volunteer Convention was to be held at Indianapolis, I packed my suitcase and went to the convention with the sole aim of meeting Kagawa.

Kagawa, knowing that I believed in prayer, asked me to gather a group of folks who had special faith in prayer to meet with him. So at six o'clock on New Year's Day, in a room on the twelfth floor of the Lincoln Hotel, fifty people gathered. We sat on chairs, on the bed and on the floor. Then Kagawa came in and began speaking in that soft voice of his:

"I cannot do much for your country unless prayer meetings are organized. I have no message with which to compete on the secular platform. When the best people come together and start prayer meetings, then the spirit will spread and revive. Before I go anywhere I simply kneel down and pray. When the Holy Spirit moves in the upper room you cannot stop it. So far as I have known, you Americans have the best stock of Christians imaginable, generous, universal-minded, big-hearted, gracious—but they are separated, they haven't their forces united. The one way to unite is in prayer. So I wish you would start prayer groups everywhere, and as far as possible link them together for the great needs of the world."

Since then Kagawa and I have been thrown together many times, and I share the opinion of many that Gandhi and Kagawa were the two greatest souls of this age.

I have always been a great believer in the orchestration of minds, especially when that orchestration of minds rises high enough to be an orchestration of souls.

I once sat down with two of my friends of long standing, Ralph Budd, president of the Burlington Railroad, and A. N. Williams, now president of Westinghouse Air Brake Company. Franklin D. Roosevelt had just been elected President, and his New Deal was the talk of the hour.

"We have no right to criticize this New Deal," Ralph Budd said, "until we can propose a better deal." And then out of a clear sky he built up a dream of all the spiritual-minded business leaders coming together for a period to work out plans for an economic order that would be fair to all and that would end the evils which have become the groundwork for communism. Ralph Budd's dreams usually come to fulfillment, but in spite of the fact that we were all in earnest about our dream, the chasm between government and big business soon widened to such an extent that the subject was never brought up between us again.

Dr. Alexis Carrel invited me into conference once and broached his dream of gathering a group of specialists, each capable of thinking in terms beyond his own narrow specialty, to integrate the knowledge of the world regarding the life and destiny of man. He felt that something must be done to save civilization. World War II and his death that followed left this dream also unfulfilled.

I was often in the home of Otto Mallery while he was working out a solution for international trade in *Economic Union and Durable*

Peace and *More than Conquerors* which attempted to get at the heart
of the whole world problem. While these dreams were only partly
successful, each one represented a seed in the ground. For one of my
basic convictions is that no dream, properly dreamed, is ever wasted.

Another close friend and partner in our camps was Joseph Tucker.
When he got word from his missionary daughter that every grain of
wheat in China was that much insurance against starvation, he dreamed
of producing combines that would thresh the wheat without losing a
grain. He went still further and organized an army of operators who
could begin in Texas and move north as the ripening season came along.
During World War II when the shortage of farm hands was serious,
the fulfillment of this dream saved hundreds of lives throughout the
world.

Roger Babson is another with whom I have long enjoyed swapping
dreams of putting God into government, into business, and–this was
his chief dream–into the church itself. He wished the church could be
kept open for services all Sunday long so that in summer the crowds
which leave the cities for the day could attend early service, even though
a brief one, before they left.

For a long time I dreamed with certain educators of establishing
a College Farthest Out where all the various branches of learning
would be correlated and their principles and laws integrated around
a philosophy of life based on absolute faith in the reality of God.
Gathering together an unusual group of teachers, we held three summer
terms of this college in a summer resort at Maple Plain and two winter
terms in a wing of the State Teachers College at Livingston, Alabama.
Our experiments proved that all we had hoped for was possible, but
alas! the Maple Plain summer resort was sold, and the close of the
war so flooded all colleges, including the one at Livingston, with war
veterans, that there was "no room in the inn" for the child of our brain
to emerge from its swaddling clothes.

However, I was able to accept this postponement of my hopes with
acquiescence because I needed all my spare time to write for a while.
So I told the Lord very frankly that we had tried to do our part toward
proving the value of our dream, and now if he wanted it to come to
pass, all he needed to do was to furnish the buildings and grounds.

Out of our college experiment, however, came another dream of a group in Florida, who hoped to establish an ideal community with the college as a center. Included in this community was a "home for the golden years" where old folks could develop hobbies, could pray as "fanner bees" and live in the Camp Farthest Out spirit the year round. Then, Mrs. Hopson and Mrs. Ritchie dreamed of converting the Hopson estate in Vermont into a healing center, and a few years later beautiful Merrybrook was born. Walter Beall had similar plans and Glenn-Haven in Florida came into being. John Lickert's dream produced Melrose Manor in Indiana.

But the greatest dream that kept pounding at my heart came out of my contacts with men of the dark races. George Washington Carver and I visioned a spiritual awakening for our nation, only to find the same year that Kagawa was engaged in launching what he called a Kingdom of God Movement for the world. All around us there are great souls moving in the same direction, inspired by the same purpose. If everyone working for God could work in love and harmony with no element of jealousy entering in, what a world we should have. To be sure, great things have to move in a slower rhythm than small things. My own little life plan had mounted to higher stages every seven years. This infinitely greater plan cannot be hurried, it cannot be pushed. It must wait upon God's own rhythms of time and tide.

BOOK EIGHT

Christ in the World

CHAPTER XXVIII

Where Two or Three Agree Together

IF ANYONE reading these chapters is under the impression that prayer is a substitute for thinking, he is greatly mistaken. There is nothing that inspires *real* thinking, clear, true thinking, like sincere praying. Indeed, right thinking is the handmaiden of all the highest types of praying.

This is especially true of prayer when it invades the arena of world affairs. We had an outstanding opportunity of testing this fact when the catastrophic depression of 1929-33 burst upon the nation. At this time over twenty thousand people were thrown out of employment in Minneapolis alone. At the end of the second year of the depression the surplus funds of the city were exhausted, the Community Chest was empty, the nest eggs of individuals had vanished. The city was bled white, and twenty thousand unemployed and their thirty thousand dependents needed help at once.

When there is no other place to turn one can always turn to God. So I got a small group of men together. Our only hope was to face the problem clearly, feel it deeply and give it entirely to the Father of Lights "in whom is no variation, neither shadow that is cast by turning." We used as our lever the following passage from Genesis 13:14-15: "Lift up now thine eyes, and look from the place where thou art northward, and southward, and eastward, and westward: for all the land which thou seest, to thee will I give it, and to thy seed for ever."

Standing squarely where we were, we worked out a definite, detailed plan for a solution of this problem by a unified, coordinated effort of everyone concerned. First we agreed about our plan, then we took it deeply into our hearts and loved it, and finally we lifted it up and gave it completely to God. While waiting for the Lord to send the right man to take the initial steps to put the plan into action, we went to a Camp Farthest Out by Lake Koronis and for many days prayed about our plan and visioned it as coming to pass.

Then the man came. Dr. George Mecklenburg, pastor of the Wesley Methodist Church, was driving home from a long journey to various cities where he had been trying to find the right solution for the Minneapolis situation when suddenly he caught the picture from us through the ether, exactly as we had drawn it up. When he arrived in Minneapolis he called us in for consultation. Immediately he appointed most of the people we suggested, and the greatest experiment of organized unemployed in the history of the country began in the city of Minneapolis. Practically all the magazines of this nation and of many other nations had extended write-ups about the undertaking, and delegations came from all over the world to study it. Had all our cities followed the blueprint of this Minneapolis plan, Roosevelt need never have instituted the W.P.A. and billions in taxation could have been saved the American public. There was no wasteful turning over of leaves in Minneapolis. Every move of every man counted.[1]

Immediately after this successful civic venture Mrs. O. P. Clark, a Republican committeewoman of California, who claimed her life had been saved by the reading of *The Soul's Sincere Desire*, came to me with a very strange request.

"I want you to write a letter to Franklin Roosevelt asking him to appoint a Spiritual Trust to consult and advise with on all important matters. A Brain Trust is all right as far as it goes, but if he puts all his reliance on a Brain Trust he will fail when the crisis comes just as Teddy Roosevelt and Woodrow Wilson failed when their great opportunities came."

"I shall gladly write the letter," I exclaimed. "But I doubt very much if my letter will ever get beyond the eyes of his secretary."

---

[1] A full account is given of this project in *Two or Three Gathered Together* (Harper), pp. 95-103.

"Pray about it and then do it. Be sure to. Can I count on you?" Thereupon I sat down and wrote to the President suggesting the idea of a small inner council consisting of such men as Rufus Jones, George Washington Carver and E. Stanley Jones. To them should be added representatives from the Roman Catholics, Jews and Christian Scientists.

I explained further,

> The purpose of such a spiritual council would not be to advise you (unless you especially asked for advice) but to pray for you and to marshall the praying forces of America behind you. There are some of us who believe that such forces are more powerful than mighty armies, both for the protection and for the extension of the ideals that America represents.
>
> We should wish that our names and our plans be kept a secret as long as possible, lest the force which we would see channeled into uses that God has planned might, through the premature exposure to the exaltation or ridicule of unthinking men, be weakened in its power or deflected to trivial and inconsequential uses....
>
> If such a council is formed it may be you, rather than we, who might receive the guidance from God how best to use it.

I knew if I sent the letter to Mr. Roosevelt direct it would not get past his secretary, so I sent it to Mrs. Roosevelt with a note asking her to hand it to the President. I received a letter from her, "I am very glad to give your letter to the President." Then in a few days I received a letter from Stephen Early, secretary to the President, saying that while the President appreciated the spirit of good will which animated the letter, he felt he could not give formal endorsement to the suggestion.

Why was the suggestion not heeded? It is too easy an answer to blame Mr. Roosevelt and to assert that if he had cooperated with such a spiritual council the war and its ensuing tragedies might have been avoided—although there is no doubt a measure of truth in such an assertion. The answer to our failure is tangled into a web of circumstance and character, more clearly apprehended in retrospect.

It is comparatively easy now to look back and realize how rapidly the repercussions of the great depression in our land reverberated around the world, giving rise to Hitlers and Mussolinis everywhere. When the have nations went neurotic over *their* hard times, the have-not nations went psychopathic and stepped off the deep end. Each year the echoes from these "psychopathic wards" across the sea grew more ominous. When unemployment struck the have nations, their brain trusts, by reshuffling the "alphabet bureaus" were able to get their food surpluses distributed in some way. But when unemployment struck the have-not nations, which had no food surplus to distribute, then armies began to march. To complicate matters still more, the have nations put up tariff barriers shutting the last doors of hope for the have-not nations. "When exports cannot cross boundaries, then soldiers will," wrote Otto Mallery in *Economic Union and Durable Peace.*

Those of us who met together to pray our way out of the world-scale depression realized that the natural sequence to a world depression is a world war; therefore, the next problem before us was how to stop the war. Again we had recourse to the promise in Genesis: "Lift up now thine eyes and look from the place where thou art northward, and southward, and eastward, and westward: for all the land which thou seest, to thee will I give it, and to thy seed forever." This time two highly intelligent men, Pickert and Baerman, came into the picture. Together we looked east and west and north and south and tried to get the *whole* view. And getting that whole view, we discovered a feasible solution, which, if it could be brought to the attention of those in power fast enough could prevent World War II.

Because the situation was so serious and time was so short, we worked ceaselessly to bring this vision into concrete form soon enough to save the day. Ralph Baerman, who had become our channel for getting the plan into book form, worked night and day, pouring the ideas into a dictaphone, most of the dictating being done in my house. This book presented the fact that the have-not nations and our own have-not farmers (who were have-nots because of the price depressing effect of their surpluses) were two parts of a single world picture, two halves of one whole problem. Handled as parts the result would be mutual disaster, but handled as one, both parts would be readily amenable to solution. It became simply a matter of finding a way whereby the have-not nations could send us their manufactured products in payment for our crops without injuring our whole industrial system.

With one hand in the hand of God we prayed about it. With the other hand on levers of action we spent time, money and energy to bring the solution to realization. I spent two thousand dollars of my own money in publishing the book while Baerman and Pickert gave their entire time to presenting this plan to farmers all across the country, and to the congressmen in Washington.

This book, entitled *The Way Out for America*, pointed out that American farmers had thirteen million bales of surplus cotton which could not sell, that forty thousand bales of that cotton lay on the wharves of Genoa while the Italian knitting mills were closed for lack of cotton, and that the reason Italy could not pay for the cotton was her inability to build up her foreign exchange in New York. Because our bankers refused to sell cotton on a barter basis Mussolini started a campaign in Ethiopia in order to get a place to grow cotton. And all the time our farmers were suffering in dire poverty because they could not sell their cotton to the Italian mills. There was cosmic absurdity in the American farmers' plowing under of 40 per cent of our cotton crop because Italy could not build up her foreign exchange in New York to pay for it!

The plan that Baerman and Pickert laid before Congress was a plan by which, on a prorated basis, Germany could export enough of her finished products to give her sufficient purchasing power to buy the farm surplus from our farmers, restoring prosperity to us and effecting salvation for her own people. Such a course of action might have ended the causes of depression in the United States of America and the causes of war in Europe. In spite of the fact that all the forces of selfishness and materialism were arrayed against us, our combination of prayer and intelligent action came within a hair's-breadth of success. The plan was pronounced sound by every administrative head and administration economist who saw it. Several gave it high praise. Two bills were prepared for Congress, one sponsored by Republican congressmen and one by Democratic congressmen, calling for the exchange of raw materials of America with the have-not nations for the kind of compensation that they would be able to make, and in a form that would not hurt our own manufacturers one whit. Had war been postponed another year these bills could have brought the solution to our problems at home and abroad, and in all likelihood would have prevented World War II.

To make the most of these spiritual levers so that we can use them with still more effect in the crises that may lie ahead, let us try to find the reasons for their success or failure. The "lever" succeeded in Minneapolis; it failed in Washington. Why? In one case we applied it to a city problem and the result was success; in the other case to a world problem and the result was failure. But in both cases the problem was very much the same: unemployment of men and breakdown of distribution of goods. One situation was merely a magnified edition of the other. When people of a city are out of employment riots occur; when people of the world are out of employment wars occur. Where there is happy employment that guarantees both freedom and security, there are no riots and no wars.

We were able to achieve this re-employment and distribution of goods in a city and the result was complete success. We were on the way to achieving success for the world problem but the net result was failure. In accounting for this failure the time element looms as a large factor. For so large a problem we started too late. A small airplane doesn't require as long a runway to take its rise as a trans-Atlantic plane requires. But as I look into the steps that were taken I see other reasons for failure.

The Minneapolis plan was initiated with much more prayer to begin with and this prayer continued over a longer period of time. The plan was first shared with a very small group wherein *perfect agreement* was secured. Then a committee of leading businessmen from my Plymouth Bible class presented it to the mayor of the city, into whose office had been brought Edward Waite, the leading judge of the city, and George Perry Conger, chairman of the philosophy department of the State University. The plan met with their complete approval and received their blessing. Then we took the plan to a spiritual camp where it was shared with one hundred and fifty praying souls, obtained their *complete cooperation* and was blessed by their longing and love. Days and nights of prayer were put behind the whole plan before it came into realization as a living, breathing thing.

In contrast to this careful maturation period, the world plan was shared first with a small group of religious-minded businessmen, all of whom believed in prayer but most of whom nevertheless lacked experience in prayer. They were conservative, meaning that their faith lacked assurance, and hence they threw over the plan a wet blanket of doubt. In other words we *spilled* the plan while in its formative stage among too many doubting Thomases. There was some trampling of it underfoot and there was some turning and rending, although all criticism was voiced in the kindest manner possible. Finally, for so large a plan, that would affect so many people of the world, there was not a wide enough base of praying people behind it. One camp full of praying people could furnish power enough for one city. We should have had a hundred camps full of hundreds of praying people to move a world. Finally, President Roosevelt did not receive the proffered spiritual cooperation as Mayor Anderson had done; he could not put his blessing upon the plan and give it the right of way.

While Baerman and Pickert and I were striving to ward off war with Germany, Stanley Jones and Toyohiko Kagawa were working out a similar plan for warding off war with Japan.

Stanley Jones said, "The idea, carefully nurtured by propaganda in the United States, that Japan was united in its desire for war was disastrously false. From the time of the attack upon China, the Japanese nation went through a deep struggle of mind and soul. It was a titanic grapple between the war party and the peace party. It was touch-and-go as to which way the situation would swing. The struggle continued to the fall of 1941. Then the militarists triumphed. Had we been wiser we would have outplanned the militarists. If we had lent aid and encouragement to the peace party in their efforts to prevent war, we could have made Japan an ally instead of an enemy. Certainly our course played into the hands of the war party."

The Japanese war party at the beginning was confident that the conquest of China could be quickly accomplished. After many years of fighting, however, they found themselves mired down in a war that was getting them nowhere and if there had been any way to withdraw and at the same time "save face" they would gladly have welcomed it. Then it was that Stanley Jones took his stand and looked from where he was, "northward, and southward, and eastward, and westward," and visioned a plan that would enable the Japanese war lords to "save face" as they withdrew from China.

He asked Toyohiko Kagawa what the Japanese needed to compensate them for taking such a step. Kagawa replied that confined as they were to so small an island, most of it untillable, they needed a place to which they could expand, a place where "they can take off their coats and work in comfort." Together Kagawa and Jones agreed that the solution to this problem was to give Japan some unused area where it could dispose of its surplus population. Their choice was New Guinea, a huge island owned by the British and Dutch, two nations that were making no real attempt to develop it and who did not need it for emigrants. The island had a population of only three hundred thousand natives, but with proper development could sustain from twenty to forty million people.

Stanley Jones proposed that the United States pay one hundred million dollars to Holland and Australia to compensate such landowners as might be dispossessed. He found the Australian minister at Washington sympathetic. "If we don't do something now about Japan's surplus population," the minister said, "we shall have to do it within ten years." When Dr. Jones interviewed the Dutch minister, however, he was told, "No part of the Dutch empire is for sale."

On November 18, 1941, three weeks before the Pearl Harbor attack, Maxwell H. Hamilton of the State Department's Far Eastern section, submitted the plan to Secretary Hull. Instead of considering this face-saving method of persuading Japan to abandon the program of the militarists, Hull handed Nomura and Kurusu the President's ten-point statement of November 26, which, says Dr. Jones, "could have no other interpretation than that of an ultimatum."

Even when confronted with the American demands, Dr. Jones reports that the Japanese representatives did not abandon hope that we would grant them the means of reaching a peaceful solution. Two days after the Hull ultimatum, Counselor Terasaki of the Embassy, in a note transmitted to Roosevelt by Dr. Jones, pleaded, "Don't *compel* us to do things but make it *possible* for us to do them.

If you treat us in this way, we will reciprocate doubly. If you stretch out one hand we will stretch out two. And we cannot only be friends, we can be allies."

There was no response, nor any relaxation of the pressure. As Dr. Jones says, "Our ultimatum put Japan in a box. She had to knuckle under or else fight us."

In retrospect Dr. Jones suggests that almost until the very end Japan and the United States were very close to peace. During the negotiations he was told by a member of the Senate Foreign Relations Committee, "It has all boiled down to two air bases in North China; Japan wants to retain two air bases and we want her to get out of China." Whether we were within two air bases of peace Dr. Jones says he does not know for certain, but in one of their last conversations Nomura told him that "it would be absurd for us to go to war over two air bases in North China. It would be very expensive for both of us."

In listing the causes of the war Dr. Jones says a principal cause was "the pressure of a war party that surrounded the president. A Supreme Court justice said during the negotiations, 'We Americans have a war party as well as Japan. They are surrounding the President and making it more and more impossible for others to see him.'"

Here again, had the President been surrounded by a Spiritual Trust, a love party instead of a war party, we could have been saved the ravages of war. Indeed, Stanley Jones and Toyohiko Kagawa, backed by men like Frank Laubach and Rufus Jones, were exactly that—an unofficial Spiritual Trust—doing its best to get the ear of the administration and cabinet officials.

Note again the perfect pattern that this plan fell into. First, Jones and Kagawa were able to take the peoples of both nations into their hearts and love them. Next they looked at the problem honestly in all its ramifications, north and south and east and west, and saw a solution clearly. Upon this solution they both agreed. In prayer they lifted this solution up and gave the plan to God. Had three hundred thousand people been praying behind them in this particular undertaking, I believe the hearts of the leaders would have been opened and a wonderful event would have happened.

Just think of this possibility in practical terms. For one hundred million dollars used for the purchase of this island, we would have been saved the expenditure of three hundred billion dollars for a war that has created more problems than it has solved. Had there been three hundred thousand actively praying people behind this project we would not now have three hundred thousand of our finest young men under ground. Yes, the lever of Genesis 13:14-15 is all powerful when applied on a scale large enough to fit the problem. Why can we not learn to turn to the Scriptures instead of to the Manual of Arms when danger threatens?

CHAPTER XXIX

The Lord God in the Affairs of Men

I TRUST my reader has discovered by this time that this is not an autobiography of me, but an autobiography of an Idea, a tremendous Idea, and that Idea is that a dream, if properly dreamed, *always* comes true, and a prayer, when prayed in accordance with the laws laid down by Jesus, is *always* fulfilled. I am referring to an unselfish dream for the good of mankind, not a little possessive one; it must be relinquished, it must be seen whole, it must be "agreed upon." But why enumerate the requirements? They are reiterated all through this book.

I know that boldly stated thus, this Idea may test some people's credulity. If I am sincere the reader will be tempted to label me a fanatic; if I am not sincere he will be tempted to label me an egotist. And yet the only sin I have committed has been to take the statements of Jesus seriously, and try to apply them in my life. All I can do is to beg of you not to be too harsh in your judgments until you, too, try applying Jesus' promises in your own life and see if the results will not equal or transcend anything that I have here recorded. You remember that in the first chapter I stated that this was not only an autobiography of me but a biography of you, dear cousin reader. If you would follow up the reading of this book with a week at the Camp Farthest Out under leaders like Frank Laubach, Glenn Harding and Starr Daily where you can see the Idea made flesh you would know what I mean.

A book was once written entitled *The Man That Nobody Knows.*

263

This book might be entitled *A Truth That Nobody Knows*. I have never been able to make anyone know this truth in one lecture or even three. It requires a week or more of living in the atmosphere of this Truth made flesh. That is the reason for Stanley Jones's ashrams, Albert Day's missions, and Gerald Heard's retreats.

I know the inertia of the Christian world regarding prayer, the one subject that is not studied in the theological seminaries. A vote taken in a Southern theological seminary revealed that 90 per cent of our future ministers believe that the Sermon on the Mount is impractical, and 80 per cent believe that it is impossible. I was with a group of twenty ministers representing the largest churches in one of our largest cities, and half of them told me that they do not believe in prayer and one of them said that he believed that prayer did more harm than good. That day I discovered that Stanley Jones's assertion is not far off the mark when he said that the spiritual life of most of our church leaders is so anemic that when anyone comes along who has a healthy circulation they think that he has a fever.

Some dear friends of mine have cautioned me against putting these experiences dealing with world situations into this book. Experiences like these they say should be kept for the few. In medieval times the ruling class thought that education should be kept for the few. In Czarist Russia they thought power should be kept for the few. We live in a Christian democracy where we are not supposed to limit either democracy or Christianity for the few. The real teachings of Jesus have been kept from the masses too long. For over half a century Marxism was kept for the few. Now it is spreading like the measles. The only serum that can combat it is the real Christianity of the real Christ. Some of us must take Christ as seriously as Lenin and Stalin have taken Marx. To some this may appear like pitting fanatic against fanatic, crackpot against crackpot, but if that is the case there is one thing I am sure of and that is that Christianity will not crack up first. This book is a challenge and an affirmation that there are many of us who are willing to bet our lives on Jesus.

In some respects our Mother Goose rhymes are wiser than our colleges and seminaries. When Goldilocks tasted of the big bowl, which represented the physical solution of problems, she found it too hot. When she tasted of the mental bowl, she found it too cold. When she tasted of the religious bowl, she found it was just right, but, alas, there was not enough of it. We have got to increase our praying army. In order to spread this faith in prayer rapidly enough to save the world we must imitate the zeal of the Communists of Russia, on the one hand, and emulate the industry and intelligence and faith of our great scientists and industrialists of America, on the other, two groups in two hemispheres who are building a brand new material world.

I opened a copy of *Colliers* magazine recently and in a full-page advertisement of a great manufacturing company I read the following slogan, "The impossible we do immediately, the miraculous takes a little longer." I asked the manager, "Do you believe that miracles are possible in industry today?" "Oh yes," he replied, "they are possible today but they were not possible two thousand years ago."

Next I stepped into a theological seminary and I saw a slogan that went something like this: "If you have faith like a grain of mustard seed, you can say to this mountain, be ye removed, and it shall be removed."

I asked the president of the seminary, "Do you believe that miracles can happen today through prayer?" "Oh no," he replied, "Miracles were possible two thousand years ago, but not today."

When I reported this to Frank Laubach, he said, "When Christian people can believe in the miracles of atomic bombs as the mightiest force in international affairs and refuse to believe in the power of prayer as a still mightier force it is no wonder that the world is in the mess that it is in."

Over fifty years ago Steinmetz, the electrical wizard of General Electric, said to Roger Babson, "We have been studying the laws of matter; fifty years from now the world will be studying the laws of Spirit. They will take Love into the laboratory and find more power in Love than there is in electricity."

For the past twenty-five years I have been taking Love and Prayer into the laboratory of my college classes, my athletic teams, and my Camp Farthest Out and there I have discovered that the laws of Spirit are stronger than the laws of Matter. Many others have been exploring the same territory and have been making greater discoveries than I have. A study of modern history will reveal many far greater miracles of answered prayer than the few that are recorded in this book. One example is the way food and drink came to the seven men in the rubber boats with Rickenbacker. Another is the account of the King of England calling for an all-day of prayer and the miracle of Dunkirk occurring the next day. But as this is an autobiography and not a history of modern times I am forced to limit my narrative to the incidents that fell under my own personal observation.

In this book I began by showing how a dream properly dreamed can solve a little personal problem, and end by showing how it might solve world problems when enough people "agree together" in dreaming the dream. I am one, for instance, who sincerely believes that had Stalin, Churchill, and Roosevelt agreed together on their war aims when the United States entered the war we would now see the miracle of the world at peace.

"Give me a lever big enough and a fulcrum to rest it on and I can move the world," said the great Greek scientist. The greatest lever there is, is the lever of Love. Love itself is the greatest power in the universe, so great that it needs no other power to protect it or sustain it. "Whether there be prophecies, they shall fall; whether there be tongues, they shall cease; whether there be knowledge, it shall vanish away," but "Love never faileth."

Let me show you how love, when properly used, never fails.

In the summer of 1939, one hundred people who believed in prayer came from all over the nation to Lake Koronis, in Minnesota, and spent many days in putting their entire lives in as complete alignment and surrender to God as they knew how. Then one evening they all united in a special prayer for the Love-way to prevail over the war-way in Europe and in the world. There was power in that prayer. A few weeks later, one hundred and fifty people who believed in the power of prayer, gathered on Star Island off the coast of New Hampshire, and humbly put their lives in as complete surrender and alignment with God as they knew how. And then came the miracle!

It happened on a night on Star Island when the camp period had nearly come to an end. A stunt night had been arranged, and a part of the program was a little "take-off" on Hitler. We gathered that evening in the mood of happy expectancy. We put our overserious, adult nature aside and let our spontaneous, childlike nature have full sway. That night we learned what Jesus meant when he said, "Unless you turn and become as a little child, ye are not worthy to enter the Kingdom of Heaven."

Hitler with his little mustache came upon the stage surrounded by his henchmen. First he commanded that a Jew be persecuted, and as he did so a "boomerang" knocked down one of his own guard. (They were doing a take-off of my talk on "Boomerangs.") Next he commanded that a university professor be interned in a prison camp, and again the "boomerang" swung back upon his own guards. Then Goering said, "You are wonderful. Where do you get your marvelous ideas?" Proudly Hitler replied, "I have a secret. I tune in to the cosmic forces of the universe. Let me show you how." And he seated himself, bending forward, till his ear touched the table before him as one catching messages not open to others. As he did so a back curtain opened and four young women with arms upraised, facing the four points of the compass, were revealed "broadcasting" the love of God to the whole world.

Hitler stirred uneasily. He seemed puzzled. Then he raised his head and said, "I am getting something different, something I never got before." Finally he sat up and said, "I am going to surprise you. But after all, I am always surprising people. Why not give them a *big* surprise while I am about it? Command the police to stop persecuting the Jews. Tell them to release all the captives from the prison camps." The guards that had been "boomeranged" began to arise. As he spoke and continued speaking, a strange spiritual power began to fill the hall. It continued to increase in power until the entire building became a veritable house of prayer.

Of course the little hall was darkened for this play. All save the actors on the stage were shrouded in darkness, and absolute silence reigned. They say that man in his highest moments drops words and resorts to symbols. So did Jesus on the Mount of Transfiguration. We were resorting to a symbol of love for all the world in a room of exalted silence.

I was standing in the back of the darkened room. Glenn Harding, our leader of singing, felt his way to me and said, "I have never felt greater spiritual power in all my life." Miss Elizabeth Lee, now the Methodist general secretary in charge of all foreign missionary work of the Methodist Board in the continents of Europe, Africa and South America, felt her way to me and said, "I *know* that something is happening to Hitler *this very hour and this very minute.*"

The next day when the *Boston Transcript* arrived from the mainland, the headlines were flashing the news of a complete change of policy by Hitler. The lead article on the front page expanded these headlines into an account of how Hitler's army, under orders to march into Poland at 4:30 in the morning for the most smashing blitzkrieg in the history of the world, was suddenly stopped. In the dead of night Hitler had countermanded the order.

On the right-hand column of the front page were the words that I shall never forget: "THOSE CLOSE TO RULER KNOW THE VERY HOUR AND THE VERY MINUTE WHEN HE MADE THIS DECISION. IT WAS TWO O'CLOCK IN THE MORNING." That was the identical hour and the identical minute, when one makes allowance for difference in longitude and daylight saving time, that Miss Elizabeth Lee said to me in the darkened room that night, "I know that something is happening to Hitler *this very hour and this very minute.*"

Hitler not only halted his soldiers before they had started, but he reopened telephone communications with Chamberlain and Daladier promising them that if they would agree on a truce, he would grant Poland a plebiscite to determine what lands they would be willing to cede to Germany. This plebiscite was to be held not earlier than a year from that date, under a neutral commission composed of representatives from England, France, Russia and Italy.

What he asked for, merely the Danzig Corridor and a little more, was a fraction of what, when provoked to war, he finally did take. In other words, all he asked for were territories which many neutral authorities thought it only just for Germany to have.

Think what this offer meant! It might have ended all threat of war for at least a year and ultimately brought about adjustment of those Versailles provisions regarding Poland that Lloyd George had always considered untenable. What might have occurred during that year to bring about peaceful adjustment of all the conflicting claims! Had we had that extra year of peace, our world program of barter and exchange might well have been approved by Congress.

I am a great believer in *prayer in action*. By that I mean not only praying for the Jordan to divide and make a path for the Israelites to enter the Promised Land, but actually walking down to the shores of Jordan till "the soles of the shoes are wet." So in 1938 while praying for peace to come about in Europe I proposed that we definitely plan a traveling Camp Farthest Out in Europe for the summer of 1940. I chose that year because it would be an Oberammergau year. My roommate of college days, Wilbur Schilling, who had been my partner in the trip through Europe in 1907, was now living in Minneapolis and his lifework was the directing of the well-known Schilling Tours. When I asked his help he was delighted at the idea and carefully planned the journey for us. We printed announcements of the trip and the itinerary. Then I spread word to my fifteen thousand readers and got them all to vision the journey with Christ going with us all over Europe and taking control. The year of 1938 was drawing to a close when we began spreading this word, and the strange actions of Hitler and Mussolini were beginning to look ominous.

"You are taking big risks," said many friends. "Likely as not by 1940 Europe will be at war."

"God led me to plan this," was my stubborn rejoinder. "I admit it doesn't sound feasible but I am sure there is *some* reason for God letting me plan it."

In August, 1939, things looked still more ominous. If Chamberlain and Daladier had had Spiritual Trusts behind them to share their problems and furnish strength and guidance I believe they would have accepted Hitler's request for an armistice and, with all these prayers sustaining them, peace could have prevailed. But without the adequate protection of prayer behind them, they dared not trust Hitler again and war was declared. Our dream of a spiritual journey through Europe faded away when Hitler's men marched into Poland in September, 1939.

Or had it faded away? Why had the Lord let us plan that journey? Something about it was real. Something about it was permanent. What could that real and permanent thing be? With a kind of childlike clarity–reminiscent, perhaps, of the imprint formerly made upon my young mind by Sheldon's *In His Steps*–I had visioned that journey now for almost two years–our party traveling through Europe with Jesus. Ah! The permanent part was Jesus. Even if we ourselves in our little corporeal bodies were barred from marching through Europe, Jesus in his spiritual body could not be barred.

Therefore, early in January, 1940, while the fighting in Europe was at its height, I began proclaiming wherever I went on my speaking journeys that there would be no fighting in Europe in the summer of 1940. When my hearers asked for definite dates I finally said that the fighting would stop on June 23 and not be resumed again till after September 1. I can never forget how startled people looked in Judge Don Allens' home in Des Moines when I first made that assertion in April, 1940.

Two months later the radio announced that the final papers for war to cease between Germany and France were signed on the eve of June 23. And no more fighting occurred in Europe until after September 1, 1940. The English, still dazed over the "Miracle of Dunkirk," are puzzled to this day why Hitler made no move that summer to invade England, which lay open and helpless before any attack.

Looking back on those early days of the war and *knowing* the modification of events brought about through prayer, I ponder on the unwrought miracles which awaited only a greater daring, a livelier assurance, a more ardent love rising from my own heart–and from the hearts of other half-disciplined citizens of the Kingdom of Heaven on earth.

CHAPTER XXX

The Third Front

AFTER Pearl Harbor came victory after victory for the Axis in one unbroken string. These victories could not be accounted for merely on the basis of better armaments, better discipline, better generalship. There was something uncanny about the way Hitler made his moves at exactly the right time and exactly in the right way. Finally I sat down one day determined with God's help to get to the bottom of the secret of Hitler's unbroken series of successes. And then it burst upon me with such force that I put it at once into an article that appeared in *Clear Horizons* for October, 1942:

> The intuitive plans, plots and strokes of Hitler are more powerful than the calculated steps of Daladier and Chamberlain because they take their inception at deeper levels. For the most powerful technique of the subconscious level is to *see* a plan *complete*—not *think* it out complete—and once this vision is seen within the inner chamber, unless equally powerful spiritual or psychic forces are marshalled against it, it will come into manifestation in the outer realms of action.
>
> The power in Hitler is not entirely accounted for by the fact that he is a creature of his own subconscious, there is the additional fact that he is the focal point through which the subconscious emotions of all Germany flow. He definitely makes himself that focus of power. To lose his contact for one hour would cripple all his capacities and effects and influences. Himself a man of

271

very mediocre abilities and of very unstable emotions—so long as he holds this door open to the subconscious of his people, and reflects it with fidelity, he is almost irresistible. His intuitive judgments, his timing of attacks, his programs and speeches may not be honest or even logical, they may not seemingly make sense, but they "accomplish that whereunto they were sent." It is as though Germany were a great tiger panting through the jungle of this world with marvelous internal coordination, releasing its lethal energy upon its prey whenever its whole being hungers, and glorying in each attack. The subdivided and separate energies of other nations moving as scores of separate entities governed by separate plans and standards of logic, honesty and culture, are as feeble as insects before this monstrous coordination that opposes them.

Then I called attention to the analysis that Dr. Carl G. Jung, the great psychiatrist, made of Hitler.

Hitler belongs in the category of the truly mystic medicine men. He is the mirror of every German's unconscious. He is the loudspeaker which magnifies the inaudible whispers of the German soul until they can be heard by the German's conscious ear. He is the first man to tell every German what he has been thinking and feeling all along in his unconscious about German fate, especially since the defeat in the first World War, and the one characteristic which colors every German soul is the typically German inferiority complex, the complex of the younger brother, of the one who is always a bit late to the feast. Hitler's power is not political; it is *magic*.

Now the secret of Hitler's power is not that Hitler has an unconscious more plentifully stored than yours or mine. Hitler's secret is twofold: first, that his unconscious has exceptional access to his consciousness; and second, that he allows himself to be moved by it. He is like a man who listens intently to a stream of suggestions in a whispered voice from a mysterious source and then *acts upon them*.

In our case, even if occasionally our unconscious does reach us through dreams, we have too much rationality, too much cerebrum to obey it—but Hitler listens and obeys. The true leader is always *led*.

We can see it work in him. He himself has referred to his Voice. His Voice is nothing other than his own unconscious, into which the German people have projected their own selves; that is, the unconscious of seventy-eight million Germans. That is what makes him powerful. Without the German people he would be nothing. It is literally true when he says that whatever he is able to do is only because he has the German people behind him, or, as he sometimes says, because he *is* Germany. So with his unconscious being the receptacle of the souls of seventy-eight million Germans, he is powerful, and with his unconscious perception of the true balance of political forces at home and in the world, he has so far been infallible.

That is why he makes political judgments which turn out to be right against the opinions of all his advisers and against the opinions of all foreign observers. When this happens it means only that the information gathered by his unconscious and reaching his unconsciousness by means of his exceptional talent, has been more nearly correct than that of all others, German or foreign, who attempted to judge the situation and who reached conclusions different from his.[1]

This ends the quotation from Jung. I quote again from my own article:

That which would bring this war to an end quicker than anything else would be the recognition of what the true nature of the war is, and the recognition of the planes upon which it is being fought. The only way to counter the powerful attacks of the enemy that are initiated on these subconscious levels is to launch a defensive movement on a higher level of the superconscious plane bringing into play the full use of the power of prayer and the full use of the power of love.

Prayer is being used frantically by individuals everywhere, but love is generally discounted as though it were a negative force, whereas everyone knows deep in his heart that hate is the negative and love is the positive power. Love is the light of which hate is the mere shadow. The power of the subconscious can be made to vanish as a shadow before the power of love, just as the

---

[1] Quoted by permission of Karl Gustav Jung

fanatical loyalty of a race finds itself powerless against unselfish loyalty to a spiritual ideal.

Even while war is on *we* can join in an about-face to *broadcast love* to friends and enemies alike. We can send *prayers* to God day and night, and *vision* the world in God's hands. Were we able to find three-million people who would unite in such a love-broadcast, I know they would accomplish what Gideon's men accomplished and just as quickly—a victory for our Lord. Then Love would take the place of hate, harmony of discord, and the Prince of Peace would take control over the governments of nations.

After writing this article I was determined to act upon it. I was absolutely sure that if a few persons who believed in this plan as completely as I did, would be willing to make a journey from one end of the country to the other, recruiting armies not to spread death and destruction but to spread love and prayer, then we could prove that love and prayer are more powerful than tanks and bombs!

Even while I was thinking these thoughts a great religious leader, a minister of the gospel but one of the doubting Thomas kind, threw a tremendous challenge into my lap.

"Your assertion," he said, "that one hundred persons at Star Island temporarily halted the war is a very dangerous one to make. If, as you say, you have the evidence of the *Boston Transcript* and of Elizabeth Lee and of Glenn Harding, and of a hundred others, that it actually did take place, God has placed upon you a terrible responsibility. How can you dare to sit back and watch Germany and Japan conquer the world?"

The speaker did not expect me to accept the challenge. He expected his words to silence me, to make me retract my statement. But that which has happened under the power of the Holy Spirit never can be retracted. Instead, I accepted the challenge.

The only way to prove a thing is to bet your life upon it. So I wrote Starr Daily and Glenn Harding and asked them if they subscribed to this doctrine sufficiently to drop everything that they were doing and give a year of their time to the proving of it by sharing with me in opening a "third front" in America.

"Russia is frantically calling for our nation to start a second front in France as soon as possible," I explained to them. "Everyone knows that it will probably be two years before our armies can be trained and equipped to start that second front. But while waiting for that second front to start, undergirded with tanks and guns, why don't we utilize this period of waiting by starting a *third* front undergirded with Love and Prayer?"

The response of Starr and Glenn was instantaneous and unanimous. They would go with me on any journey for the Lord that I cared to undertake and follow any program that I wished them to follow.

> It is my opinion [I wrote to them further] that Hitler up until now has been outmaneuvering Daladier and Chamberlain because he functions on a deeper level. He is out there in the "no man's land" of the psychic, surrounded by astrologers and delving in the occult, trusting to the magic of his subconscious mind. As long as the world fights back at him on the dog-eat-dog, jungle level, and as long as we trust merely to the mental powers of men, Hitler will continue to keep the advantage he already holds. But the moment we get enough people, an entire army of them, to mount to a higher level, the level of the spiritual which is as much higher than the psychic as the psychic is above the mental, the power of Hitler will be short-circuited and every move that he makes will bring the war more rapidly to an end.

Glenn Harding and Starr Daily were with me one hundred percent in this point of view. I gave up my position at the college and the other two cut all their ties for the year and we started forth upon our journey. With no gold or silver in our purses, with no job, no employer, not even any group or organization to sponsor us, we started forth, We soon saw that our journey, unwittingly and spontaneously arranged not by our own design but by the plan of God had taken the form of a cross.

Starting at the headwaters of the Mississippi, in Minneapolis and St. Paul, we went down to Chicago, then to Andalusia, Birmingham, Montgomery and Mobile, this span constituting the vertical section of the cross. Then back to St. Louis, Kansas City, Lincoln and Denver, and back again to Chicago; and then on to Washington, Norfolk, Boston, Hartford, New York and Philadelphia, returning again by way of Cleveland to end in Chicago, in which city we found the center of the cross, Three successive Institutes of Prayer were held there, one at the beginning of our trip, one when midway through it, one at the very end. Then followed an interval of summer camps and after them a series of Prayer Institutes in Portland, Seattle, San Francisco, Los Angeles and San Diego.

Our message was very simple: Turn to the paradoxes of Jesus, reverse the world process, lift up your eyes to the hills, and see God's plan unfolding before you; look away from the negatives of suspicion, hate and fear, and fix your gaze upon the positives of faith, hope and love that can redeem the world. We tried to show people that Love can sweep out hate as darkness has to flee before Light; and that all evil—even war—can be transmuted into good. We knew that war and all the causes of war could come to an end if such a concerted vision could be held by a million people. It was wonderful the way this faith gathered force wherever we went, and what tremendous reservoirs of spiritual power we discovered waiting to be unified, organized and used!

We called our Institutes of Prayer not Retreats but Advances, and instead of using high-pressure advertising for our meetings and demanding guarantees of expenses, we trusted entirely to praying friends for arrangements and to the free-will offerings of the people to carry us safely along and keep our home fires burning. Coming as we did to each city without any fanfare or ballyhoo, in every city we naturally drew only the earnest, devoted souls, the "remnant" as Isaiah would call them, upon whom rest the hope of the nation. Great numbers we did not reach. But we reached enough to prove to ourselves beyond a shadow of a doubt that prayer and love can save the world.

So many answers to prayer occurred on this journey that it would require another book to relate them all. All I need do is to refer to the statements of both Roosevelt and Churchill that all our battles before November 1, 1942, were defeats and all our battles after that were victories. We do not claim any credit for victories for the simple reason that *we never once prayed for victory*. But this journey did prove beyond a shadow of a doubt that if enough people mount high enough in their states of consciousness to a place where they can look upon their foes with forgiveness and love and ask the Lord and His righteousness to prevail, then the Lord will turn the tide in favor of that side which *deserves* to win, and in His own good way will bring the war to a close.

Two years later this power of corporate prayer to influence leaders in government was revealed in striking fashion.

Twelve men were meeting in Washington on January 1, 1945, for three days of prayer for the United States and the world.

"Let us pray for the administration," John Magee said.

"For whom especially shall we pray?" Glenn Harding asked. "All power stems from one man," said Walter Judd.

"Then let us see Christ in Roosevelt," said Starr Daily.

Frank Laubach picked up a picture of Jesus from a table and placed it beside a picture of Franklin Roosevelt on the mantel. Then we all stepped into the silence. Presently someone began to pray. I opened my eyes and saw a sight I shall never forget. Rufus Jones was on his knees giving expression to one of the most moving prayers I have ever heard in my life. I know it went straight to the heart of God.

As he prayed, the phone rang in an adjoining room where our hostess, Mrs. Aymar Johnson, cousin of Franklin Roosevelt, was resting. When she answered it a voice said:

"This is the secretary of Franklin Roosevelt. He says he feels a great love flowing out to you and your house and he wants to convey that message to you now." Then followed a long and happy outpouring that was unusual in the annals of the White House. When word came to the room where we were praying, someone exclaimed impulsively, "This incident reveals that Roosevelt was 'on the beam.'"

Germany stepped out of the war in the spring of 1945. When the season of the Camps Farthest Out began, Japan alone was at war with us. Here loomed another opportunity and another responsibility. Germany had made her surrender amid an atmosphere of hate and confusion and despair. Consequently hate, confusion and despair would stalk her footsteps in the aftermath of reconstruction and rehabilitation for years to come. Would it be possible for these camps, dedicated to the expression of love and prayer, to create an atmosphere in which the surrender of Japan might be made a creative, redemptive experience for herself and the entire world?

I had hardly raised that question when Glenn Harding came forward with an inspired suggestion. "Our government is telling Japan that we will accept nothing less than *unconditional surrender*. Jesus has told us that it is only as we *give* that we shall *receive*. Only as we forgive our debtors can we expect to have our own debts forgiven. According to that, the quickest way to bring Japan to give unconditional surrender to us would be for us to give unconditional surrender to a power greater than ourselves. It comes to me that our camp can be the spearhead for bringing that to pass, by making unconditional surrender to God."

"That is God Himself speaking through you," I cried. "It comes to me that after three camps have made that surrender and made it an absolutely unconditional act, that Japan will end the war."

We made the surrender at Estes Park and at Maple Plain and when the Camp convened at Koronis the same experience was planned as the climax of our program. The spiritual orchestration had attained a beautiful height when we reached the night set apart for an all-night of prayer. On that night all of us made unconditional surrender to Christ our Saviour, the Prince of Peace. Just as we were rising from our knees at six o'clock in the morning, ready to close with a final song, someone came rushing into the chapel crying, "Japan has surrendered!" We came marching out of the chapel singing the Hallelujah Chorus.

I cannot leave this theme without one final word about the future. Should there be another war, there will be no defenses against total destruction that can be worth the name, excepting defenses of Love and Prayer. Therefore, if in my time another war looms as a seeming certainty, I shall call for an army of three hundred thousand people for three months. What would I do with these people? How would we marshal our army? We would divide them in groups of three hundred and assign them to specially prepared training camps from one end of this nation to the other where, under staunch spiritual leaders, they would devote their time to the study and exercise of the power of prayer.

Thirty million people gave time and overtime—twelve million in combat lines and eighteen million in production lines—to end a war in *sweat, tears* and *blood.* Does it seem an unreasonable request to ask for only one-tenth of that number to give their time for only three months instead of three years to end a war in *Prayer* and *Love?*

Moreover, we would not ask for the healthiest, finest young men, the cream of our nation and the hope of our future; we would be content with old or middle-aged folks, yes, with the blind and the halt and the lame. But they would have to meet one requirement—a more demanding requirement than any other army ever had to meet—*they would have to have an absolute faith in the power of prayer.*

BOOK NINE

Green Pastures

CHAPTER XXXI

A Seed in the Ground

THE journey that I had just completed on the third front revealed to me that my place was no longer in the college. My classroom henceforth was to be located wherever need was great. Lincoln Avenue, that I had traveled for so many years, had truly been transformed into the Lincoln Highway. Now that my wife was in heaven the whole United States had become my home. This constant coming and going on spiritual missions was gradually turning the whole country into my own front yard. Just as in my boyhood I knew the streets in Des Moines and every hill on the outskirts, so I now knew the streets of Mobile and Montgomery, the hills around Chattanooga and Birmingham, the avenues of Washington, and the winding trails of Boston. The canyons of New York, and the Loop and the boulevards of Chicago were like old friends to me; the palm-lined streets of San Diego and Pasadena, the perpendicular streets of San Francisco, the quiet avenues of Philadelphia and St. Louis and the thriving, energetic thoroughfares of Pittsburgh and Kansas City were a part of the path I climbed. But why should I tarry to describe the highways and byways of Seattle, Cleveland, Portland and Detroit and my own beloved Twin Cities? Suffice to say that every journey takes me deeper into the heart of my country. At the end of every trail, awaiting me at every station, are little praying bands of my "brothers and sisters" and eager, seeking groups of my "sons and daughters." These are my people; this is my nation. At last I have a right to take them into my heart and bless this nation as a patriarch blesses his people.

Now that I knew my own country so well and loved it so deeply, I felt an urge to know the world better that I might take it more understandingly into my heart and love it more profoundly. And so the postponed journey that Wilbur and I had planned for 1940 took place in 1948. As we had taken our first journey to Europe together, we were happy to take this journey together. A party of forty accompanied us.

But how different this trip was from the one we took as college boys in 1907! Our first interest was no longer sightseeing. In Paris, for instance, we saw again the famous portraits in the Louvre, but this time we were more impressed with the living portraits of hungry people in the streets; we saw the magnificent tomb of Napoleon, the killer of men, but our thoughts strayed off to the simple tomb of Pasteur, the savior of men; we saw hundreds of fountains flowing at Versailles, but were more impressed with the fountains of longing in the hearts around us.

In pagan France where there are one million Protestants and eight million Catholics and all the rest indifferent or atheists, we found the most vital Protestant group was the CIMADE, Comité Inter-Mouvements Auprès des Evacués, supported by Church World Service, which was doing a work very similar to the American Friends Service Committee. Our richest contact with that movement was made through Elizabeth Perdruiset who heroically worked with the underground during the war saving many lives, and is now saving both lives and souls working among displaced persons. We had the privilege of breaking bread with a large group of these displaced persons in a hostel where she presides just outside of Paris.

In the secret chapel of St. Catherine of Siena, we bowed our heads in reverent prayer. When our little party stood on the high hill of Assisi and looked over the vast landscape that had often filled the eyes of St. Francis, I offered a prayer of gratitude for that gentle, intrepid soul who belongs to all of us. As we descended the hill our scholarly Roman Catholic guide said, "In all the years that I have conducted parties to this shrine, this is the first time that any group, Catholic or Protestant, ever offered a prayer. I never knew before that Americans were interested in spiritual things."

Our last day on the continent of Europe we drove to the Peace Palace at The Hague. It was not the hour for visitors, but by the grace of God, the doors were opened for us and for a group of Danes who arrived just as we were entering. On the grand staircase halfway up, where the stairs divide to the right and left, I paused before a statue of the figure of Justice with her blindfold removed and her sword tossed away—a gift that the United States had presented to the Palace. Then I turned about and beheld on the second floor above me the gift of Argentina—a replica of "Christ of the Andes," the figure that stands in the high mountains symbolizing peace between two great nations. Our band had gathered on the stairway to my right and the Danes on the stairway to my left. I asked both groups to pause; and then I inquired of the Danes if they had someone who would be willing to offer a prayer. A volunteer immediately stepped forward and took his stand beside me. There we sent up a prayer first in English and then in Danish for the peace of the world.

When the Dane had finished his prayer, he turned and took my hand and said in broken English, "All through the war, people of my country were praying that you Americans would come some day and liberate us from our captors. We feel that your band of praying people are doing that now in the most real way of all."

And so we sent up prayers wherever we went: in a corner of Notre Dame Cathedral; in the little chapel of St. Catherine of Siena; on the high hill of Assisi; before da Vinci's "The Last Supper" in Milan; in the Sistine Chapel of St. Peter's in Rome; in the Catacombs; on the Appian Way; in the pulpit of Calvin's cathedral in Geneva; in the headquarters of the World Council of Churches in Geneva; in the Amsterdam hall where the World Council of Churches had just completed its great conference; and in the little chapel at Canterbury where St. Augustine brought inspiration to the Christian religion in Britain in A.D. 595. We shared messages with the Waldensians in Italy; with the Swiss in Geneva; with the British in churches in London, Glasgow and Liverpool, and with the Guild of Health at Swanwick, England.

There were two significant things about this trip. First, the vast amount of prayer that preceded it, prayers in which we held uppermost the longing that the Spirit of Christ might accompany us and abide and remain. The other significant thing was that on this trip we were able to lay the ground wires and prepare the way for future spiritual odysseys and traveling Camps Farthest Out in the years ahead. These journeys will be distinguished by their emphasis upon the week-long sojourns and retreats which our groups will hold with English groups at Lee Abbey, with Italians in Waldensian centers, and with French and Germans in their countries and, we hope, someday with Russians.

Having made this spiritual pilgrimage to Europe, the urge came to make a similar journey to Asia. Even while writing these pages three letters have come to my office begging me to bring a similar spiritual odyssey to Japan. "We are translating some of your writings into Japanese," said one letter, "and can arrange a welcome for you all over Japan. Come next cherry blossom time."

My son Miles, who is taking off my hands the mass of detail involved in arranging for leaders and correlating the work of the Camps Farthest Out (which at this date have grown to seventeen over all of the United States) will take over the planning of these spiritual odysseys abroad.

In the meantime, the Macalester Park Publishing Company, which I had established as a mere post office address for folks ordering my little pamphlets, had been growing and almost before we knew it, had become a small business on its own. Every three years we had had to move to larger quarters until finally we had completely outgrown the building we were occupying. But, alas, at this juncture we could find no place to which to move. For many months we drove about St. Paul and Minneapolis looking for a suitable building to rent. As a final resort we began looking for old residences. Then one day our mailman, Walter J. Hodgins, who had been regularly delivering our ever-increasing packets of orders, paused to chat and remarked, "I overheard you folks saying you were looking for another location. It is too bad you don't want to *buy* a place. My uncle, who owned the mortuary two blocks up the street just died and my aunt is anxious to sell."

"We can at least look at the place," I replied. Then we were in for the surprise of our lives. Had the building been especially designed for our particular purposes from the very beginning, it could not have more perfectly fitted our needs. In order to buy it, however, we would have to purchase two other stores that went with it, one of which had been vacant for years.

Clear guidance came to buy the entire place, a positive green light. We had no difficulty borrowing the funds, and in a few days I sent a check for the full amount. The vacant store beside us was immediately occupied as an ice cream parlor, and the other store continued as a beauty shop. The rent from these two stores paid all the taxes, all the interest on the investment, all the cost of heating the three buildings, and in addition, covered all the regular costs of upkeep. The entire rent on our own quarters could thus be applied on the principal. So while the two stores adjoining ours keep people's insides happy and their outsides beautiful, our third of this little trilogy is dedicated to making people good.

Besides the front office for Manager Dunham and a private office for me, there are three spacious rooms that will take us ten years to outgrow, providing ample room for our clerical staff, our editorial staff and our shipping staff. And under these rooms there extends a vast dry basement with capacity to store one hundred thousand books. To fill our cup to overflowing, there is a beautiful Prayer Room—our Prayer Tower. When we outgrow this building five or ten years hence, all we will need do will be to cut a door into the ice cream parlor and ten years after that, another door into the beauty parlor. Someday it may even be necessary to build a second story, if the calls for prayer continue to increase in volume. For the only direction possible for a Prayer Tower to grow would be up.

While the Macalester Park Publishing Company is a mail order house for distributing books on prayer and the deepening of the spiritual life, it is not so much a house of business as a house of prayer. Every morning at ten o'clock, the workers all gather in the Prayer Tower for a session of prayer, and at three in the afternoon the Prayer Tower staff holds a similar session for all who have been writing in for help. All day long workers are reading and answering letters asking for prayer, or for books on prayer. And those who wrap the packages to send out are putting their love and blessing into them as they pile them into the mail sacks to go on their missions of healing and inspiration to those who ordered them. And as the staff of *Clear Horizons* assemble the material for each issue they find themselves actually glowing under the inspiration of some of the material submitted. And whenever a world crisis arises and we send out a call to all our subscribers to unite their prayers for God's solution to prevail, the response is so immediate that our hearts cry out, "Oh that believers were numbered in millions instead of in thousands so that their united prayers could save the world!"

CHAPTER XXXII

Give All

IN AN EARLIER chapter I pointed out that we are all related, having a common set of great-greats somewhere up the line of our inheritance; and I am sure that most of us have been molded by many of the same cultural elements so that you recognize your childhood's fancies in the games Page and I used to play and you relive your own struggles of married life and professional attainment in the incidents which helped to bring me to maturity. But it is the Idea which really makes us kin. Perhaps there is no other valid kinship.

Indeed, experience magnetizes this kinship so strongly that any mere fact of blood relationship seems weak in comparison. Whenever we meet another individual who shares the Idea, our hearts rush out to him; we fall upon him ecstatically, even though our enthusiasm must conform to conventional outward patterns; we want to follow him around hungrily, to draw out his experience and thus to reaffirm our own. There is nothing more thrilling than for a group to come together in a laboratory of the Spirit and there discover for themselves that a dream, if properly dreamed, nearly always comes through, and a prayer when prayed in accordance with the laws laid down by Jesus, is remarkably fulfilled.

No matter how different the denominations we belong to or how varied the ritual or the creed, such a group can always find union in Christ. Each of us may be traveling a somewhat different path and hence remarking on other scenery but immediately, as soon as we begin to pool experience, we recognize that we have shared much the same rigors and caught some of the same vistas. God "left not himself without witness" is the experience of any true seeker, any place, any time. If my kinsman has trod his path more firmly than I, and followed it closer to our common goal, then I hope he will reprimand me with all the severity he knows because I have lagged behind. The lack is not in the Idea to which my days are pledged but in my own faltering footsteps. Looking back, I wish I could reclimb those stretches where I have faltered. When comes the day that we know even as also we are known, I am sure that our greatest embarrassment will lie in all our faltering; we will be chagrined that we asked too little, claimed half-heartedly, paced off our pre-emption with too short a stride. We will stand amazed before our stingy acceptance of God's great grace and laugh aloud at our lack of credulity. I never yet met a man of prayer who felt he had claimed too much for God. Also I never met anyone who had consistently tried out the promises of Jesus and found they did not work.

For those who work at the Idea, whatever their methods, I have only profound respect. To those who speak negatively without experimentation, and to those who proclaim loudly to all who will listen that prayer can be no more than self-delusion, an intellectual opiate or an escape device, all I ask is, Have you ever really and sincerely and humbly stepped into a real laboratory of prayer? To them I would speak a small parable:

I went to a lecture hall to hear a famous orator tell of the wonders of radio two thousand years ago. As I left the hall, filled with amazement that such wonders should have been, I asked one of the audience, "Does he give these lectures often?"

"Oh, yes," the stranger replied. "Every week. And there are thousands of orators all over the country filling auditoriums with the same theme."

"Tell me where I can obtain a radio," I asked.

"Nobody uses radios now," he replied. "'It would be the height of bad taste. They were in style two thousand years ago, but not now."

In the meantime a little group had gathered and had heard the conversation. One of them named Frank Laubach broke in at this point.

"I have set one up and I use it."

"He does, indeed," a bystander added with enthusiasm. "'Through it he is able to influence quite a sector of the world's population."

"It is a tremendous instrument," Frank Laubach went on.

"'Through it I've been able to reach people who speak many different tongues. And Starr Daily here beside me has used one that changed him from an incorrigible convict into a saint of God. Agnes Sanford and Roland Brown use theirs to help bring healing in almost unbelievable ways."

So I turned from one to another of those he pointed out and asked, "'But why don't you write about these present uses of the radio? Then other people could hear the glad tidings and get radios of their own."

"We did write about our experience," Agnes Sanford said. "'But publishers were loathe to take them. They said some people might try to use their radios without following the directions and then they'd be disappointed and they might even doubt if radios ever did work two thousand years ago."

"That's right," Starr Daily added. "'They also said that because so few used radios today it would be very unconventional for anyone who did use one to tell of any of the actual messages that came through. In a world where static is still possible, they said that people who claimed to have got a clear message would sound egotistical."

Then said Frank Laubach, "I repeat, why do people believe in the miracle of the atom and refuse to believe in the miracle of prayer?"

"They believe in the atomic miracle," I said to him sadly, "'because so many thousands of them worked in some capacity or other in the atomic laboratories and then saw the results. When as many get to work in laboratories of prayer—"

But I did not need to finish the sentence; not to one who has worked in such a laboratory.

Skepticism of the validity of prayer on the part of those who make no claim to a religious interest in life is relatively easy to explain. It is the skepticism of Christians in regard to prayer that defeats the

Kingdom. Actually there is a more serious disease than skepticism bleeding the Christian world; that disease is inertia, and skepticism is only one of its manifestations. Gerald Heard has pointed out that it is not so much our credulity which is put under strain by belief in prayer as our characters. Thousands of Christians are too lackadaisical to try out the disciplines essential for making prayers come true.

According to Doctor Whiston's recent book, *Teach Us to Pray*, the one subject not studied in theological seminaries today is prayer. Ask five professors in such seminaries why Jesus is reported as having left the crowd to go off to pray and the answers of four will be that he went to get away from the telephone, to catch up on his sleep, to plan his strategy, to analyze his own motives and destiny. The fifth will say that the writers of the gospels merely reported the superstition of their times. How many professors in theological seminaries come to mind as men who openly discuss the disciplines of prayer—the demanding, consistent discipline of body and appetite and sleep which produces the alert passivity that makes true prayer possible? How many times during a seminary year do students hear their spiritual superiors discussing the value of prayer in the night, the rules for successful intercessory prayer, the single-mindedness of true meditation?

Anyone who becomes interested in the *power* of prayer will soon enough find out its requirements of selflessness, of forgiveness and lack of resentment, of unremitting determination to bring to pass the good for which one prays. More people outside the orthodox churches will understand this contention than conventional church members. And yet it is to the people within the churches that one still looks longingly for kinship. After all, they are the ones who have made at least verbal acceptance of Jesus as Savior. At least once in their lives—at the time of confirmation or baptism—they have looked at the age-old questions: Who am I? What is my destination? Does life have meaning? Dare I believe in God the Father and in the transforming love which Jesus brought into the world? Sometimes with conventional acceptance but often with heart-searching acquiescence they have once taken a stand for Jesus' way of life. Why not the whole way? Why not have enough faith in the record to give it a try?

It comforts me—in a goading, energizing fashion—to recall that there were seven persons to whom Jesus gave special approval and each of them went the whole way. Each gave all he had in some special capacity. The widow gave all her money; the Syrophoenician woman gave all her pride; the Samaritan gave all his gratitude; the Roman Centurion gave all his will; John the Baptist gave all his body, his zeal; Simon Peter gave all his mind; Mary of Bethany gave all her heart. It may sound dogmatic, even conceited, to shout against the wind of the times, "Here is a thing I know. I who am nobody special speak out to you who are wise: Give all! Hold nothing back and reap the promises of God." But so I do shout. So I speak. So I write. So I try to live. I stumble; I get in my own light; I bump against my own inconsistencies; I defeat my own message. But it remains my message. The flaw is in the messenger and not in that which is being proclaimed.

Now it is difficult to achieve a high degree of surrender alone. It is almost impossible for one to give all until all give all. That is the glory and despair of the Christian faith, that we are our brother's keeper and he is ours; nobody can step into the Kingdom alone.

It is difficult enough to step into the kingdom no matter how much help we get. Sometimes we do almost despair. How shall we ever get all the contradictory images of our subconscious into complete subservience to the Christ? This problem is of course the old struggle of developing hinds' feet. The best most of us can do is to get three feet to track; the fourth wants to go its willful way. But just as the misjudgment of an inch may throw the hind who is climbing a precipice into the chasm below, so may one recalcitrant ego-desire hold us back from entering the Kingdom. Nevertheless I have stood on the edge and looked in and been so enamored by that Kingdom of Love which I have glimpsed that nothing else seems worth the trying except to stick to the path and ascend as I can. Browning wrote that "a man's reach should exceed his grasp. . ." My own experience would largely substantiate that claim. But on the other hand there is that amazing command, "Be ye therefore perfect, even as your Father which is in heaven is perfect." Jesus would not have set us a fool's goal. I know from experience that he meant what he said whenever he proclaimed, promised or commanded. In admonishing us to become perfect he meant that having the very nature of God, being in very fact His sons, we have the potential to achieve whatever we can dream. The only condition, I believe, is the ability to give all.

Now the desire to give all and the ability to give all are not the same although the desire is necessary, of course, before the ability can be developed. Ability has to be learned, earned, developed, grown into. I believe the ability to give all will come if the desire is unremitting, steadfast, consuming. I make it sound like a nerve-straining process and so it is, but at the same time it is no struggle at all but a joyous voyage of discovery. In order to give all one just has to give all! If it sounds easy, just try it. If it sounds difficult, try any other course once you have had a taste of the adventure.

Sometimes people come to me with all sorts of problems of the Way. They say they have achieved considerable success at prayer and in many cases feel that their prayers are answered, and then again they seem to get no answers and no feeling that there is Anyone to hear; they are lost in a dryness. Sometimes I discuss technicalities with them. Are they sure they have made peace with their brother before coming to the altar? Are they doubting the wisdom of their own desire? Is their prayer for the good of all? Have they relinquished the method of fulfillment to the Father? Again, people sometimes tell me of miracles of healing that have been wrought through them and then comes a time when they are unable to heal. So we discuss ways of cleansing the channel, the constant healing of the healer, the relationship of one's own physical well-being to the well-being to be wrought in others, necessity for anonymity, difficulty of being surrounded by the doubt of others, healing in sleep. There are many other problems of prayer which naturally come to my door; one who makes such protestations as I make as to the power of prayer is constantly asked to prove his words. In common parlance it is the everlasting business of put up or shut up. And the challenge is a fair one. And so I am drawn into much discussion, some of which is highly profitable. The laboratory work still to be done is beyond our present assessment because we have scarcely got into the ABC of understanding this power we are attempting to handle. But—

Now this is a large *but* and needs to be italicized in the minds of us all. But the basic answer to every problem of prayer is the same answer: GIVE ALL. Hold back nothing. Insist on being used entirely of God. Feel ourselves transmuted into love, without reservation or adulteration or hesitation. "Give me a lever long enough, and a fulcrum strong enough, and single-handed I can move the world," said the great Greek scientist. The greatest lever there is, is the lever of Love and God Himself is the fulcrum. Insist on this lever and this fulcrum and insight will come for whatever the particular problem may be. It may come through meeting a friend who has the right word at the needful moment; it may come through picking up some written word in an entirely unexpected source; it may come through direct insight. But come it will. Those are no chance words of Jesus, "Seek, and ye shall find; knock, and it shall be opened unto you." They are just as much law as the proclivity of water to seek its level. Both laws can be counted on to work every time. Whenever love of God and man consumes the willful ego, then problems open out to disclose their hidden meaning, their blessing.

These words come rightly as the closing paragraphs of this biographical sketch because they are the goal of whatever days or years still lie before me. If I had tried to include in this small compass all of my own failures there would have been room for none of the assurance of success which is so much more important. It is profitable for me to know why on specific occasion my reach exceeded my grasp. But it is more profitable to know why on some occasions my reach and grasp were one. And that is my goal—that the reach and the grasp shall be the same. We have the word of God Almighty that it may be so. We have the roles for making it so. We have the pattern in Jesus. We have the available strength in the abiding Holy Spirit. What, then, are we waiting for? Let us arise—now—and be about our Father's business.

A Concluding Chapter

By
Marcia Brown

CHAPTER XXXIII

The Last Seven Years
"Hail and Farewell!"

IN the closing paragraphs of the preceding chapter, entitled "*Give All,*" Glenn Clark revealed that these final words that he was sharing were the goal of whatever days or years still lay before him. He recalled again Browning's proposition that

"A man's reach should exceed his grasp, or what's a heaven for?"

He acknowledged that he could benefit from knowing why on certain occasions his reach *had* exceeded his grasp. But he knew it was more profitable to know why on some occasions his reach and grasp were one.

Glenn Clark had come to focus his mind, heart and soul beyond Browning's beautiful dictum. He reminds us of Jesus' amazing command, "Be ye therefore perfect even as your Father in heaven is perfect."

In this statement recorded in Matthew 5:48 Jesus opened wide to believing, yielding, loving "reachers" for the Kingdom the potent fact that they can have the very nature of God. Therefore they have the potential of grasping all that He has, achieving all that He wants and may actually become all that true sons of God are.

Yes, what Jesus commands *can* be obtained and experienced. All of it. He never promises or commands the impossible. It becomes possible with Him, through Him, in Him. It is the way of the Kingdom of Heaven coming from invisibility into visibility—even on earth as it is in Heaven.

Glenn Clark said in *A Man's Reach*, page 295,

> "And that is my goal–that the reach and the grasp be the same. We have the word of God Almighty that it may be so. We have the rules for making it so. We have the pattern in Jesus. We have the available strength in the abiding Holy Spirit. What then are we waiting for? Let us arise–now–and be about Our Father's business."

The book, *A Man's Reach,* was published in 1949. However, Glenn Clark lived another seven years–and the ever expanding, yet deepening, hopes and dreams of his last years and the God enabled accomplishments through him were never chronicled by him. He died early Sunday morning, August 26, 1956, at age 74. The few individuals, or the countless number of individuals, who *had* caught, *were* catching and *would* yet catch God's dream for the world because of the word, the mission and the spirit of this sincere, prayerful and humble teacher of the mysteries of the Kingdom and coach of athletes of the spirit all owe God infinitely in gratitude.

Glenn Clark was a co-teacher and co-coach with Jesus. He knew that if he could but erase himself enough to stay in true and right relationship with the real Master, Teacher and Coach that all who would "hear" and come close enough to Him would reach for, catch and spread the Kingdom. He was therefore trusting us who still have God's gift of time, even here and now, to *give all*–and "arise and be about our Father's business" wherever, whenever, and however He guided.

In re-reading a portion of *A Man's Reach* just now, the portion that tells about Glenn Clark's ancestors, I noted a comment he made about one ancestor, Jonathan Edwards, a famous philosopher, theologian, writer, moralist, and leader of the movement known as "The Great Awakening" that swept New England in 1734 to 1743. Later he became the first president of the college at Princeton. Glenn Clark said he treasured Edwards, not because of all these facts that history treasures highly but because of the beautiful home-life and the devotion that existed between husband and wife, and that the children of such a union, conceived in the love of God as well as in the love of man and woman are the kind of children who will ultimately nourish the life and spirit of their nation unto the thousandth generation.

I recalled Glenn Clark's comments about the home he grew up in. He said the marriage between his father and mother "proved to be marvelously happy and the home that resulted was one of the most heavenly homes ever established on this earth." How often he referred to the healing, nourishing holy love that ministered to him through his father and mother. How vital was the love between him and the younger brother, Page. How heavenly the relationship among all the children. I knew three of those children after they became adults: Dot, Helen, Mabel. That spirit of love had invaded, and remained, in them, too.

I knew Glenn and Louise Clark personally. I had my first contacts with them at a Camp Farthest Out at Lake Koronis, Minnesota, in 1935. I was a young minister's wife—very much in love with my husband, very happy with our little son, and very eager that our home be like heaven. It was during the Depression and I fortunately had a good position in a profession I liked very much. The salary was fantastic for those days. But the minister's wife part of my life overwhelmed me. I was very shy. I had never had the opportunity of knowing a minister's wife or of knowing *how* she was supposed to function in the church, among other ministers and wives, in the homes of church members, in Sunday School teaching, in counseling, or in praying with people. I became intrigued with the obvious relationship between Glenn Clark and Louise. He wasn't a minister but he was a spiritual leader. I particularly noted his wife's quiet manner, her "spiritual" cooperation in all that was going on, the sincere interest and joy evidenced as she listened to her husband's talks, her shy, yet not shy, mingling with people, the counseling she did, the love and commitment she revealed. I learned so much from what I saw.

Before going to that camp I had heard "chatty talk" about *rivalry* between a minister and his wife; and the *jealousy* of the wife because so much of his work was with *other* women or fixing up other people's problems. But the statement that alarmed me most was "Many a minister is forced to leave his pulpit because of a difficult wife." I didn't want to be "difficult."

In this spiritual husband and wife team I had proof that all could be heavenly. And I had a pattern.

Yes, my husband and I are so grateful that Glenn Clark and Louise were in the Jonathan Edwards tradition of love, devotion and dedication to each other and to God. Their children–Helen May and husband Kermit, Marion and husband Norman, and Miles and wife Virginia–are living illustrations of how that spirit carries on in the next generation.

How vast and how enduring is the inheritance we all have now and for generations to come because of the beautiful, loving, heavenly homes of the Jonathan Edwards' of this world.

I am beginning to see an additional significance in Glenn Clark's statement that he treasured more, in his heart, the beautiful relationship between Jonathan Edwards and his devoted wife and the home they established–so saturated with love of God and love of husband, wife and children instead of treasuring in his heart his ancestor's other tremendous acts.

Glenn Clark himself was tremendously interested in the nature of a man more than in his exploits. Is the nature one of love, joy, peace, patience, meekness, forgiveness, faithfulness, goodness? Are the thoughts of his heart becoming like God's thoughts, and his ways like God's ways? Is that reach of the soul grasped? Is that fruit visible? Then prayers are answered! Hopes are realized! Dreams implanted by the Spirit are coming through!

Glenn Clark expended himself–through teaching, coaching, speaking, writing dozens of books and booklets, counseling, encouraging, praying–that the life of the individual, the nation, and the world might be all that the Father, Jesus and the Holy Spirit wants and enables. As it is in Heaven.

Glenn Clark told of his experience at the time his wife, Louise, was so seriously ill. He spent his days going from his home to his classes at the college, and then to be with Louise. Her condition remained very grave. He was distressed. He started going from minister to minister, seeking strength, comfort, assurance. He wasn't begging their prayers for Louise's healing. He was giving her to God. He was looking for a man who could minister to *him* like the man described in Isaiah 32:2 "And a man shall be as an hiding place from the wind and a covert from the tempest; as rivers of water in a dry place, as the shadow of a great rock in a weary land." He couldn't find such a man.

Out of the experience was born the resolve TO BE, HIMSELF, LIKE THE SHADOW OF A GREAT ROCK where the weary, needy and distressed might come—and in coming find the TRUE WATER OF LIFE, the TRUE ROCK, and Peace.

He became that kind of a man. And thousands of people found their way to him. I know of no one since the days of Jesus who was more available for counseling and prayer. Or who had so many prayers answered. Perhaps the greatest blessing a camper experienced in a Camp Farthest Out was because Glenn Clark was so willing to listen as campers came to him for help. Then he would ask them to kneel beside him and he would pray—so simply. So genuine. So humble. The camper would leave—so often with the burden lifted. They were new people trusting God with everything.

During the last seven years of his life Glenn Clark published a major, full-length book each year. There were also three smaller booklets: *The Other Dawn, The Way To Victory In International Affairs, The Holy Spirit.* These were in addition to his busy schedule of speaking in camps, retreats, churches; managing the Macalester Park Publishing House and the overseeing of the Camps Farthest Out movement in the United States and overseas; a heavy correspondence, maintaining his own spiritual life through study, meditation and prayer—plus being a friend to those who sought his help through counseling and prayer and benefiting from spiritual and friendly fellowship from those who could help him.

Because his books more or less followed each other in a developing sequence of ideas, and his interest and activities were in the same pattern, I am linking year, book, and activity or projects together in this unfolding story of the man.

The book published in 1950 was *What Would Jesus Do?* a sequel to

Charles M. Sheldon's inspirational *In His Steps* that became translated into 45 languages with an estimated 40,000,000 copies sold. Sheldon's book swept the world with a tremendous challenge to walk in His steps, doing what He would do in confronting any situation. .

Glenn Clark met Dr. Sheldon in 1946 while giving a series of talks on prayer in Sheldon's former church, the Central Congregational Church of Topeka, Kansas. It was there that the famous book had been written and read chapter after chapter on Sunday evenings to the young people of the Christian Endeavor Society.

Glenn Clark wrote in "Clear Horizons," Fall issue 1950:

"Ever since Charles M. Sheldon's *In His Steps* came out fifty years ago I have been dreaming of writing a sequel to it in which the grandchildren of the leading characters of that famous book would again face the challenge raised by that book.

"Now the fifty years are up and that dream has been fulfilled. The sequel under the title *What Would Jesus Do?* will make its official appearance October 15, 1950. The city of Topeka, Kansas, where the scene of the novel is laid has planned a premier or coming out party for the week of October 15-20, backed up by the churches, the newspaper, the mayor and even the governor of the state."

In the next issue of Clear Horizons, Winter 1950-51, Glenn Clark reported the results. A score of outstanding Camp Farthest Out leaders assisted in the day meetings held in Sheldon's former church. Among these leaders were Rebecca and Wally Beard, Genevieve Parkhurst, Starr and Marie Daily, Roberta Fletcher, Vivian Osborne, Roland and Marcia Brown, Grace Curry, George MacCausland, Ethel Dow, Karl Menninger and Glenn Clark. Some gave messages, some conducted healing sessions, some led prayer groups, etc. All came back repeatedly to the theme *What Would Jesus Do?* in a world crisis like this?

Evening meetings were held in the packed great Civic Auditorium with Edgar Guest, Bishop Richard Raines, Bishop Bromley Oxnam, Dr. Daniel Poling and Starr Daily the speakers on consecutive nights. Glenn Clark was the speaker for the final night.

Glenn Clark in telling about the first evening said,

"Streams of people were filling the upper galleries; outside hundreds were being turned away... I pinched myself several times to make sure I was actually sitting there—that it was not a dream from which I would awake. And then I knew it was a dream—a dream come true. Something within this dream was real, was tremendously real. These people were not coming to listen to Edgar Guest, but were coming to listen to the Holy Spirit; they were not coming to honor me but to honor Christ."

He confessed, "One of those vagrant thoughts came to me that are so human and yet so childish that we are ashamed of them the moment they come; 'what a perfect final chapter for my autobiography, *A Man's Reach*, this would have been!' And then a big thing happened. A Man's Reach as the story of a man's life came to a close. Yes, a man's reach ended and God's reach began. From that moment and all through the week that followed, I faded completely out of the picture and a heavenly power entered in that God, and God only, can direct. Seeds were sown that week that may grow into a Kingdom of God movement for America and the world."

Each succeeding evening was stimulating, wonderful, super: Bishop Raines, Dan Poling, Bishop Oxnam, Starr Daily.

The final night Glenn Clark was the speaker,

"'The audience gave wrapt attention throughout, I wondered how many in that vast throng, most of them strangers to me and my message, would respond to the appeal that I intended to make at the close. . . and then turning to the audience: 'How many of you will make the pledge here tonight that during this coming year whenever you undertake anything you will ask the question, What would Jesus do?' I waited in silence for a moment and the hands began to go up all over the hall.

"Near the back of the great hall sat two stalwart working men, clad in clean overalls, magnificent specimens of manhood, each over six feet tall with weather beaten faces. When this challenge was put to them they turned and looked at each other straight in the eye, their profiles revealing that they were father and son. They remained thus without moving for some time and then the father gave a slight nod and they both raised their hands. This spirit swept the hall."

And what came out of all these meetings besides a lot of tremendous messages from voices new to many? In addition to a lot of praying, a lot of upraised hands, a lot of enthusiasm? I don't know. Perhaps nobody knows except Jesus. I do know that He was at work and He works toward changed lives—a new order in the world—a permanent ever expanding Kingdom with Him in control. I saw Him breaking through. I was there. I am still asking myself the question, What would Jesus do in this or that situation? And then endeavoring to do likewise.

Perhaps this same question should be repeated in these current times. It is another generation.

The book published in 1951 was *God's Reach*. As indicated a few paragraphs back, Glenn Clark said while sitting on the platform that first evening at Topeka, "A man's reach ended and God's reach began." That was the first time he gave a name to experiences that had been forming spiritual roots for several years. Just as a seed starting the process of germination needs favorable conditions of moisture, oxygen, a suitable temperature usually after an adequate period of rest. It is planted. First the seed starts to swell. A root tip emerges—growing downward—anchoring the seedling to be and absorbing moisture and nutrients. A lot of development is going on in the root area unnoticed on the surface of the soil. Next the stem starts growing upward. As it emerges from the soil people say, "My seeds are beginning to grow." The roots *had* been doing their work in the dark. The plant *had* been developing, unnoticed, until it broke through—upward. Glenn Clark had spent years getting spiritual roots established, absorbing moisture (Water of Life). The temperature (love) was right. So was the rest (abiding in trust). Suddenly he became aware of a new factor—something tremendously real. He discovered he no longer had to do the reaching—as if everything depended on him. For God was reaching—had reached—him. Now he could look back and recognize God had been in the reaching him process for a long long time. All the time.

On the jacket of the book *God's Reach* is a subtitle, "An Analysis of

Spiritual Growth." On the inside front flap it says,

"This is a book for adventurers with God. . . . No adventure is more compelling than the search for God, and no discovery is more satisfying than the realness of God. Pondering on the lifetime of discovery through prayer Glenn Clark surveys all that he has learned and gives his results and conclusions in a most lucid manner.

"Beginning with the three dimensions of space he probes into the mysteries of the seven dimensions of God. He says the culmination of all our early and heavenly endeavor is Oneness—with one's neighbor, oneness with God the Father, and oneness with Christ."

He also brings out some applications to the problems of life: with friends, finances, health, guidance, etc. He closes the book dealing with Stillness, the Perfect Pattern, Eternity and Everlasting Life.

Someone commented about Chapter VI, *"The Law of Alignment,"* picking it out as wonderfully capturing the imagination. Someone else commented on the last chapter, Chapter XXI, *"Beyond This Life Lies Life Everlasting"* as a "must." Both chapters are very helpful.

This book prompts some very creative thinking. Portions of this you could spend a long time with to understand. The "stretch" of the mind and faith is good.

The book published in 1952 was *Come Follow Me.*

In Glenn Clark's Thanksgiving Letter written near the close of 1952 he says:

"It has come to me with redoubled force this past year that this is all we have to do: Abide in Christ and let His precious words, especially His two great commandments to love God and men, abide in us and live in us, and all will be well. In other words, seek first the Kingdom of God and harmony with our fellow men and all these things will be added unto you.

"I followed that principle this year and the greatest book I ever wrote was transcribed through me: *Come Follow Me.*"

I smiled when I read these last words. He had referred to other books he had just written in more or less the same way. His statement about its being his greatest book *could* be very true. Also it certainly contains within it the best glimpse into Glenn Clark's inner desires and of his close relationship with Jesus. He was *trying to reveal Jesus* as he had come to know Him and as other people *might* come to know him. I am sure he didn't realize how much of himself he was also revealing.

The inner flap of the jacket of *Come Follow Me* says:

> "This is a dramatic adventure in stepping outside of Time and becoming a friend and intimate of Jesus and the disciples 2,000 years ago. The author expresses a wish, 'Take me to Jesus,' and lo and behold, he is in the company of Jesus of Nazareth.
>
> "In general the narrative follows the sequence of the Gospels. But, in the tradition of the Gospel of John, it is the personal gospel of the author. The result is reverently personal and sacredly intimate.
>
> "The story flows smoothly and swiftly. The drama of Jesus comes alive, the disciples are real people and the report is striking enough to have happened in this day and age."

This book reveals a very important facet of Glenn Clark's biography. It reveals his search for fundamental truth and the *One* who said, "I am the Way, the Truth and the Life."

It is a very inspirational book. The chapter "Quelling Storms" was selected to be printed in full in a Fall issue of Clear Horizons 1952. A comment from inside the cover of that magazine says:

"There are more storms than those of wind and water. There are storms of passion, politics, etc., that demand our attention."

Another chapter, "A Mountain Top," is my particular favorite.

I would say the book is a "must" for those who teach the Gospels— who want to make Jesus come alive to others. It is not a competitor of the Gospels. It is an inspirational complement.

What was Glenn Clark doing in 1952? He was living with Jesus, obviously.

He also had a very heavy speaking schedule which took him to churches and retreats of many denominations. He was also a speaker in fifteen Camps Farthest Out. Many of these were new camps in the process of being introduced.

1953 brings another important book entitled *Be Thou Made Whole*. Back in 1940 Glenn Clark had published a very helpful book relating to the field of healing, *How To Find Health Through Prayer*. Following the writing of that book his interest in healing had continued to expand. He invited individuals whom he knew to be powerful in the field of healing and prayer into special conferences where they could share convictions and experiences. It was in these conferences held in the 1940s and early 1950s that such people as Agnes Sanford, Louise Eggleston, Ruth Robison, Genevieve Parkhurst, John Gaynor Banks, Starr Daily, Roland and Marcia Brown, Rebecca and Wally Beard, Glenn Clark and others began "pooling their secrets." A "Healing Movement" spearheaded by these same people was soon in the process of beginning. Through the subsequent years most of them authored outstanding books in the field of prayer and healing. Some of the books had great acceptance and are still best-sellers. John Gaynor had founded the *Order of St. Luke the Physician*. Many of the above mentioned people were charter members of the Order.

The book *Be Thou Made Whole* is not divided into chapters to be just read but into "lessons" with suggested exercises to be carried out. The original intent was for it to be the basic material for a correspondence course in prayer and healing but it was revised and put into book form for the interested general public. The material is presented in the inspirational style of the author, contains underlying principles, some mention of technique, and exercises to follow that give the reader something specific to do.

The book is particularly designed for anyone who is in ill health and anyone interested in helping in the healing ministry.

Throughout 1953 Glenn Clark also continued his other interests—bringing messages about *prayer* and *living the life* as indicated in the Gospels and other portions of the Scriptures.

In 1954 the book *Windows Of Heaven* was published, a very

beautiful oversized book very appropriate for gift giving. It contains twelve weeks of daily meditations. Each one-page meditation has opposite it a very meaningful full-page photograph taken by the sensitive and professional photographer, Lucien Aigner. Some of the photographs are portraits of well-known leaders in the Camp Farthest Out movement: Carola Williams, Starr Daily, Norman Elliott, Frank Laubach, Glenn Clark, Roland Brown, Marcia Brown, Glenn Clark and Mary Lou Elliott, Glenn Harding, and Gertrude deKoch Keene.

Most of the meditations are select inspirational portions of Glenn Clark's published writings. In addition some are taken from his unpublished writings.

This book is an excellent one for coffee table display. Everyone would appreciate it.

1954 was the year that a resolve Glenn Clark made back in 1952 to build a Belt-of-Prayer Around-the-World came into fruition. This is the story:

In the Fall of 1951 a long distance phone call from his home brought the news that Mary Lou Elliott, his only granddaughter, had leukemia with only a few weeks to live. The following hours were of shock for he and the nine year old Mary Lou had a great comraderie going between them—most precious.

He said that when he accepted the probability of losing another of his loved ones as a part of an unknown divine plan he found a measure of peace.

Mary Lou did not die in a few weeks. God arranged for her to be with them for another six months. The story of those last months and weeks together, if published, would be very precious. Glenn Clark hoped to write it sometime.

February 8, 1952, he was in a Camp Farthest Out in Florida. He awakened very early that morning and recorded in his notebook that he was preparing to give his only granddaughter back to God. When she was gone he would let nothing deter him expending himself that the spirit of heaven might be brought into every phase of life. He would battle the skepticism and cynicism of intellectuals. He would work tirelessly that law-makers might be spiritually aroused and dedicated to the cause that the laws of the land conform to the laws of God. He would champion the idea that men in authority need to have people close to them who believed in love and prayer and guidance—that the decisions they made would be good and right—guided from above.

Later that morning a message came that Mary Lou had stepped into heaven while he was writing his resolve in his notebook.

Then and there a NEW idea came to him that he had never before contemplated. He would increase his activities beyond the boundaries of the United States or the shores of North America. He would make a speaking trip completely encircling the world with the deliberate purpose of building a Belt-of-Prayer around the world.

His love for Mary Lou and Mary Lou's love for him had become as a catalyst that propelled him into this widened program of giving himself in the name of love, for the blessing of the whole world.

These are thoughts that came to him:

For God so loved the world that He gave...

Jesus so loved the Father and the world that He gave...

Glenn Clark loved God and Mary Lou so much that he would give his energies, himself, all he had, for the world, too.

The Round-the-World Belt-of-Prayer journey started January 2, 1954 and was completed in mid-May the same year—four and one-half months in length. He started writing detailed reports of the fascinating experiences almost immediately—sending them to his office in St. Paul so his family and praying friends could know what was happening. It wasn't long before he realized he had material for a book. Since the book titled *On Wings Of Prayer* was not published until 1955 I will not say much about the journey now. Just this—he did not make the trip alone. He took with him Roland and Marcia Brown, both of whom had assisted him through the years in establishing many new Camps Farthest Out and who had taken major roles in camp leadership. The three of them had traveled widely together in this country, Hawaii, Mexico and Europe sharing program responsibilities as a team. They were each filled with joy as they anticipated watching Jesus at work each step of this new journey. Yes, they enjoyed working together. I am sure of these facts for I am number three of the team, Marcia.

At the end of the trip Glenn Clark returned home much more relaxed, more enthusiastic and more sure of God's ways to PEACE than he had been when he started. He wrote,

"I have just completed the most thrilling experience of my life, building a Belt-of-Prayer around the world."

On Wings Of Prayer, the account of the Belt of Prayer around-the-world tour, was published in 1955. The book is far more than a travelogue, interesting and different as a travelogue might be that at no point includes the agenda of the usual guided tourist tour with the endless walking through museums, cathedrals, lovely gardens; shopping, fancy hotels and restaurants where fellowship is with other tourists. This trip included more simple living, meeting with people with desires like yours who eagerly, though for some a bit shyly, gather for your coming. And you gather in places that are designed for THEIR living or learning or worshipping. How beautiful the women! Yes, and how beautiful the men! How precious the children and the teen-agers! What eyes! What fantastic fellowship! It was truly a wonderful trip.

The book is a beautiful combination of factual reporting of experiences in all kinds of places and situations; of conditions which rarely get much press or TV coverage back home; and of inspirational facets that are so often present for those who have eyes to see and ears to hear. The book inspires praying people to want to pray—because they are made a bit more aware and a bit more understanding.

In places it calls attention to political or economic situations where much love and prayer would help.

It tells of prayer groups and praying people that are becoming as links in a belt—a prayer belt encircling the world with love and compassion.

The book also names people, good people. Some of them are teachers, ministers, missionaries, Y.M.C.A. secretaries, doctors, and young people.

To mention a few of those he had closer fellowship with in the various countries: the group of 230 choice people in England who assembled for the first five-day Camp Farthest Out outside North America, 33 of them clergymen and ministers; tea and prayer with Princess Wilhelmina in Holland; the very promising young Baptist minister in Germany, Arnim Riemenschneider, who was the German interpreter; the long time missionary, Dewey Moore, in Rome; Waldensian groups in Florence; the Presbyterian ministers in Cairo: Ibrahim Said, Menis Abdul Noor and Sam Habib; the very helpful friends he found in Bishop Cubain and Najib Khoury in Jerusalem; ministers and missionaries in Beirut. And deeper into Asia: India with K. K. Chandy and Bishop Appasamy; Ceylon with Selvaretnam and the doctors Walpols—such beautiful friends; Baptist missionaries in Singapore, Bangkok and Hong Kong with Christian centers and schools; the Philippines with Bishop Sobrepena; Formosa with Lillian Dickson—a former student of his at Macalester College; Japan with Merrel Vories and Toyohiko Kagawa; and Hawaii—beautiful Hawaii. He called it,

> "All one glorious trek of discovering and fellowshipping with devout and serious souls all around the world who are working and praying for peace and a spiritual awakening for all people."

Part II of the book deals practically and spiritually with ways of solving the problems of the world—as timely today as when he wrote it. His insights are keen. His suggestions are so right. His conviction that the way of love and prayer is the only way for peace is so true.

It seems that Glenn Clark always had the longing to see unity, harmony and peace everywhere. During the interval between the first and second world wars he was encouraging people to constantly remember there was a needy world beyond the oceans and south of the Rio Grande River. He frequently led the camps in praying for the world—and would lead groups in the experience of "broadcasting love" to the peoples of the entire world. This continued with greater urgency during the Second World War and on into the frustrating Cold War years—even as long as he lived. During the Belt-of-Prayer trip he was out there in the world, on location, praying and broadcasting love with every step on the ground and from every flight in the air.

For many years he had been actively advocating the formation of a Department of Peace in the Government. He had endeavored with the assistance of Frank Laubach and others in the Washington, D.C. area to interest political leaders saying, "We have a Department of War and we have become adept in waging and winning wars. But we have not been winning Peace. We need a Department of Peace to lead the thinking of our nation in how to win and maintain peace at home and throughout the world." One idea Frank Laubach advanced was to initiate a *War of Amazing Kindness*. Prayer would be essential. These ideas were relayed to governmental leaders but were not considered seriously.

Finally Glenn Clark decided *he* could initiate a movement toward permanent peace through an acceleration in the spread of prayer groups, through spiritual seminars on ways to peace, and through the Camps Farthest Out. He hoped that other movements such as the Ashram movement of E. Stanley Jones, the Prayer and Spiritual Life Movement under Thomas Carruth, the Disciplined Order for Christ movement established by Albert E. Day, and for that matter every church group, would join in such a movement. All of it should be under the leadership of the Prince of Peace. It would begin with the "grass roots" and might eventually sweep Washington, D.C. and the world. Through 1955 he increased his dreaming about the tremendous potential of such a movement and the possibility of its happening. Some people felt that we were already in the midst of the greatest prayer movement in the history of the world. If so, it could be even greater.

Glenn Clark invited nine of his co-workers to a "summit" type of prayer conference, which was held the autumn of that year on Petit Jean Mountain, Arkansas—to ask God to weave all the threads of a new prayer and peace movement into His perfect pattern for accomplishing His purposes for the world. The group shared ideas for implementing such a movement through the projects and programs Glenn Clark had initiated. He outlined details on a blackboard. Everyone began to get a clearer picture of what God's plan in this direction would be.

America's first *Congress of Prayer* was held in Washington, D.C. December 6-8, 1955. It was the culmination of dreams and plans of many religious leaders. It was not highly organized under the control of any denomination or organizing board, but was a "grass roots" program welling up from the prayer groups of the nation. The emphasis was on prayer. The people came from 31 states. The Lord chose leaders such as Catherine Marshall, Frank Laubach, Elton Trueblood, Edward Elson, Billy Graham, Thomas Carruth and Glenn Clark. Meetings were presided over by Judge Luther Youngdahl, Albert Shirkey, Charles Wesley Lowry, Clifford Richmond, Ward Hurlburt, Norman Elliott and Paul Wilkinson.

At the close of this national prayer congress folk on every hand were saying "This is the greatest thing that has hit Washington."

A year later a Congress of Prayer was to be held in London—welling up out of their "grass roots." Wonderful!

1956 saw the concluding year of Glenn Clark's life. He had been told by a doctor to take it easy. He enjoyed the way the advice was worded, "If you need to get something from upstairs, stand at the foot of the stairs and look up. Think twice about it before climbing the steps. Perhaps you won't need it." By February 1956 he knew he would have to slow down and began cancelling appointments.

The book published that year was *God's Voice In The Folklore*. He had anticipated writing this book for years. It would be a large book interpreting the nursery rhymes, folk-tales, fairy-tales, fables, myths, legends, allegories, etc., of the world. He had discovered deeply spiritual meanings and messages hidden in this vast body of sayings, tales and legends which seemed to arise from the imagination or the soul of peoples in their more primitive times and which were passed, orally, from generation to generation. Because the stories were basically the same in area after area throughout the world, even where the people were remotely separately geographically, Glenn Clark began researching the whole field of folklore. Where did the stories originate? From the deeply imbedded longings of the soul? A wisdom that came from within? In the course of time his one large book became so large he decided to divide it into four volumes. The book came off the presses in November after his death. It was the first of the contemplated volumes. For that matter it was his *last* book.

He would frequently bring a spiritual interpretation of a nursery rhyme, fairy-tale, or perhaps from *Alice in Wonderland* or *Homer's Odyssey* into a talk—much to the delight of his audiences. An illustration:

> Jack be nimble,
> Jack be quick.
> Jack jump over
> The candlestick.

The candle stick was being used as a prop in a game—an exercise in cleverness. *But the purpose of a candle stick is to hold a candle—lighted—to show the way.*

Jesus wanted *candles* on candle sticks to give light to all in the house. He condemned the leaders of his day for giving excessive importance to the outside of platters, the outer frames, the candle sticks—instead of lighting the inner wicks. Jack, the one who should have been in the light-spreading business was too involved in clever platter polishing or candle stick jumping.

In the Spring of 1956 Glenn Clark arranged for what he called his "Forty Days in the Desert." It was a period reserved for stillness, reading, writing and regaining strength. He had a cabin all to himself in Arizona with access to the near-by home of friends.

He had already been focusing in on two words which summed up much of his thinking. One was HARMONY—a word that to him was a blending of love, forgiveness, agreement and unity. The other word was RELINQUISHMENT—a word that meant letting go and letting God—with radiant acquiescence.

While there on the desert two more words sprang to life and infiltrated his heart, mind and soul. One was INFINITE: unlimited, immeasurable, inexhaustible, endless. He wrote,

> "To lift your love to Infinite love, all you need do is to take one step–but it is a very long step–yes, we call it an Infinite step–all you need do is to forgive those who have despitefully used you, and love–yes, and actually love–your enemies." Jesus had Infinite love, Infinite faith, Infinite trust, Infinite humility. "Jesus changed the word finite to Infinite in His life and vocabulary, thus making all the victories and blessings of the Christian world possible for us."

The other word was HUMILITY. He had taken a copy of his book *Come Follow Me* to the desert, rereading chapter after chapter. The paragraphs became "living" conversing and fellowshipping with Jesus. He became increasingly aware that the power of Jesus' life rested primarily in one word–Humility. He had been inspired by Andrew Murray's great book HUMILITY (Fleming H. Revell Co., New York and London.)–particularly with the idea that at their roots, faith and humility are one. That an individual can never have more of true faith than he has of true humility. That true lowliness of mind and the heart of humility are to be seen in the relation of one individual to another–in the treatment of one individual of another.

Jesus said, "…for I am meek and lowly of heart." The truest lowliness of the mind and the truest example of the heart of humility are to be seen in the relation of Jesus to His Father, and in his relationship with and treatment of, everyone–always.

So Glenn Clark learned what humility was through watching Jesus–the one who said, Come! See! Find! Receive! It became the sincerest desire of Glenn Clark's soul to *be* humble, like Jesus, in all ways–always.

He flew back to St. Paul near the first of May. In the desert he had found many blessings in stillness, done much writing, received loving care from the few who knew where he was. He said that he felt like he had passed through a celestial filtration. Any dross of his life was filtered out. That which heaven permitted to pass through was purified, and tremendously useable for the Kingdom.

Several months earlier Glenn Clark had learned that his friend

Sherwood Eddy, the great Christian evangelist so well known on three continents, now 86 years old, was to rejoin the Sherwood Eddy Seminar that summer and lead a group of 43 notable ministers, lawyers, educators and other professional and business people into Russia. Glenn Clark wanted so badly to go. He wanted to pray for Russia and the peace of the world from inside Russia. The tour would begin June 20. He planned to go.

He came to Chicago in early June to finish work on Volume I of *God's Voice In The Folklore*, contact a printer, and make outlines for the next three volumes. It became evident his physical strength was diminishing. I took him to the same doctor who had treated him the previous year. He checked into a hospital that evening–very low blood pressure and red blood count–so low that the doctor was amazed he could get around at all. He received some transfusions. However, he wasn't cooperating in giving the technicians the necessary time to discover the cause of his difficulty. He was too eager to get out. His condition improved with the transfusions and he received reluctant approval to do the Russian part of the tour. The Seminar group was already in Europe!

July 9 he arrived in New York City and was met by his son-in-law Norman Elliott and a friend. They spent a delightful evening together and the next noon saw him off to West Berlin where he joined the tour. July 16 they had an exciting interview with President Tito of Yugoslavia, in his summer palace. They flew into Kiev, Russia on the 17th. Keeping up with a tour group is not easy, even if the program is fascinating, and theirs was: collective farms, factories, museums; conference with the American ambassador, two American correspondents, some Soviet officials; the mausoleum of Lenin and Stalin, Red Square under the walls of the Kremlin, churches, a synagogue, worshipped in the principle Russian Orthodox church, had a tremendously moving experience in the largest Baptist church crowded with 2,000 persons seated and standing in every available spot.

While climbing stairs into the dining room of the hotel in Leningrad on July 26 he collapsed. The woman house doctor put him to bed to rest. The next day–their last day in Leningrad–he was much better.

That Friday evening the group assembled in two large connecting bedrooms of the hotel to evaluate their impressions of the Russian experiences. Following that Glenn Clark gave a talk to the group on his life's experiences and the power of prayer. All were deeply moved.

The next day they journeyed by slow train to Helsinki, Finland. While in a retreat outside Helsinki, Sherwood Eddy gave the final spiritual message. Glenn Clark listened attentively.

They flew from Helsinki over Copenhagen to Paris and from there via Iceland and Gander to New York on July 31. And on to Chicago where Roland Brown met him at the airport and took him to his home. While there he again entered the hospital—more transfusions.

He arrived back in St. Paul Sunday morning, August 5. Norman Elliott met him and took him home. Trying as the trip had been, Glenn Clark was happy about it. His long dreamed-of mission of prayer had been accomplished.

He spent every day of that week at his office. In addition to trying to catch up on a multitude of other details he completed a final chapter to a manuscript on which he had been working.

He insisted on a special Board meeting Friday evening, August 10, of the Foundation Farthest Out, an incorporated, non-profit body made up of a few very capable, loyal friends who were overseeing, and assisting in other ways, the spread of his work—particularly the Belt-of-Prayer Around-the-World and other "out of the U.S.A." work. He invited the Mel Reynoldses from Florida, the Fred Markhams from California, the Roland Browns from Chicago, Norman Elliott (son-in-law, editor and new president of the Glenn Clark-founded Macalester Park Publishing Company) and his secretary Mrs. Glen Stowe to join the group. He was eager to hear, and have the others also hear, the report of a nine month Belt-of-Prayer world tour Roland Brown had completed in July. The meeting stimulated him. The meetings continued Saturday and Sunday. The Board saw some excellent colored slides of the world trip that vividly brought the Belt-of-Prayer right into the room. There was opportunity for him to meet separately with individuals and couples about other specific projects. And some opportunity for "dreaming about the future." The closing was a lovely picnic at the home of the President of the Foundation Farthest Out, Charles Stone.

Monday morning, August 13, he was extremely tired, too weak to get involved with a day's activities. Shaving was too much work!

That noon he entered the Northwest Hospital in Minneapolis. He had four transfusions in the next few days and for a while they proved strengthening.

It wasn't until three or four days after entering the hospital that his condition was diagnosed as Multiple Myeloma—a condition resulting from the failure of the bone marrow to produce blood platelets.

During the first days in the hospital he talked about many things—planned the trip that autumn to England where he would hold camps in England, Ireland, Scotland and Wales followed by a great Congress of Prayer in London, possibly in Westminster Cathedral. I was to accompany him to assist in the programs. He added, "If I am not able to travel in time to take in the camps, I will at least go to London for the Congress of Prayer. If I can't give all my talks I can sit on the platform and listen while you read to the entire assembly some portions I will select from my book *The Three Mysteries of Jesus*. It has the message I want to share with Britain in the Congress of Prayer."

(No, he didn't recover to make that trip.)

He talked about books he wanted to have reprinted; about ideas that were coming to him he wanted to develop. He talked about people—many people he had been associated with. And we prayed for them.

He wanted to be read to. *The Three Mysteries of Jesus* was his first choice.

Three of us spent much time with him: his daughter Marion, Ruby Roskilly a long time friend from Minneapolis, and myself. One afternoon a nurses' aid stepped through the open door. We were all in the room at the moment. She smiled at him and said, "Is there something I can do for you?" I expected him to answer, "No thank you, all my needs are being taken care of." But he didn't! He said, "Yes, just love me." The nurse answered "Of course I will. I do." We almost gasped! The next morning on arrival we went straight to him and said, "Has anyone been in here yet this morning to tell you they love you?" He stared! Then we said, "Then we will. We do." From then on we made sure he *knew* he was loved.

After about the seventh day in the hospital he spent more and more time sleeping followed by times of sharing with great alertness. Norman Elliott came in during one of the waking-up periods and bending over him said, "Have you been on a journey?" He smiled and answered, "Yes, a fabulous journey." One morning Marion brought his grandsons for a short visit. His smiles lingered long after they left.

As time went on the weather turned warmer. The hospital staff brought in an oxygen tent to provide more comfort. Helen May Olsen, his daughter from Beloit, Wisconsin came. His son, Miles Clark, was arranging to come from California. Friends from the area dropped in—quietly—and we all knew—prayerfully: Alma Fisher, Judy Glen Stowe, Marie and Clate Dunham, and others.

During the last days the periods of consciousness were fewer. There wasn't any pain. There hadn't been any pain. There was a sense of peace and a knowing that God was fully in charge in a beautiful way.

I could not stay in St. Paul indefinitely since I had an appointment I must keep in Alabama. So Friday morning, August 24, I said "Goodbye."

What a powerful instrument he had always been for the Lord. What a tremendous personal friend to so many. God was so good.

Saturday noon I telephoned the hospital from Chicago to find out how he was. Amazingly the nurse reported in detail. He was sinking into a deepening coma. Then she said members of the family were in the room. Would I like to speak with one of them? Miles Clark's voice came over the wire. He had arrived that morning. It was so good to hear him and to know he was with his father.

I told Miles I would be leaving immediately for the drive southward. I would plan to spend the night at the Cairo Hotel in southern Illinois.

Very early Sunday morning, August 26, while it was still dark outside there in Cairo, the phone call came from Miles that his father had let go here and he and God were off on another journey together.

Norman Elliott, in an article entitled "See You in the Morning" published in the Fellowship Messenger, gave this beautiful comment:

"Isn't it just like Glenn and all he stood for and thought, that his parting was accompanied with gentle rain, tender breezes, and lightning flashes. The lightning flashes were not the knife-like cutting of the heavens, but rather like a light bulb that was intermittently turned on and off in a darkened room."

Glenn Clark was now indeed one with the Father and the Lord whom he loved so much.

Doctor Forrest L. Richeson in presenting the Memorial Tribute to Dr. Glenn Clark at the Macalester Park Presbyterian Church, August 29, 1956, said:

"There are moments in life when words seem so inadequate to interpret the true feelings of the human heart. Indeed, it is difficult if not impossible to crowd a life like Dr. Clark's into the narrow compass of mere words. There was such endless breadth, depth, and height about his life. A life spurred on by divine urgings. A life finding its motivation in the spiritual needs and hopes of mankind."

Miles Clark has recently published a book entitled *Glenn Clark, His Life And His Writings*. It is the life of an outstanding man and father as seen through the eyes of his son at various stages in the son's life—a son who is now also a writer and is an editor of a weekly newspaper. It is a story of a boy's, teen-ager and young adult's growing understanding of his father that climaxes in great appreciation. A beautiful book.

More about the man, Glenn Clark. He would sometimes describe himself as a full-time *"preacher,"* a full time *teacher* and a full time *coach*. He would say that as a "preacher" he could never tell if what he was saying was going in one ear of the listener and out the other. As a "teacher" he had an advantage over himself as a "preacher." If he suspected it was going in one ear of his students and out the other he could give an examination and they would have to write it all back to him. But as a "coach" he had an advantage over the "preacher" and the "teacher." He didn't pass out paper and ask the boys on his track team to write out "how to jump the hurdles." He would take them out on the track field and they would prove they knew how by doing it—and winning.

Glenn Clark was also a *prolific writer*—publishing more material each year than most professional writers do in three years.

He was a man with *great insight* or sensitivity. He could sense the worth or potential of an individual that even the individual himself was unaware of. He could help draw it into fruition.

He had *great imagination*. And because of the way he used it you could call it *a heavenly imagination*. Creative ideas were constantly claiming his attention. His books revealed the creative way he could put creative ideas together. And the ideas became translated into living.

He had a *great sense of humor*. Sometimes he talked about the creative power of humor. His listeners often saw this demonstrated. He loved good jokes and enjoyed hearing them and telling them. He claimed to have the best collection of good stories since Abraham Lincoln. Some of his jokes were asked for again and again. Who could ever forget the story of "Mrs. Bedbug." Or the point he was making when he told it.

He had his own particular *style of speaking*. Sometimes haltingly. Sometimes not finishing his sentences. Sometimes he didn't want to finish them with words—he found a gesture or a bit of dramatizing would do it adequately—and unforgettably.

He *founded a publishing house*. Originally his purpose was to publish little leaflets and booklets he was writing. Later he published large books as well. Many of them were his own but he published other authors, too. It had excellent editors in himself and Norman Elliott. It also had a mail-order and over-the-counter book sales business.

He *founded the Camps Farthest Out* in 1930–a world-wide movement since 1954 that is still expanding in 1977. The history, nature and purpose of the movement is described in *A Man's Reach,* chapter XXI.

He was the *founder of the Foundation Farthest Out, Incorporated.*

He was the *founder of the Koinonia Foundation,* Baltimore, Maryland.

Glenn Clark didn't think of himself as a person with special powers in praying for the sick but letters kept coming to him requesting prayer. He couldn't cope with the increasing numbers of requests so found some perfectly qualified people to set up a program which became known as *The United Prayer Tower.* Its first home was in a very special room in the Macalester Park Publishing Company. Alma Fisher was in charge for many years. They had a special period every morning for praying for the individual requests. Glenn Clark joined them when he was in town. The United Prayer Tower took care of the prayer request correspondence. They also had a prayer ministry to the individuals and churches of the area as requested.

He *organized the first Alcoholics Anonymous* group in his area, and attended the sessions although he could not be a member of the group. He never drank.

He was *always a church member.*

He became an *Elder in the Macalester Presbyterian Church,* St. Paul, he attended so many years of his life.

At the same time he was the *teacher of* a *large Bible Class* of the Plymouth Congregational Church, Minneapolis. He would dismiss the class a bit early and rush over to his Presbyterian Church in St. Paul–arriving soon after the morning service began.

* * *

This list could go on and on. How do you complete a list that serves as a portrait of a person who is linked to an inexhaustible God who has convinced you that you can do all things through Christ who enables you? So you make that the slant of your life.

I close with this that he wrote. You can find it in *The Three Mysteries of Jesus*, pages 32 and 33.

"Hawthorne tells in the story of the Great Stone Face how a legend grew up in the little village at the mountain foot promising that some day a man would come who would look like the Great Stone Face with its sweetness and peace and strength reflected in his countenance. A little boy who loved this great image was always looking for this promised man to come. First one, and then another stranger came to the village but they never met the test. Then events led the little boy to leave the village, and not till years later did he return. But when he did, the whole village went out to welcome him for he bore upon his countenance the strength, the courage, the sweetness and the majesty of the Great Stone Face."

Glenn Clark was like that little boy. He loved Jesus. He was always looking into the faces of people confident he would find someone like Him. As time passed others who knew him saw upon Glenn Clark's countenance the strength, the courage, the sweetness and the majesty of the One he had been looking at all his life.

Writings of Glenn Clark

1906 *The Art of Living.* Des Moines: private. Bible lessons. 34 pp.

1921 *The Master Key of Reading Character.* Privately published. Six volumes. Applying body characteristics to understanding oneself. 295 pp.

1922 *The Manual of Short Story Art.* New York: The Macmillan Company. Developing creativity in creative writing. 282 pp.

1926 *The Soul's Sincere Desire.* Boston: Little Brown and Co. The lost art of Jesus: prayer. 114 pp.

1926 *Twelve Parable-Miracles of Answered Prayer.* New York: The General Board of the Young Men's Christian Association. Modern parables. 34 pp.

1928 *Fishers of Men.* Boston: Little, Brown & Company. 101 pp.

1929 *Power of the Spirit on the Athletic Field.* Privately published. 48pp.

1930 *The Thought Farthest Out.* St. Paul: Macalester Park Publishing Co. 57 pp.

1931 *Water of Life.* St. Paul: Macalester Park Publishing Co. Fiction. 300 pp.

1932 *The Lord's Prayer.* St. Paul: Macalester Park Publishing Co. Study of the Lord's Prayer. 57 pp.

1932 *Personality in Essay Writing.* New York: Ray Long and Richard R. Smith. 242 pp.

1933 *Song of the Souls of Men.* St. Paul: Macalester Park Publishing Co. Spiritual poetry. 60 pp.

1934 *The Land We Vision.* St. Paul: Macalester Park Publishing Co. 38pp.

1935 *Islands of Light.* St. Paul: Macalester Park Publishing Co. 26 pp.

1935 *Power in Athletics.* St. Paul: Macalester Park Publishing Co. 47 pp.

1936 *Fruits of the Spirit.* St. Paul: Macalester Park Publishing Co. 14 pp.

1937 *I Will Lift Up Mine Eyes.* New York: Harper & Brothers. Guide to richer living. 178 pp.

1937 *Footsteps, Voices and Silences in College Halls.* St. Paul: Macalester Park Publishing Co. 58pp.

1939 *God's Minute Man.* St. Paul: Macalester Park Publishing Co. 27 pp.

1939 *Beatitudes of Married Life.* St. Paul: Macalester Park Publishing Co.

1939 *Divine Plan.* St. Paul: Macalester Park Publishing Co.

1939 *The Man Who Talked With Flowers.* St. Paul: Macalester Park Publishing Co. Biography of George Washington Carver. 62 pp.

1939 *Gold, Frankincense and Myrrh.* St. Paul: Macalester Park Publishing Co. 20 pp.

1940 *The World's Greatest Debate.* St. Paul: Macalester Park Publishing Co. Debates between Patrick Henry, James Madison; Robert Y. Hayne, Daniel Webster; Stephen A. Douglas, Abraham Lincoln. 214 pp.

1940 *The Slingshot of David.* St. Paul: Macalester Park Publishing Co. 21 pp.

1940 *How to Find Health Through Prayer.* New York: Harper & Brothers. 154 pp.

1941 *Armor of the Soldier.* St. Paul: Macalester Park Publishing Co. 16 pp.

1941 *Does God Hear Prayer?* St. Paul: Macalester Park Publishing Co. 28 pp.

1942 *Two or Three Gathered Together.* New York: Harper & Brothers. 154 pp.

1942 *Three Mysteries of Jesus.* St. Paul: Macalester Park Publishing Co. 45 pp.

1942 *The Way, the Truth and the Life.* New York: Harper & Brothers. 179 pp.

1943 *The Truth Shall Set You Free.* St. Paul: Macalester Park Publishing Co. 22 pp.

1944 *Home of Love.* St. Paul: Macalester Park Publishing Co. 60 pp.

1944 *The Third Front.* New York: Harper & Brothers. 232 pp.

1945 *The Secret to Power in Business.* St. Paul: Macalester Park Publishing Co. 24 pp.

1945 *The Senior Partner in Business.* St. Paul: Macalester Park Publishing Co. 50 pp.

1946 *The Man Who Walked in His Steps.* St. Paul: Macalester Park Publishing Co. Biography of Charles Sheldon. 60 pp.

1946 *The Man Who Tapped the Secrets of the Universe.* St. Paul: Macalester Park Publishing Co. Biography of Walter Russell. 90 pp.

1947 *The Way of Love.* St. Paul: Macalester Park Publishing Co. 44 pp.

1947 *Touchdowns for the Lord.* St. Paul: Macalester Park Publishing Co. Biography of Dad Elliott. 43 pp.

1948 *Collaborating With Eternity.* St. Paul: Macalester Park Publishing Co. 32 pp.

1949 *Man's Reach.* New York: Harper & Brothers. Autobiography of Glenn Clark. 314pp.

1949 *Under the Shelter of His Wings.* St. Paul: Macalester Park Publishing Co.

1949 *Together.* Privately published.

1950 *What Would Jesus Do?* St. Paul: Macalester Park Publishing Co. Fiction. 286 pp.

1950 *From Crime to Christ.* St. Paul: Macalester Park Publishing Co. Biography of Starr Daily. 63 pp.

1950 *The Other Dawn.* St. Paul: Macalester Park Publishing Co. 24 pp.

1951 *God's Reach.* St. Paul: Macalester Park Publishing Co. 223 pp.

1951 *The Way to Victory in International Affairs.* St. Paul: Macalester Park Publishing Co. 21 pp.

1952 *Come Follow Me.* St. Paul: Macalester Park Publishing Co. Fiction. 206 pp.

1953 *Be Thou Made Whole.* St. Paul: Macalester Park Publishing Co. Lessons in healing. 161 pp.

1954 *The Holy Spirit.* St. Paul: Macalester Park Publishing Co. 23 pp.

1954 *Windows of Heaven.* New York: Harper & Brothers. 188 pp.

1955 *On Wings of Prayer.* St. Paul: Macalester Park Publishing Co. 258 pp.

1956 *God's Voice in Folklore.* St. Paul: Macalester Park Publishing Co. 213 pp.